VIRTUAL REALITY NOW

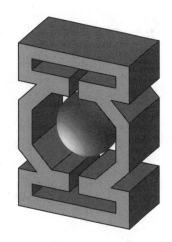

A DETAILED LOOK AT TODAY'S VIRTUAL REALITY

BY LARRY STEVENS

MIS:
PRESS

A Subsidiary of
Henry Holt and Co., Inc.

First Edition—1994

Library of Congress Cataloging-in-Publication Data

```
Stevens, Larry 1947-
    Virtual reality now : a look at today's virtual reality /
Larry Stevens.
       p.  cm.
    Includes Index.
    ISBN 1-55828-255-2 :
    1. Human-computer interaction.  2. Virtual reality.  3. Computer
industry.  I. Title.
QA76.9.H8574  1994
006-dc20                                            94-38357
                                                        CIP
```

Printed in the United States of America.

10 9 8 7 6 5 4 3 2 1

Development Editor: Micheal Sprague   **Technical Editor:** Jono Hardjowirogo
Copy Editor: JoAnna Armott   **Production Editor:** Anthony Washington

Associate Production Editors: Maya Riddick and Audrey Smith

Table of
Contents

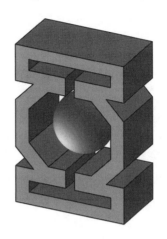

A Virtual
Primer

Wearing a headset that looks like a bicycle helmet with wires streaming from the top, thick goggles, and skintight gloves, all tethered to a computer system, the participants move around in front of a screen. They pace left and right; they bend down and mime picking up imaginary objects; they walk a jagged line like drunks failing a sobriety test, and then bob their heads, watching some apparition invisible to the rest of the world. To understand the gyrations of these people, one has to realize that they are, for the time being, not in the same world as the onlookers. Instead, they are in a virtual world, one that is viewed in their goggles, heard from stereo headphones in their headset, and manipulated with their gloved hands. They are moving around geometric shapes, picking up rocks, walking though woods. None of that exists outside their artificially stimulated senses. But, as in the real world, each change in the position of their body or the orientation of the position of the participants' head or body results in a corresponding change in the view from their goggles and in the sounds in their earphones. The system is a relatively simple example of a range of research activities and products that are called *virtual reality* (VR). This is all taking place at the IBM Thomas J. Watson Research Center in Hawthorne, NY, where a rudimentary but fascinating VR system is currently in place.

Starting around 1991 or 1992, VR has attracted a good deal of attention both in the popular media as well as among researchers. VR conferences, bulletin-board services (BBS), newsletters, books, magazines, university courses, and research centers began to proliferate. All the popular news magazines as well as business publications featured at least one cover story on the subject. *Scientific American* published a number of articles on VR and so did *Playboy*. Trade magazines wondered what this new technology would mean for their particular business. Even one congressional committee held a hearing on the subject.

What is this technology that seems at the same time so important and fascinating and yet so allusive in terms of practical applications?

It would be convenient to be able to define VR in a way that everyone would agree on. Unfortunately, the term is much fuzzier than, say, E-mail or desktop publishing. The term VR is used in different ways by many different people. Basically, VR is a combination of computer graphics and simulation technologies. In its most ambitious form, the goal of VR systems is to create an artificial environment that is indistinguishable to the user from a real environment. VR may be viewed as a video game, but one that involves all your senses (or, at the least, most of your senses). A simple TV-screen video game may totally engross your mind, but your peripheral vision allows you to see the housecat scamper across the floor. And the sound of traffic or people walking in the next room are constant reminders that you are playing a simple game in your living room.

A VR system completely engages your vision and hearing. Peering through special glasses and wearing stereophonic earphones, nothing outside the virtual world reaches your eyes or ears. VR systems, in their purest form, would also affect senses that standard video games ignore. You'd be able to touch and feel objects. You'd be able to feel the cold and the heat. You might even be able to smell or taste things. Your interaction with the virtual world would be more natural than that with a video game, that normally requires a joystick or mouse. In a virtual world you might use your feet to walk. In some cases, the VR experience allows you to do those things which, because of finances or courage, you could never do in the real world. You could drive a race car at lightning speed, climb to the top of a snow-covered mountain, or practice firing sophisticated weapons. VR systems also allow you to do things impossible in the real world, no matter how rich or courageous you are. For example, it would allow you to see inside the human body with X-ray glasses, shrink yourself smaller than an atom to explore the world of molecules, visit a planet on a distant solar system, or walk around homes that haven't yet been erected.

Many of these VR worlds are similar to the real world. They are familiar houses, roads, and parks. Others are places that we may know about, but could never travel to. They may be planets or the interiors of patients' blood streams. Other VR worlds are complete fantasies, having a basis in fiction, not in any reality we know of. VR participants might also navigate the virtual world in a familiar or unfamiliar way. He or she might use a joystick to move through the world or simply incline their body in the appropriate direction. Alternatively, travel in the virtual world might be more exotic. For example, we might be able to fly from place to place merely by pointing our finger in the location we intend to move. Some VR worlds have nothing to do with location. A VR based spreadsheet, for example, might allow us to float around the bars and pie slices of charts created from the data we had previously inputted. A VR program meant to assist in project management might allow users to manually move arrows and other indicators in flowcharts listing project priorities.

SUSPENSION OF DISBELIEF

The ultimate VR system would create its illusion by providing a complete range of sensory experiences including sight, sound, touch, smell, and taste. And the system would also allow more than one user to experience the same illusion. Of course, even if that amount of sensory control were possible, the user would still know he or she is in a virtual world, not a real one. Accordingly, one requirement of an VR system is to assist the user in his or her attempt to reach a suspension of disbelief. The user should, as quickly as possible and for as long a period as possible, be able to ignore the VR interface—the apparatus—and concentrate on the experience.

A number of issues affect the ability of systems to offer this suspension of disbelief effect. One of the most important is that the display provide a perspective from the user's point of view. This viewer-centered perspective is actually a concept developed by Renaissance artists. It refers to an image taken by a camera situated along the axis extended perpendicular from the center of the canvas. But still, artists need create only one perspective for their canvases. In VR systems, there is a need to change the perspective as the user changes his or her position. So many VR systems incorporate some form of sensor that continuously monitors the viewer's position and causes the display to change its images accordingly.

Suspension of disbelief is also affected by the speed at which the VR image changes to accommodate a reorientation of the user's head or body. If the user turns to the right and there is a lag time before the image changes, the user is rudely reminded that he or she is in an artificial world. The suspension of disbelief is also affected by the number of senses that are involved. Most of us live in a world of sight, sound, smell, touch, and taste. Whenever any of those senses are not affected by an experience, we feel something is missing. Just as the old soundless 8mm home movies seemed so artificial compared to today's video recorders, the suspension of disbelief is affected by the quality of the graphics. If, in order to reduce latency and include sensory experiences without overburdening the processor, the system provides "cartoony" graphics, our belief in the victual world is seriously lessened.

▣ FAR FROM THE IDEAL

Where is this VR system that allows us to suspend our disbelief? Nowhere. Who manufactures the VR system that enthralls all our senses, provides realistic sight and sound and no latency? No one.

VR technology, unfortunately, is still far from reaching its ideal state. Serious problems, both in terms of hardware and software prevent us from receiving a pure VR experience. So we have to make compromises. Some systems make major compromises, creating VR systems that are little more than video games. Other systems try to provide the full experience, but fall short in one or two ways. As noted, the term VR is at best a fuzzy one. The reason is that it has to encompass both the systems that are similar to video games and cost less than $1,000 and the more sophisticated ones that cost over $100,000. Today, the term VR is used to denote any system in which the user is able to interact with a simulated environment. This environment may range from a simulation appearing on a computer monitor to a system that includes an array of sensory stimulators.

THE HISTORY OF VIRTUAL REALITY

In order to gain an understanding of where we are today, it is helpful to look at the history of the technology both in fiction and reality. Suprisingly, VR is closely linked both to the development of calculating machines as well as the development of mechanical devices, such as automata.

Viewed one way, VR can be traced back to the automata of the ancient Greeks. Archytas of Tarentim (c.400-350 BC) was reported to have developed a pigeon whose movements he controlled remotely using a jet of steam or compressed air. In China, at about the same time, inventors had created an entire mechanical orchestra that could be controlled by operators sitting yards from the instruments.

Calculating machines such as Charles Babbage's Analytical Engine were attempts to simulate reality in numeric form and then manipulate that reality to learn the results of different forces. In the 1890s, a punch-card system was used to represent population in order to complete the census in a reasonable period of time. During World War II, the first computer was developed to decipher intelligence as well as to assist in missile research. Rocket trajectories, airflow patterns, and other characteristics of rocket engines were simulated on computers before the prototypes were actually developed.

VIRTUAL REALITY IN FICTION

As with most technologies, fiction preceded fact in VR.

◇ In the 1932 novel, *Brave New World*, Aldous Huxley described "feelies," movies which allowed the viewers to feel the action taking place.

◇ Isaac Asimov explored the subject of virtual environments in his Robot series. The books in that series featured positron brain that operated in virtual worlds.

◇ Arthur C. Clarke, in many of his books, talked about "cyberspace" created by orbiting satellites.

◇ Frank Herbert depicted, in a few of his books, a "human cyberspace" that could be explored through the unlocking of genetic code.

◇ In a 1951 story called The Veldt, by Ray Bradbury, two children lure their parents into a movie-like attraction that involves all the senses.

◇ The first fictional description of true VR may have come from William Gibson, an American who moved to Canada during the late 1960s. VR, or "the matrix" or "cyberspace" plays an important role in Gibson's trio of 1980s novels, *Neuromancer, Count Zero, and Mona Lisa Overdrive.*

In William Gibson's books, the stories take place in the 21st century. Humans are crammed into sprawling and deteriorating metropolises. Young toughs, rather than holding up convenience stores or gas stations, steal data from computer banks. Money gained from these thefts are not spent on drugs but Simstim, or simulated stimuli which are actually VR systems to which many people are addicted. To enter the system, addicts plug computers into jacks implanted in their necks.

Possibly the most well-known fictional VR system today is the Holodeck from the TV series *Star Trek: The Next Generation*. This system is used primarily as an R&R environment which allows the crew of the Starship Enterprise to visit historical periods or fantasy worlds. The VR environment is controlled by a computer that translates voiced commands into scenarios. These scenarios can be peopled with lifelike characters that seem to have volition. In fact a computer bug occasionally causes the characters to go awry, threatening the Holodeck user. The Holodeck requires no special gear such as goggles, earphones, or tracking devices connected to the user's body. Rather, all the mech-anism is hidden somewhere in the room, providing what may be called "unencumbered VR," a system not yet available in reality.

▣ NON-FICTIONAL VIRTUAL REALITY ORIGINS

The roots of non-fictional VR in a form that might be recognized as VR today may be traced back to the early 1940s. An entrepreneur by the name of Edwin Link joined forces with Admiral Luis DeFlorez to develop flight simulators in order to reduce training time and costs. The early simulators were complex mechanical contraptions and the illusion of flight was relatively poor in the early models. But the increasing power of computers and image technology have, by today, made these simulators very realistic. The cockpit display images exactly simulate what a pilot would really see. The mocked-up cockpit turns and rolls on a moving platform—almost exactly simulating what would occur in a real plane.

These original simulators required that the user sit in front of a computer or TV screen, which normally represents either a window or a set of gauges. The room is built to look like the equipment or vehicle the user is being trained on: a cockpit, bridge, or power-plant control room.

When a VR system requires that the user view the virtual environment though a screen, it is called Desktop VR or a Window on a World (WoW). Its origin can be tracked back to 1965, when Ivan Sutherland published a paper called *The Ultimate Display* in which he described the computer display screen as "...a window through which one beholds a virtual world." He challenged scientists to create images that would justify the computer screen as window analogy.

While WoW systems may represent an earlier form of VR, they are still considered an important part of the VR family today. In the newer VR systems, more of the environment exists only as software and is displayed in goggles and represented as force feedback joysticks or other sensing devices. An advantage of these systems is that without the requirement to build large rooms or mock cockpits they should be less expensive to build and maintain.

The next step in virtual display is the video mapping approach. This merges a image of the user's silhouette with an on-screen two-dimensional computer graphic. In order to accomplish this, the user has to wear some device that provides input to the computer as to his or her physical orientation. *Artificial Reality and Artificial Reality* II both published in the 1960s by Myron Kruger described such systems. A few TV game shows have used variations of image mapping techniques. For example, Nick Arcade, on cable channel Nickelodeon, places young contestants into video games.

Immersive VR systems, when and if they can be perfected, represent the final step. In theory, these systems should, from the users perspective, exactly replicate reality. In other words, the user should not be able to discern whether the world he or she is interacting with is real or merely virtually real.

▣ VR Equipment

Presently, the majority of immersive VR systems use a head-mounted display (HMD). There are three parts to most HMDs. The visual display is results from stereoscopic eye pieces, normally tiny LCD screens, positioned over the eyes like glasses. Sound is provided though stereo audio output positioned at the ears. And finally, most HMDs provide a means of tracking the viewer's head position to allow the system to change the display to suit the user's perspective.

An alternative to HMD is the binocular omni-oriented monitor (BOOM). If the head mounted display's display looks like goggles, the BOOM looks like a periscope. It is suspended form an articulated arm, which is actually a tracking device. The viewer peers into the BOOM to see the VR images.

A final display alternative is the use of large projection displays that surround the viewer. This method, called CAVE, has the advantage of limiting the amount of apparatus the user has to be attached to.

The first HMD-based systems were prototyped in 1968, by the same Ivan Sutherland mentioned before, who is now a vice-president at Sun Microsystems. That prototype was a HMD that showed computer-generated images that changed correspondingly to the position of the head. Soon after the development of the HMD, systems that provided force feedback, which simulated the sense of touch, were incorporated into the system. Force feedback allowed users to move around a computer-generated world. If the computer image representing the user bumped into an object, the joystick would respond accordingly.

In the 1960s, Michael Noll at Bell Labs developed a force feedback joystick, Raymond Goertz at Argonne National Laboratory, and John Chatten at Motorola created a commercial system that used force feedback. The purpose of the early system was to view inside "hot cells" which contained radioactive materials that had to be handled for experimental purposes or for processing for use in nuclear power and medicine. The HMDs displayed images from remote, close-circuit cameras.

The above project is an example of telepresence, a form of VR which links sensors in the real world with the senses of an operator—human or robotic—in a remote location. Besides handling nuclear material, telepresence devices have been used by fire fighters to control robot fire suppression equipment, for deep sea and volcanic exploration. In the near future, such systems might be used for space exploration.

PROCESSING POWER

In order for VR to provide an experience of actually being in a virtual world, systems have to provide photographic quality, real-time, interactive 3-D graphics. That requires powerful processors with lots of memory. True interactive systems with high resolution graphics is very difficult to attain with any existing computer. With machines costing less than around $150,000, it is impossible. Still, the cost of processor power, dollar per millions of instructions per second (MIPS) has been dropping steadily. By one estimate ,the power of microcomputer chips (the Intel 80386 to 80486 to Pentium and the Motorola's 68030, 68040 and now Power PC) has doubled every 18 months. If that trend continues, the power of desktop machines will equal that of current mainframes by the turn of the century and of supercomputers a few years thereafter.) In fact, some believe that the term MIPS will be replaced with giga instructions per second (GIPS, where giga is billion) by the year 2,000.)

The cost of memory has also been dropping since the introduction of desktop machines. Although RAM chips have stabilized at over the last year or so, new chips that contain large number of bits will likely begin a new downward spiral of costs. In any case, the cost of memory is not so high even today to be the prohibiting factor in creating VR systems.

With the increasing power of desktop computer chips and the introduction of floating point processors and graphics accelerators. the generation of photographic quality, 3D graphics has become easier. New breakthroughs in graphics generation may be on the way. For example at the University of North Carolina's Pixel-Planes systems has a processor dedicated to each individual pixel (picture element).

⊡ VR AND ARTIFICIAL INTELLIGENCE

In some ways, VR has replaced artificial intelligence (AI) as the goal of far-thinking computer engineers and dreamers. A true AI system had been defined as one in which you could type in questions and the typist would not be able to determine if the responder was a person of a computer. Similarly, the true measure of VR is whether the user is able to distinguish the VR from reality.

Will VR technology ever reach that goal? At present, no one knows the answer to that question. However, AI, without every truly reaching its original goal, has presented us with important computer solutions in terms of expert systems, optical character readers, and medical equipment.

VR also doesn't necessarily have to reach its ultimate goal of completely replacing reality in order to do human kind ultimate good. It has already provided us with entertainment that is nothing like we've ever seen before. Simulations are already saving companies and governments billions of dollars in training costs. And VR computer-aided design programs are helping architects see an entire house before it is built.

For anyone interested in the technology, perhaps the question shouldn't be how far will it go? Rather we should look at all the applications which become available at each step of the way towards creating true VR. Each of those applications should be evaluated as to its importance to human endeavor. The true measure of VR, in other words, may be what it actually spawns, not whether it meets a set or particular goals.

🔳 Who's Doing What

While many companies and institutions are experimenting with VR systems and developing prototypes, commercial products are still relatively rare. The reason for that is, while full-featured VR may be possible in terms of technology, the cost of such systems makes it less impractical for most applications.

To see what is actually being sold, let's look at the Meckler's 4th Annual VR Conference held in 1993. There were only 52 exhibitors. And while attandance almost doubled from the prior year, the total number of 4,000 attendees was nothing to crow about.

Four contributors won the Meckler's conference award:

1. SRI International won for its Sensory Science and Technology Center, which developed a VR simulator for NASA-Ames Research Center to train airport marshals to direct pilots as to where to taxi their planes. The simulation taught how to guide a four-engine jet aircraft.

2. Sense8 won for its WorldToolKit "world building" software. WorldToolKit, a leading VR software, integrates a simulation manager, a real-time renderer, an object manager, animation sequences, input sensors, and graphic display devices. Sense8 products work on a wide number of platforms and the company has developed strategic alliances with Crystal River Engineering, and Intel. We have included a demonstration of this remarkable software with this book. For more information, see Chapters 30 and 31.

3. Polhemus won for its Fastrak sensors, a motion tracking system, which provides tracking of multiple targets in real time. This is the device that allows VR systems to know the location and position of head, hand and, in some cases, the entire body.

4. Robert Jacobson, Ph.D., of Worldesign won for developing a theoretical foundation for VR systems.

Some of the commercially available products on display are also worth noting, since they point to the direction where VR is going:

◇ **Origin Instruments** displayed a lightweight, very simple display system. Called DynaSight Sensor, the system consists of a pair of clip-on sunglasses with an adhesive retroreflective dot stuck on the bridge. The DynaSight Sensor is placed onto of a display screen which contains a polarized window. The Sensor tracks the users head motion and changes 3D color image on the screen.

◇ **RPI, Inc**. displayed its $9,000, 3D, eyeglass-sized, head-mounted display. It uses high-resolution LCD panels. While the current models sport only 200x400-pixel resolution, the company hopes to increase the resolution to 1,000x2,000 shortly.

◇ **Silicon Graphics Inc.,** displayed its Onyx parallel-processing supercomputer, The machine, that cost from $200,000 to $600,000 can generate nine different images in nine stereo displays simultaneously.

◇ **SimGraphics, Inc**. displayed its "Facial Teleoperator Master Control" that allows for the development of VActors (Virtual Actors) . The product is a helmet with wire probes or spokes connecting the top of the helmet to various parts of the user's face. As the users talk or makes a facial expression, the wire probes sense the movement of the facial skin on your face. The data is transmitted to a computer that is able to tell a computer-generated face to make the same facial gesture. The company says the product will speed up production time for annimations.

◇ **The University of Pennsylvania** displayed its anthropomorphic data set that it developed over many years for NASA and U.S. Army. This figure, called Jack, has 71 segments, 70 joints, and a 17-vertebra spine. Te university also provides software to assist in the positioning of Jack. The software allows for voice input such as "turn left," or "raise your arms." The software runs on Silicon Graphics Workstations.

◇ **Tier 1, N-Vision, and Liquid Image** all had their head-mounted displays on display. They are now designed to take most of the weight off the user's nose.

◇ **Viewpoint Animation Engineering, Inc.** was hawking hundreds of well-detailed, scanned, 3-D images of animals and commercial objects such as computers, owls, a skull, and a printer. Each image (which range from $100 to $500) is segmented so VR developers can use a rendering program to apply colors and textures to them. The company will supply the images in virtually any graphics program format.

VR Business

According to a workshop entitled "Investment Perspectives" held at the above meeting, an estimated $50 million has been spent so far on nonmilitary VR. Most venture capitalists at the meeting said that while VR has the potential of providing a 2500% return over three to five years, they are holding back before jumping in with both feet.

Since investors believe that the entertainment industry will lead the commercial VR markets, many are waiting to see if entertainment VR takes off as many hope. Next, these investors will look into other areas of promise: science, finance, education, manufacturing, medicine, and military applications.

Still, a number of brave companies are putting their money with their entertainment eyes. W Industries, based in Leicester, England, sold around 300 of its Virtually machines, costing from $32,500 to about $125,000 apiece, to amusement arcades in 17 countries in 1993. (The company's five year goal is to have half its profits coming from VR at the end of that period.)

Sphere, Inc., a computer-games maker, has created a new division called CyberStudio, which sells software for VR entertainment systems. Electronic Arts, another games maker, recently formed a joint venture with Matsushita, Time Warner, and AT&T. Their plan is to design and build VR entertainment systems. And Virtual World Entertainment, which operates VR entertainment centers in the U.S. and Japan, was recently bought by an investment firm Shamrock, which is associated with the Disney family.

While many large companies are reluctant to tip their hand about VR investments, news reports abound with tentative or even more than tentative steps. For example, Chrysler and IBM are reportedly working together on virtual cars that will speed up the design process. Boeing is already using VR models to help in the design of tunnels and interiors of it airplanes. British Aerospace plans to use VR data to fighter pilots.

Autodesk says it recently sold a workstation to a footwear manufacturer that plans to create VR shoes to help in the design and marketing process. Autodesk recently released development software to allow users to write CAD applications for engineers, and architects. Called Cyberspace Developer Kit, and selling for $2,500, is touted as "complete toolset for 3-D visualization and simulation."

Division (Bristol, England) is working with the University of York, IBM and Glaxo to develop models of molecules in order to learn how they fit together.

On the personal computer and workstation arena, area, Apple, IBM, Sun, and Silicon Graphics are also investing in VR R&D.

Japanese corporations have targeted VR as a key technology of the future. Many Japanese firms have stated publicly that they see VR as a way to meet the needs of its customers—from purchasers of vehicles to consumer electronics.

Sony is investing heavily in VR entertainment systems. Other Japanese firms, including Matsushita, Toshiba, and Fujitsu are working on commercial VR systems for use in design and marketing and other business applications.

At the University of Tokyo, researchers have set up a well-stocked laboratory to experiment with VR technology. The lab is developing high-resolution goggles, sophisticated sound systems, and software that can manipulate 3D graphics.

At the Fujitsu Human Interface Laboratory in Kawasaki, Japan, researchers are immersing VR users in a fishbowl populated with mushroom-shaped forms and behemoths, all of which can be controlled with hand gestures.

While the fishbowl program is fun for those who get to use it, the more important issue is that the process of programming the four computers which control it is teaching engineers how to create viable VR applications.

Augmented Reality

Augmented reality differs from virtual reality (VR) in that it doesn't attempt to replicate the real world but rather to superimposes itself on it. So, instead of obscuring the real world, these systems attempt to illuminate it. They do this by displaying to the user instructions, diagrams, or other graphics, but all the time allowing him or her to see the real world. Virtual reality systems attempt to replace as many of the user's experience of the real world with computer generated graphics, sound, and touch.

Accordingly, augmented reality systems require special glasses or headsets which have a see-through (or earphone with a hear-through) display. In fact, the first concept of the head-mounted display (HMD) was of a see-through model. Ivan Sutherland, a VR pioneer, described an HMD in which each eye viewed a miniature CRT, that displayed synthesized graphics. Using an optical beam splitter, the human-produced graphics were merged with real-world images. Since then, other technologies for see-through vision were developed. One method is a transparent LCD that allows the user to see a virtual image and then adjust the eye focus and look beyond it to the real world image.

Private Eye, another method used by Reflection Technology's, Inc., is a miniature TV screen mounted on a headset. This system allows you to direct the display downward and use a mirror beam splitter. By looking through the beam splitter, the user sees a combined image of a virtual and a real world. Augmented reality is normally used to assist in the performance of a task in the real world. It might highlight certain objects, add arrows or schematics, or display balloon-type instructions. Say a worker is tasked with the job of drilling a screw in a particular location in a component part. He or she can line up the edges of the virtual image with the edge of the part and use virtual guides to position the screw onto the part.

If a worker has to perform a number of activities that require instructions that may be difficult to memorize, the augmented reality system can display floating help screens. Surgeons, too, can use augmented reality systems. In a number of trials, doctors have superimposed images from X-rays or from magnetic resonance imaging machines onto the patient's body. The result is a window on the patient. This window allows the surgeon to see inside the patient for the purpose of performing traditional or endoscopic surgery.

An interesting augmented reality system was recently developed at the Columbia University Computer Science Department, where researchers developed a system to assist end-user maintenance for a laser printer. This testbed provided information on relatively straightforward operations, such as refilling the paper tray and replacing the toner cartridge. However, once this simple augmented reality system is perfected, researchers plan to develop systems for more complex tasks.

The system displays diagrams and instructions which users can superimpose on the real-world view of the laser printer. The advantage is that it eliminates the need to shift one's gaze back and forth from the manual to the printer. It also eliminates the difficulties involved in translating line drawings in a manual to the object in the real world. The project is called Knowledge-Based Augmented Reality for Maintenance Assistance (KARMA). The system was developed using what is called by VR and augmented reality engineers "knowledge-based graphics." Specifically, KARMA is based on Intent-Based Illustration System (IBIS), a rule-based system for creating illustrations.

IBIS is built by specifying a list of "communicative goals," each of which specifies something the picture is to accomplish. For example, the goal of one diagram may be to show a property of an object. Since the user's viewpoint is constantly changing, IBIS continuously examines the illustration and alters it in order to reach the illustration's communicative goals. For example, if an object is obscured when you install the toner cartridge, IBIS can decide not to render the obscured object at all, to render it as partially transparent, or to use a cutaway view.

To show how rule-bases graphics works, let's look at the instructions for use of the paper tray. The design rule specifies the use of a "highlight" strategy. The style rule indicates that if the tray is within the view volume, it should be marked for rendering. This entails highlighting it with solid lines and labeling it. If the tray is completely within the view volume, a text label identifying it appears at the tray's center. If it is not completely within the view volume, the label is contained within a balloon-type instruction filed with a line pointing to the tray's center. If the tray is only partly in the view volume, the obscured part is highlighted with a dotted line.

In order to illustrate an action, the system often implements a "move strategy." The move strategy causes a moving arrow to depict the tray's trajectory. The illustration of a completed action is accomplished by a "ghost style" strategy, which depicts the component's position after a desired action is taken. In this strategy, the component in the desired position is depicted using double dotted lines. For example, the ghost style is used to indicate how to pull up the lid's lever and then open the lid fully.

Besides programming the system on different styles of displays, the researchers had two other challenges:

◈   The graphical image had to change in response to the user's head motion.

◈   Each image had to be registered correctly with the real world object it was illustrating.

To accomplish these goals, the researcher employed trackers that measured head position and orientation and trackers that sensed the presence, position, and orientation of objects on the laser printer.

The head and object servers, which receive data from the respective trackers, maintain the integrity of the object and head motion information. They then edit the display list so that the display is appropriate for the real-world head and object conditions. (Each object server continually edits the position and orientation information associated with its object. The head server updates the display list which controls the viewing specifications.)

In operation, the program creates its augmented reality display to satisfy the initial set of goals. Next, it uses its evaluators to determine if the goals have changed or if the head or object trackers have sensed a change in orientation or position. Then, it determines if a new graphical image is needed to satisfy the requirements of the changing situation. Finally, it replaces the graphical image (if necessary).

In order to maintain real-time alterations to the augmented reality world, the system uses multiple processors. The head server tells the display server when to render each image. However, the head server, which merely has to determine head location and orientation, has a lighter task than the display server, which has to render the image. Accordingly, researches had to find a way to avoid bottlenecks. They did this by having the head server, after it transmits data for the current frame to the display server, pause until the display server sends a message that the frame was rendered.

▣ IMAGE REGISTRATION

Registering the augmented reality image with the real-world image requires actions by the user. First, the position the user will be working has to be known by the system. Next, the user has to physically adjust the display on his or her head. Finally, he or she has to adjust his focus and viewing angle so that the virtual object corresponds with the real-world object.

Another problem was related to shortcomings in the Private Eye viewer. A small portion of the display may be sometimes obscured from the viewer. In order to compensate for that difficulty, the researchers had to request that each user first adjust the size and position of a rectangle frame in the viewer until it is large as possible. The dimensions of that area are communicated to the program, which recognizes it as a "safe area" within which all displayed graphics will be visible.

Another problem was the need to constantly manually change Private Eyes focal length. Since KARMA's graphics are overlaid on objects close to the viewer, relatively short changes in distance require changes in the viewer's focus controls. KARMA is, of course, only a first step. Its researchers point to a number of areas that have to be studied further before a commercial augmented reality systems such as KARMA is viable:

◇   The development of a model of how performance will be affected by different 3D illustrations.

◇   Support for visible-line and visible-surface determination. This would determine how a projected line fragment should be rendered, based on the surfaces that obscure it.

◇   To study how graphics in combination with speech and nonspeech audio can be used to instruct the user.

◇   The development of see-through displays that are far smaller and lighter, have higher resolutions, and have a wider field of view.

◇   Finally, systems need more accurate and less cumbersome tracking mechanisms. Tracking is much more difficult with augmented reality than in VR systems primarily because alignment is essential. A tracker must therefore be accurate to a tiny fraction of a degree.

◇   Lag time also has to be very low. In a VR system lag time is a primary problem of illusion. To feel the full impact of the virtual world (to suspend disbelief), response time has to approach zero. But the consequences of slower response time is merely lowered verisimilitude or, at worst, a bit of dizziness. In an augmented reality system, any delay may result in a component part or other real world object being misidentified. Or the instructions meant for a previous real world object may cause the user to treat the new real world object incorrectly.

◇   The system has to be able to track the user as well as send images over a long range. With VR systems, the illusion of movement can be accomplished by changing the image. Users fly miles in virtual worlds while their real bodies remain confined in a small area that is easy to track. In an augmented reality system, the user locomotes by walking.

One major difficulty augmented reality systems is that the user remains in control much more so than in VR systems. In VR, the processor and graphics engine is always in complete control of what the user sees. The user can change the view only by moving within the virtual world housed in the program. With augmented reality, the user is able to see the real world, which is totally out of the control of the program. In augmented reality, for example, the user may change the viewing angle or remove or install components. Each of these actions requires a corresponding change in the augmented reality image the user sees.

VR systems also achieve their communicative goals by itself. Everything they need to convey to the user is accomplished though the display. Augmented reality, on the other hand, requires activity by the user. For example, if the system needs to specify some detail on an object that is not in the user's range of filed, the system has to instruct the user how to find and remove the needed object.

Artificial Intelligence

Artificial intelligence (AI) has as its goal the creation of machines that can think and act like inelegant humans. There are a number of similarities between AI and VR. The most obvious of which is that VR has taken over from AI as the technology sparking the most media attention. In the 1980s, any journalist who wanted to dazzle his or her audience with what computers will be able to do in the near future described a system that incorporated AI. The journalist would depict robots who could do housework, help children with homework, mow the lawn, and fix the car. Expert systems would allow a single expert, say in a rare form of surgery or in a particular period of history, to send his or her "brain," an expert system that contained his or her knowledge, all over the world. Vision systems would be able to interpret real-world events and summarize the scene for the visually impaired or for military intelligence officers. And natural language systems would allow computers to understand human language when typed or spoken and would be able to summarize news events.

By the late eighties, much of the general population grew tired of hearing about artificial intelligence. One of the reasons may have been that the systems, when developed, were not quite as fascinating or robust as the general media accounts suggested they would be. Expert systems became available for everyone from doctors to parents. But they were limited-domain systems. The all-purpose problem solver or all-purpose expert system has yet to be created. In fact some so-called expert systems are so low-tech that they are not easier to use or more knowledgeable than a good reference book. Robots abound in industry and upscale toy stores. But they can't do housework or work in unrestricted construction sites.

By the 1990s, reporters began looking to VR as a way to fascinate their readers with the wonders of technology. In film and magazines, systems in which someone could build a dream and then enter into it drew the imagination of a generation that began its adult life experimenting with psychedelic drugs and is now desperately trying to prevent their children from doing the same. Certainly, AI has not failed. But in terms of general expectations, what John and Mary Q. Public hopes to see from AI systems, it has failed.

The connection between AI and VR is also a curious one. While VR tries to take fantasy and computer graphics, and expand them so that they replaces reality; AI tries to take something that's real and make it artificial. VR takes the artificial and tries to make it real.

Another connection between AI and VR is that many of the technologies developed for AI systems are now, or may soon be, incorporated into VR. Speech recognition is a perfect example. Developed as an interface to expert systems, speech recognition will allow users to ask their computers questions just as they might ask a doctor or their professor a question.

By and large speech recognition is now on the brink of being truly functional. Continuous speech and user-independent systems are now commercially available. These systems will soon allow users to communicate with their VR systems in a more natural way than by using a keyboard.

Robotics is another example. With telepresence a user can control a robot that may be in an environment miles away. Since the user can see, and more importantly for VR, feel what the robot is experiencing, telepresence may be considered a branch of VR. Much of the early telepresence work has been developed by AI engineers.

WHAT CAN AI OFFER TO FUTURE VR PROJECTS?

Peter Williams, a well-known VR expert, sees other uses of AI technology in VR systems. He suggests using expert system to determine which objects have to be created in the virtual world at any given time. This expert system may reside in either an on-line or off-line workstation. The expert system could also be used to predict when the VR system will be overloaded with images. The system may thus experience rendering bottle-necks causing the system to fall behind a real-time requirement. To do this, the system would have to consider a wide number of dynamic variables including animation density and visible geometry limits.

In a prototype expert system for VR, Williams has developed rules that examine the VR environment off-line. It attempts to determine overload based on the expected usage. New iterations of the project will integrate the knowledge base into the on-line VR application itself.

Expert systems might also be incorporated in the process of choosing how to populate the VR environment, always being mindful of the processing power available. For example, you can create trees in your modeling and rendering packages. Then ask the expert system to scatter those threes across the landscape. The system then would place trees on every grassy area. But the number of trees would be based on how much memory and CPU power is available. And trees that are closer to the user would be rendered in more complex ways than those which are further away.

Expert systems may also be employed in an attempt to predict latency on a real-time basis. Since that prediction has to be based on usage of the root database as well as the rendered output, fuzzy logic techniques—an AI discipline—might be employed.

VIRTUAL TURING TEST

Artificial intelligence can be used to assist in the process of creating VR systems. But VR researcher David Barberi suggests one way in which VR can be used to benefit artificial intelligence by testing systems to determine if they are truly artificially intelligent.

According to Barberi, VR can be used to enhance the famous Turing Test. In 1950, artificial intelligence pioneer Alan Turing proposed the following as a test for programs to determine if they are worthy to bear the name "artificial intelligence." The test is based on the assumption that human possess intelligence. Therefore, if a human can't tell if the subject he or she is interacting with is human or machine, then the subject is intelligent.

For this test, the human judge sits at a computer terminal and types questions to the subject. The questions can be on any subject, not just on subjects predetermined ahead of time. By evaluating how the subject answers the questions, the judge then must determine if he or she is communicating with a computer or a human. If the human judge (or judges) guess wrong at least half the time, the machine in question is artificially intelligent.

Barberi has suggested a means of applying VR to the Turing test. Here are the steps for the "Barberi" VR test for AI. (Barberi prefers to call it the "Virtual Turing Test") Create a completely immersive virtual world for the judge and the subject (the computer being tested or the human). The world will contain virtual objects—viewed from an HMD or other means.

The judge interacts with the virtual world in the normal way: seeing, feeling, and hearing through various VR devices. The judge can change his or her viewpoint by head rotation. walking or the common VR finger pointing method..

While the actual subject is either a human or a machine, in either case, the judge sees only a computer generated image. this may be a computer graphic image of a human who is in another location. Through position tracking devices, every action of the human is replicated in real time by the computer graphic. When the subject talks, the sound is digitized and, to the judge, appears to originate from the mouth of the subject's virtual copy.

Alternatively, the computer graphic may be controlled entirely by an artificial intelligence computer. As in the original Turing Test, the judge tests the subject to determine if it is human or machine. However, unlike the original Test, this new enhanced version allows the judge to physically interact with the subject. For example, the judge can reach over to the subject and attempt to hit it on the head. The image would then, presumably, attempt to move out of the way.

The judge would base his or her decision on how well the computer image handles three basic functions: visual and audible communications, correct biomechanical movement, and awareness of its environment. Barberi points out that the last of these items is the easiest for current VR systems to accomplish. Since the computer is generating the virtual world, it knows where every object in it is located.

However, the computer would have to be careful not to give the computer-generated image more information than it should have. For example, if the judge picks up a book without the subject viewing the action and then holds the book behind his or her back, the computer should not be able to know what is hiding behind the judge. If the judge asks, "What do I have in my hands." and the computer image answers "a book," the judge might surmise the subject is the computer.

Correct biomechanical movement, while not so simple to determine as awareness of the environment, can also be created using today's VR technology. The system would have to have precise knowledge about how humans are able to move. The simulation would have to scrupulously follow the confines of the human body (e.g., by not bending in ways that real humans cannot bend.) it would also have to be limited by physical reality. (It should not be able to disappear, for example.)

The hardest part of the test would be the subject's ability to have comprehensive communications with the judge. Communications would not only require spoken language, a tough enough task, but also unspoken cues and body language. The system would have to have complete understanding of such things as hand gestures, eye movement, facial expressions, and even involuntary factors such as blushing.

Barberi concludes that this Virtual Turing Test is an improvement over the original test in two ways.

◇   It replaces the limited communications, which was confined to typing in the original test, to one in which the judge and subject cohabit a more comprehensive and natural environment.

◇   The judge can base his or her decision not only on the subject's typed words, but on spoken speech, non-verbal cues, and body language.

Despite these enhancement, the Virtual Turing Test maintains the spirit of the original Turing Test. The human judge still has to use his or her intelligence to test the subject. The judge has no way of telling if the subject is human or not other than by interacting with it. And most importantly, the goals of the two tests are the same: to test a simulation of human action to determine if it is real enough to fool a human judge.

Cave Dwellers

The CAVE is a room-sized cube surrounded by display screens, which surround the viewer. CAVE is acronym (of some sort) for Audio-Visual Experience Automatic Virtual EnvironmentÑa type of VR interface that eliminates the need for special glasses or earphones. In its simplest form, a CAVE system is similar to the OMNIMAX surround theaters or some flight simulators that project images on four walls. More sophisticated versions of CAVE combine the display with head- and body-tracking devices, which control the perspective and images that appear on the display screens. The Electronic Visualization Laboratory at the University of Illinois at Chicago (UIC) has developed an experimental CAVE system. Its current implementation uses up to five screens: three walls, a ceiling, and a floor.

Below are some of the more interesting implementations of CAVE :

◇ Regional-Scale Weather in Three Dimensions—A three-dimensional display of weather systems over a region of North America.

◇ **Graphical Planning for Brain Surgery**—It projects three-dimensional models from MR.-derived images directly onto the patient.

◇ **The Visible Embryo**—It takes the viewer on a "trip through a human fetus."

◇ **Fractal Exploratorium**—It allows viewers to investigate chaotic forms (fractals) from different perspectives.

◇ **Bio Modeling**—An interactive modeling of biological macromolecules.

◇ **The Evolving Universe of Galaxies and Stars**—It uses a database of images as well as real-time computations from a remote CRAY to allow users to "fly" or to travel through an evolving universe .

In order to create an immersive CAVE environment, researchers at UIC have four primary goals:

1. Computation of viewer-centered perspective projections
2. Deployment of viewer tracking equipment
3. Synchronization of displays
4. Overcoming any resulting projector and tracking limitations.

⬡ VIEWER-CENTERED PERSPECTIVE

The CAVE requires special perspective projections to simulate viewer-centered perspective. These projections are offset to simulate stereo, and thus require knowledge of the viewer's orientation. The viewer-centered perspective is accomplished through the use of an "off-axis perspective projection." The simplest method of attaining off-axis perspective is to begin with a standard on-axis perspective. Next, all points are sheared in a direction parallel to the projection plane. Finally, points are scaled along the axis perpendicular to the projection plane.

VIEWER TRACKING EQUIPMENT

Information about the position of the viewer's head is necessary so that the image can be adjusted if the user decides to tilt his or her head. If the image doesn't adjust to head rotation, not only will the illusion of reality be lost, but the stereoscopic effect may be lost or inverted (depending on the degree of rotation). Knowledge about the position of the viewer's eyes is needed to ensure that the stereo disparities line up at the edges where two projection planes meet. The position and orientation of the user's head was tracked using a 3SPACE Polhemus "Isotrack" sensor, whose transmitter is mounted on the StereoGraphics glasses. Like all tracking systems, this system results in some time delay or lag when the user moves quickly. The lab is currently working on extrapolation techniques in an effort to reduce the interactive delays.

CAVE vs HMD-BASED VR SYSTEMS

While CAVE systems require a lot more space to see than HMD-based VR systems, they do offer a number of advantages, such as:

- ◈ Field of view
- ◈ Panorama
- ◈ Representation of the user
- ◈ Intrusiveness
- ◈ Looking around objects.
- ◈ Image refinement
- ◈ Multiple users

FIELD OF VIEW

The field of view is the area the user can see without moving his or her head. The field of view of cathode-ray tube (CRT) based VR systems are based on the size of the screen and viewer's distance from the screen. For example, a 19-inch diagonal CRT viewed from a distance of 18 inches will produces a 45 degrees field of view. Cinerama and IMAX theaters also have varied fields of view based on the size of the screen and the distance of the viewer from the screen. However, because the screens are so large, they provide relatively wide fields of view compared to CRT screens. HMDs have fixed fields of view which are listed in the manufacturer's specifications. Most HMDs have fields of view which range from 100 to 140 degrees. The field of view of the CAVE display—all the screens combined—is 360 degrees. (Of course the field of view for each screen varies in a similar fashion as does field of view of CRTs or large screen theaters.)

PANORAMA

While field of view is the total image the view can see without moving his or her head, panorama is the total image which can be viewed with head movement. CRTs normally provide no panoramic view of the VR scene. For that reason they are often in used "Windows on the World, " VR systems in which the user seems to peer at the virtual world through a window.

In theory, HMDs provide complete panoramic view. However, in practice because there is normally a lag time between head movement and a change in the image, users have to move very slowly and smoothly to maintain the illusion of seeing a real world panorama. Since CAVE systems display all the views simultaneously, if the user pivots there will be no need for a change in the view. In that way, the panaromic view is preserved. In some cases, however, the user may take a step at the same time as he or she pivots. The screen image will have to adjust to the new perspective. CAVE systems will then experience the same delay problems as with HMDs. However, because the display is normally required to change less than the view of a HMD, the lag time is often not as noticeable.

REPRESENTATION OF THE USER

Many VR systems include a representation of the user or users in the display. For example, an image of the user's hand may appear in front of his or her face. In a complete immersive HMD-based VR systems, users would be able to look down and see their feet or view other body parts. In order to accomplish this, the system has to have detailed body-part tracking—not merely head tracking or head and arms tracking—capabilities. While this technology is available, the processing time for tracking as well as rendering makes such systems difficult to develop.

In CAVE environments (as well as CRT-based WoW environments) the user can see his or her real hand and feet. Therefore the need to track and render body parts is eliminated. Of course there are downsides to this approach. For example, the body part can obscure any physical object in the virtual world even if that object is closer to the user than the body part. .

INTRUSIVENESS

Intrusiveness of a VR system indicates the extent to which it isolates the user from his or her real senses. HMD-based systems, which block the view of the real world with LCD screens, are highly intrusive. Some augmented reality systems use HMDs that provide a transparent display through which the user can see the virtual world superimposed on the real world. While these augmented reality systems are less intrusive than standard VR, the also isolate the user to a great extent. Some users report that they feel uncomfortable or even become slightly ill after spending extended periods in immersive VR systems. The CAVE interfaces are completely non-intrusive. In these environments, the viewer's senses has equal access to the real and the virtual worlds.

LOOKING AROUND OBJECTS.

Different VR viewing technologies vary greatly in their ability to allow users to move around an object in order to view it from different perspectives. HMDs are best at providing this ability. Since the user has no view of the real world with most HMDs, the optical device can display any view of any object at any time.

CRT-based WoW systems provide only very limited ability to look around an object. Using head tracking devices, they can allow a user to move around the screen, viewing different perspectives as his or her change the viewing angle to the screen. But when a CRT screen is viewed from the side, the visible area becomes much smaller. CAVE has poor look-around capabilities. Its look-around capabilities only works for distant objects.

IMAGE REFINEMENT

In order for VR systems to keep up with user movement, many systems use a combination of coarse and fine modes. When the user is in motion, the course model, which requires less processing time, is employed. Using a coarse mode reduces lag time at the expense of resolution. As the user remains stationary, the image gradually becomes finer. HMD requires the user to remain still for the refinement process to commence. The CAVE interfaces merely require that the viewer's location remain fixed; the head location can change.

MULTIPLE USERS

Many VR applications would benefit from having the ability to include two or more users in the virtual world. The benefits to entertainment VR of multi-user or multi-player systems are obvious. But serious applications can benefit as well. Surgeons using VR for endoscopic surgery will find it easier to collaborate if the system allow the entire surgical team to enter the virtual environment. And trainees who are learning to use machinery that in the real world requires more than one operator will find a multi-user VR simulation closer to reality.

HMDs do allow for multi-users. But the cost in processing time and resources is high. In CAVE VR systems, all viewers who can fit in the room are able to view the display. The problem with CAVE systems for multi-users however is that giving each user his or her own perspective is difficult. One solution is to use shuttered glasses. Each user would see the screen only when his or her perspective is depicted on it. So if there are two users, each will see the screen 1/2 of the time. If there are ten users, each would see it 1/10th of the time. For this reason, CAVE systems are limited in how many users can experience the VR world without the image becoming too choppy.

Virtual
Hazards

Motion illness is a common malady not only among travelers in the real world but those in virtual worlds as well. Many times, users who spend more than a half an hour wearing an HMD complain of eyestrain, headaches, or dizziness.

As VR research moved into the commercial arena and workers use systems for longer periods of time, a new phenomena, "simulation sickness," is being identified. Whether or not a participants experiences simulation sickness and the extent of the symptoms seems to depend on the length of time in the simulation, how immersive the system is, and the quality of the VR experience. Also, simulation sickness occurs most often when the VR system is motion oriented and less often when the 3D image is generally non-moving.

So far, few studies have scientifically studied the phenomena. So the reports are anecdotal and subjective. Whether the discomfort comes from merely wearing a heavy apparatus on the head, viewing a stereoscopic display, experiencing lag time, or some other reason is unknown.

Many researchers insist the primary cause of simulation sickness is that the body experiences a delay from the time it responds to a stimuli and the time the virtual world reacts to that response (latency period or lag time).

A common example is when a user rotates his or her head, there is usually a split second delay before the corresponding image appears on the display.

At least one study, however, provides initial evidence that there may be some cause and effect relationship between viewing stereoscopic displays and medical problems. Researchers at the University of Edinburgh asked 20 young adults to "ride" a stationary bicycle through a virtual country while viewing the scenery through a stereoscopic display. After 10 minutes of light exercise, the subjects were tested for distance vision, binocular fusion, and convergence. Over thirty percent of the participants performed worse on those tests than on similar tests performed before the bicycle ride. Additionally, over half the participants reported symptoms of headaches or blurred vision.

The study speculates that the primary reason for the problem is the difference between the image focal depth and the actual distance from eye to the display. Normally, when one views a close-up image, the eyes converge, rotating inward slightly. The opposite happens when one views a far away image: the eyes diverge. With stereoscopic display, the eyes want to converge to accommodate the short distance. But the focal plane of the display is long. Accordingly the eyes have to strain to diverge when it normally would converge. One solution to this problem would be to use monoscopic HMDs for all applications where stereoscopic is not absolutely necessary and for all applications in which the participants will be viewing the virtual world for long periods of time.

Olaf H. Kelle at the University of Wuppertal, Germany, has been experimenting with different focal depths of stereoscopic displays. He has reported that when the focal depth is set at 3 mm only 10% of his users reported eye strain.

Another idea is to have users regularly remove the HMD to adjust their focal depth and to blink a few times. Actually, the same precaution is often suggested to heavy users of any video display terminals (VDTs). Studies have shown that when viewing a monitor for a long period of time, subjects blink less than when they view the natural world.

It is still too early to know how pervasive a problem this will be. For the present the vast majority of VR experiences are short or confined to entertainment where a bit of vertigo is part of the fun and excitement. However people who are using VR to in their daily jobs: stock brokers, engineers, architects, will not want to have to feel dizzy each time they don an HMD,

Further research on this will be necessary to ensure that VR doesn't become a new workplace hazard.

Virtual Vision

VR systems differ in the kind of display they provide users. Some systems' window on the world (WOW) use a simple monitor. Others, such as CAVE systems, project the image onto an entire wall. But the majority of VR systems, and all immersive VR systems, provide users with vision through a head mounted device (HMD).

▣ HEAD MOUNTED DISPLAYS

Most HMDs use two displays, eyeglass-sized screens, to offer stereoscopic imaging. In a few cases they use a single large display. At present, most HMDs suffer from low resolution, narrow range of field, poor or nonexistent stereoscopic vision, general awkwardness, and relatively high cost. But improvement in all those areas is at hand.

Possibly one of the most important factors that will bring VR out of the laboratory and into homes and offices is cost. Although a few low-cost HMDs now sell for as low as $1,500, higher resolution devices, those needed for commercial and scientific applications, cost over $75,000. Accordingly, most companies that bring in VR systems will want the expensive HMDs to be shared among users. This may go against the grain of today's typical computer user. Shared systems were fully accepted just a few years ago, but the revolution in personalcomputers has fostered a strongly held paradigm of one-person-one machine. Few business people will be interested in relying on a system that they have to log on to and can use at only specific times in the day.

Now, as the number of HMD makers increases, the competition is beginning to drive prices down. Firms are beginning to recover their research and development costs incurred from their earlier models, and new versions are becoming less expensive. In some models, though, lower cost is being made possible by using less expensive material. Sega, for example, says it will develop an HMD for home use that will cost between $500 and $1,000.

Those lower resolution devices, of course, will not meet the needs of architects or others who need more than cartoon-looking images. The price of the $90,000 HMDs, on the other hand, will gradually drop, but still won't be found in many homes providing the display for video games. Most experts think that VR users will fall into three broad categories:

1. Home based products, at the low end, may well sell for $200 to $300 but will provide resolution similar to that on arcade video games.

2. The middle level market will be dominated by HMDs that cost from about $1,500 to $15,000 and will be used for those who need good representation of images but do not necessarily need to have users believe they are viewing a real world. Users of these HMDs will include architects and product designers who want "walk-though" capability to see how interior elements fit together; doctors viewing the results of X rays, sonograms, or lab tests; and researchers wanting to view molecular structure from all angles.

3. High end HMDs, which will offer 1,024 by 1,280 VGA resolution will be used primarily by the military to provide realistic simulations. These will cost over $75,000.

New HMDs have improved image quality and lowered cost by providing color images from monochrome CRTs.

The color wheel and the liquid crystal shutter rotate red, green, and blue filters between the display and the optics. The CRT display converts the standard NTSC composite input signal into separate red, green, and blue fields, which, when synchronized with the filters, provide a color image.

Improvements in field of view is also on the way. Older HMDs offered only 40 degrees of view. New models offer fields of view as wide as 112 degrees. Of course, the wider the field of view, the higher the cost.

Although HMDs siill mess up your hair when you put them on, they are becoming more comfortable. Older models weighed in at about 6 pounds compared to the trim 3 ounces of some newer versions.

One way the HMDs were able to lower their poundage is through the use of smaller, lighter LCD displays. Some manufactures' displays have dropped in size from about 2 inches to a half an inch.

The smaller LCDs allow manufactures to use less material in their HMDs. Improved design also has lowered the bulk as have the use of lightweight composite material. This minimal-material design also makes it much easier to put or remove the HMD. Some models go a step further in providing hinges or pivoting devices that allow user to flip the helmet up affording an escape from virtual reality without removing the helmet.

ADJUSTABILITY

Because mass produced HMDs have to fit so many different sizes and shapes of heads, there is a need for adjustability. Most current models offer at least some degree of control over the fit. Many have knobs on the side that allow the user to control the size of the interior of the helmet. Besides the shape of the helmet, another important adjustment is the focal length of the lens and the distance between the two lenses. All new HMDs provide knobs or push buttons for these adjustments.

At least one HMD model has a detachable headband that allows individual users to own their own headband while sharing the HMD. Because the headband is adjustable, this method eliminates the need to readjust the HMD each time it passed from user to user. It also eliminates the hygienic objection of wearing something that has been on another person's head.

None of those design features, however, eliminates the problem of messing one's hair, a major objection for people who have to put on and take off their HMD many times during the day. Some HMDs eliminate the need for users to put on and take off the device by providing "view-through" capability. This enables users to see the real world when there no image is being displayed on the eyepiece. Some systems use a transparent display enabling users to toggle between virtual and real worlds by focusing their eyes. Unfortunately, at present, all models that provide his view-thorough capability do so at the expense of resolution—the virtual display appears less vivid and somewhat faded.

Still the view-through models are needed for augmented reality, where the virtual world complements the real world rather than replaces it. In such a system, a surgeon can overlay an X ray image onto the skin of a patient thus providing what appears to be a window into the patient's body.

Although certainly high-end HMDs provide a view that suggests reality to the user, there are problems with the goal of creating systems whose view appears real. Just as artificial intelligence systems are no match for the human brain, HMDs are no match for the human eye. One a clear day, the human eye can discern objects less than one inch 100 yards away. Even the best LCD displays currently offer resolutions of less than one-tenth that. The resolution of HMDs will, of course, improve, but the technology itself has limits. LCDs are composed of individual picture elements (pixels), tiny dark, light, or colored dots on a piece of plastic or glass. No matter how many pixels you squeeze into the small area in the HMD, the image cannot be as clear as that in a real world, made up of complete shapes. Additionally, the optics required to display a large field of view (typically 180-degree-by-120-degree) exaggerates the pixels, making all images appear textured.

Cathode-ray tube (CRT) screens, which are similar to the technology of standard computer monitors, provide better resolution. A good deal of work has been done to miniaturize them, and there are now HMDs that sport CRT eye pieces. But even these cannot reach the resolution afforded by the human eye. By one estimate, a CRT screen can at best discern an image 3 1/2 inches at 100 yards.

A final problem is that even if a display device could be made with the resolution approaching that of the human eye, the computer may not be able to keep up. Creating real-time computer images at current resolutions is difficult for today's computers. Higher resolution devices will take an even heavier toll on processors, to say nothing about I/O and storage devices.

Although there are many hurdles that VR developers will have to overcome, many of them relate to one problem: multimedia files are extremely large. One minute of 8-bit digitized monaural sound, for example, requires 660K. CD-quality, 16-bit stereo eats up 11M a minute. Video is even worse. In order to match television-quality video, a monitor would have to display full-screen 640 x 480 resolution images at 30 frames per second (FPS). Each second of display requires a 27.6M file.

The large file size generates problems in three areas: storing the data, moving the data, and processing the data. Currently, most VR developers try to solve the problem by reducing file size in some way. This necessarily requires some sacrifice. One way to reduce file size is to reduce the image size. This, of course, is not possible in immersive VR that uses HMDs, but it can be used for window on the world systems. A second way to limit file size is to decrease the frames per second rate. To a certain extent this is a reasonable solution. After all, the European television standard, PAL displays only 25 FPS. But even at that rate, a minute of video uses almost 1.4G. Once the display falls much below 23 or 24 FPS, a fast-moving object may appear jerky, like in an early Charlie Chaplin movie.

A final way to reduce the file size is to reduce color pitch. Photographic quality images require so called "true color" or 24-bit color. These systems, which require 24 bits to define each pixel, offers millions of colors. By limiting the display to 256 colors, the image needs only 8 bits per pixel. Unfortunately, 8-bit color usually gives a cartoon-like look to the display.

Various hardware solutions are being developed to address the file size challenge. One of them is merely evolutionary. The cost of DASD is dropping. High capacity, high-speed drives now offer storage for less than one dollar a megabyte. So even multiple gigabyte drives are within reach of many users.

New bus standards, such as Intel's Peripheral Component Interconnect (PCI) and VL-Bus—a peripheral interface standard established by the Video Electronics Standards Association (VESA)—enable data to move around the computer and peripherals faster. The bus is the way data is moved around internal components and peripherals. Older bus standards, such as Industry Standard Architecture (ISA), Micro Channel Architecture (MCA), and Extended Industry Standard Architecture (EISA) expansion buses, were not intended to handle large multimedia files, and VR applications tend to overwhelm them.

IBM's original PC, released in 1981, used an 8-bit 4.77 MHz bus. That progressed to the AT's 16-bit 8 MHz bus. Now called the ISA bus, the AT's bus provides a throughput between 4 and 8 megabytes per second (MBps). MCA and EISA are considered advanced buses because they allow short bursts as high as 33 MBps with EISA and potentially faster with some MCA-based buses But they have trouble handling sustained periods of large throughput, something that would be necessary in many VR systems.

To prevent a bottleneck, PC developers hooked the graphics display control circuitry directly onto the CPU's local bus. This solved the throughput problem. But local buses were typically based on a proprietary system, that could only be purchased from a specific vendor.

In 1993, VL-Bus, a peripherals interface standard was established by the Video Electronics Standards Association (VESA). Although the VL-Bus provided a standard for high throughput local bus, it has several problems in its current configuration. For one thing, it is specifically a 486 bus. For Pentium-based VR systems, a buffer has to collect the data from the CPU, effectively slowing Intel's fastest chip to the speed of a 486. Additionally, the VL-Bus is, at 33 MHz, slower than Pentium local-bus speeds of 60 MHz and 66 MHz. Finally, on VL-Bus designs, the CPU doesn't operate independently when a VL-Bus device is active (this might change in future configurations).

One of the ways PCI is able to beat VL-bus in performance is through its capability to work concurrently with the CPU. A PCI bus running at 33 MHz has burst speed of 132 MBps and 80 MBps for long data transfers. This speed, which is 10 times that of an ISA system, enables the PCI to transmit 24-bit true-color graphics at 30 FPS. The future looks even brighter. The current PCI specification is evolving from 32-bit bus to 64 bits. When peripherals supporting that specification are ready, the data throughput rate will double to 264 MBps. This will enable systems to display HDTV (high-definition television)-quality images and do real-time 3-D rendering. But although higher capacity drives and faster buses will help, the problems created by multimedia data file size won't yield to those solutions entirely. Accordingly, compression and decompression will be required.

Compression and decompression hardware or software are known as *codecs*. The two primary differences between codecs are whether they are symmetric or asymmetric and whether they are hardware or software based. A symmetric codec can compress as quickly as it can decompress for playback, making it the best choice for real-time video capture. An asymmetric codec takes much more time to perform the compression step. An example of an asymmetric codec is the Motion Pictures Experts Group (MPEG) standard. This stores only the information that changes from the previous frame. By adding the task of determining what data has changed, this standard is relatively time-consuming. At present, all compression and most decompression for multimedia applications are accomplished by hardware, namely digital signal processor (DSP) chips.

Most DSPs are manufactured by Analog Devices, AT&T, Motorola, and Texas Instruments. Besides compression and decompression, DSP chips are used to convert analog data, such as video, into digital data. The advantage of using a DSP for processor-intensive multimedia work is that the full power of the DSP is available for the function. The alternative is to perform the decompression using the system's general-purpose CPU. But in that case, you don't know what other functions it might be called upon to do at the same time. DSP chips will increase in power to meet challenges of multimedia. Texas Instruments, for example, recently announced MVP (multimedia video processor), which contains four ADSPs (advanced DSPs). TI claims it can deliver two billion operations per second. The chip has not yet been implemented in any product, but Xerox, Sony, and Matrox are planning to implement it in image and document processing, face recognition, and voice input and control systems.

The main problem with DSPs is that they require users to add an extra card for the particular application. But DSPs can do nothing that a general purpose CPU can't do. They don't run at a faster clock rate and they can't handle calculations that a CPU can't. Although at present, the compression of multimedia files requires a DSP codec, Intel offers a software-based solution for decompression. Its Indeo is a software-only video playback that does its work on a 486 or Pentium. Indeo is supported by Microsoft's Video for Windows, IBM's OS/2 and Video In, Apple Computer's QuickTime for Windows, and Novell's NetWare.

But although Indeo is software, it exists because of the growing strength of processors required to run it. It works on a 486, but it works better on a Pentium, and it will work still better on the P6 (Pentium's successor). For example, with a 486DX2-66 with full-screen 640 X 480 resolution, the playback speed is only 10 FPS. The same resolution with a Pentium gives a speed of 20 FPS.

One solution to the immense processing problem is to employ an eye-tracking device in the HMD. By providing data to the processor about where the user is looking, the computer will have to generate a high-resolution image only for the small area that our eyes are able to focus on. The area in the peripheral vision can be displayed at low resolution. This would more closely resemble the way the human eye sees. Ideally, such eye-position-based displays could be shrunk to the size of a pair of contact lenses and mounted on the eyeballs.

⬚ BINOCULAR OMNI-ORIENTATION MONITOR

Although helmets provide the unrestricted freedom of movement sought after by VR enthusiasts, many users, who view VR as a tool and not entertainment, need something much lees encumbering. An architect, for example, who uses VR for design work may want to move in and out of the virtual world many times during the day. Such a person would hesitate to don a bulky, uncomfortable helmet.

One alternative is Binocular Omni-Orientation Monitor, or BOOM2 from Fake Space Labs (Menlo Park, CA). BOOM2 looks like a small periscope, which contains a high-resolution binocular screen. Because the mechanism is larger than an HMD, it avoids many of the problems inherent with miniaturization, the resolution is sharper and lag time less than with HMDs. Despite its large size, viewers can still see in any direction and interact with the virtual world with as much flexibility as when they wear an HMD.

Although BOOM2 can use standard VR input devices such as gloves or joysticks, most users control it though button pads placed on either side of the unit. The button pad can be programmed to be the only navigational device, or it can be used in conjunction with other devices. At present,

BOOM2 is being used in industrial and scientific applications. Normally, the user intersperses VR sessions using BOOM2 with real sessions on a workstation. But in a few applications, BOOM2 may actually replace the workstation monitor as a viewing device. Another application for BOOM2 is as a viewing device for a telepresence system. A remote camera on or near the robot sends images to the BOOM2 viewer. The user controls the robot's actions through BOOM2's button pad.

NASA Ames Research Center uses BOOM2 (and a newer version BOOM3, just released) to study aerodynamic flow. NASA hopes to eventually use the system as a replacement for wind tunnel applications, in which aircraft of various sizes are placed in sealed chambers. Air current forced though those chambers simulate the exact flow pressures incurred against the aircraft flying at different altitudes. Normally, a mechanism in the tunnel emits an airborne dye to enable researchers to view the airflow. The BOOM2 version of the application eliminates the need to create an actual model of the aircraft and transport it to the tunnel site. The engineer enters the virtual world and points his data glove, which causes virtual smoke to be emitted. Next, dye is added to the virtual smoke, replicating the functioning of a real wind tunnel.

BOOM2 also is being used by the US Army Corps of Engineers for a waterways visualization project and by SRI Research, Inc. to create a VR world in which scientists interact with molecules.

Although BOOM2 has not caught on for entertainment applications, a few games, including a space flight game, have been developed for it. BOOM2 boosters feel that games developed with the product will have more appeal to arcade owners than HMDs where concern over hygiene is often an issue.

HEAD TRACKING

Although head tracking is not actually part of the VR vision system, it provide essential input to that system. Therefore, head tracking devices are part of virtually all HMDs. Although tracking devices in general are discussed in Chapter 10, following is a discussion of some of the challenges of HMD-based trackers yet to be solved.

The most daunting problem with current tracking devices is the delay inherent. The tracking device has to transmit data to the computer used for image-generation, which then transmits the image to the HMD. Even with high end HMDs and processors, the latency period can approach 100 milliseconds (ms). When we move our head at a moderate rate, we can rotate about 50 degrees per second. A jerk of the head may be closer to 300 degrees per second. In order to keep up with even moderate movements, response time has to be reduced to about 5 ms—very far from today's systems. The result of the time delay is not only the lack of a sense of reality but also disorientation and dizziness. This is especially troublesome for those who engage in long VR sessions.

Trackers have to increase in accuracy in terms of measuring head position. Small errors in the measurement of the head orientation can also be disorienting. The most promising head tracking system is currently being developed at UNC Chapel Hill. Optical sensors mounted on the HMD correlate their position using panels of infrared beacons in the ceiling above the user. Because the locations of the beacons are fixed, the processor can use them to make measurements of head orientation. The system can compute head motions of under 2 mm and can update images in 15 to 30 milliseconds.

◉ GLASSLESS 3-D

At present, head-mounted displays still lack the resolution and speed found in more conventional computer display. Accordingly, some VR researchers have advocated the use of glassless 3-D displayed on a conventional monitor. These systems display a 3-D image without the traditional 3-D glasses with different colored lenses.

Studying the use of 3-D display of data might have benefits beyond providing VR systems. 3-D is also the most effective way to help people understand information. Nearly half the human brain is devoted to processing what the eyes see. People grasp data in the form of a 3-D object or scene far more quickly than they can make sense of columns of numbers or flat, two-dimensional charts.

Until about 10 years ago, you couldn't visualize data this way unless you had a supercomputer. Because it required an expensive computer, the field of glassless 3-D was primarily the preserve of scientists at federal research centers. They attempted to use 3-D to explore what happens when galaxies collide or a missile strikes its target. The development of high-powered desktop workstations in the 1980s made it possible to apply visualization to manufacturing. Using CAD (computer-aided design), engineers could create on their screens products from airplanes to zippers and test their designs even before building a prototype. With CAM (computer-aided manufacturing), they could electronically direct machines to build their products.

Now graphics workstations are becoming as inexpensive as personal computers once were. Silicon Graphics unveiled a $4,995 workstation, called Indy, that has about the same imaging power as a Cray supercomputer that cost $8 million in 1976. Even ordinary personal computers will soon have processors that will turn them into powerful 3-D graphics machines in their own right. In the next few years super microprocessors—like Intel's Pentium and the PowerPC chip being developed by Apple, IBM, and Motorola—will bring about a tenfold increase in the power of PCs. "By 1998, every PC will have 3-D visualization capability," says William J. Caffery, vice president for technology at the Gartner Group, a Stamford, CT, consulting firm. Carl Machover, a computer graphics consultant in White Plains, NY, expects the market for visualization hardware and software to grow from an estimated $2.1 billion this year to $4.9 billion in 1998.

A number of approaches to creating glassless 3-D have appeared, although only a very few are presently commercially available. These systems can be categorized into those that use optics and those that use flat panel technology.

▣ OPTICS

Almost everyone who was a youngster before the days of computer games is familiar with stereoscopic displays. The popular View-Master viewing device provides 3-D image by presenting different images to the viewer's left and right eye. More modern versions of this technology, which originated last century, use special screens which can be placed in front of CRTs. Called lenticuolar optical screens, they project the left and right images to the proper eye. Typically the user sits directly in front and close to the screen. The separate images for each eye are displayed either sequentially or simultaneously. The screen unscrambles the images and directs them to the correct eye.

An alternative is to use a fresnel lens, a flat lens with convex ridges that focus light similar to the way a magnifying glass focuses light. A different image is focused through each of those convex areas and transmitted to each of the viewer's eyes. The main problem with all of the above systems, according to Jesse B. Eichenlaub, a three-dimension graphics researcher, is that the field of view is very narrow. Although these systems free the viewer from the need to wear special 3-D glasses, they still confine him or her to a very restricted area. Unless you're positioned precisely over the section of the lens from where the image is projected, the effect will be lost. Because of this problem as well as the bulky nature of the device, there has been little commercial use of these optics-related devices.

The one optical device manufactured for commercial use is the Spacegraph from Bolt Beranek Newman in Cambridge, MA. The Spacegraph is a flexible mirror that changes its curvature every 1/30th of a second. When this is combined with a CRT that sequentially displays cross-sections of the image, a 3-D effect is generated. The BBN system provides software that enables you to develop a 3-D wire frame that works with the Spacegraph.

FLAT PANEL TECHNOLOGY

Dimension Technologies, Inc. (Rochester, NY), has a flat panel autostereoscopic display. The product uses LCD display panels that take advantage of parallax, a well-known phenomena in which you see a slightly different view based on the position of each of your eyes. The phenomena can be most easily seen if you place your eyes close to a book page and place a pencil in front of your face. By closing first one eye then the other, you see different text. By keeping both eyes open, you can see through the pencil.

In the Dimension Technologies system, the LCD image is partially obscured by thin lines, which have the same purpose as the pencil in the example. Because of the way the lines are positioned, the right and left eyes see completely different views of the same object, thus creating a 3-D effect.

This system has overcome the narrow field of view problem by including a means of sensing the position of the viewer's head. By adjusting the display to account for head movement, the 3-D effect isn't lost unless the viewer drastically changes position.

Although a major advantage of glassless 3-D is for use in virtual reality systems, John O. Merritt, a consultant with Storage Dimensions, Inc., notes other benefits:

1. It provides enhanced image interpretation capability, allowing you to determine what objects are.
2. It can improve image quality and make up for defects, such as low gray scale or low resolution.
3. It helps the viewer filter out "visual noise."
4. It can help the viewer focus attention on objects in a specific depth plane. For example it can help you ignore foliage in the foreground and attend to humans in the background.
5. 3-D images have more luster.
6. Terrain perception is improved.
7. It eliminates confusion often associated with wire-frame CAD.

RETINAL DISPLAY

VR display systems, in order to mimic human range of field will need an enormous number of picture elements (pixels). By one estimate, at least 8,400 horizontal by 4,800 vertical may be needed. Placing that number of pixels in HMDs or VR glasses using standard technologies would result in devices that are cumbersome, heavy, and uncomfortable. One solution being developed at the Human interface Technology Lab at the University of Washington in Seattle is the Virtual Retinal Display (VRD). By scanning light directly onto the retina, the system eliminates the need for display equipment. The system uses special optical device to scale the image and relay it to the pupil. It also uses eye-tracking device to couple the exit aperture of the scanner optics to the aperture of the eye (the pupil). The eye tracking device is not necessary to ensure that light enters the eye but rather to enable the system to change the view of the image as the eye moves. The system can work with a single scanner or scanners working in parallel.

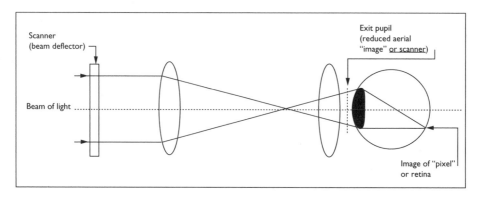

Figure 6.1 A simplified version of a Vertial Retinal Diplay.

The current prototype at the Laboratory allows for the use of a scanned image with resolution equivalent to a pixel density of 1,000 X 1,000. This provides an 80 degree range of field. The Laboratory's five-year goal is to create a system that provides a stereoscopic view with full range of field, full color, and a resolution of 4,000 by 3,000, in a small enough package so that it can be placed on a standard set of glasses and cost less than three hundred dollars.

▣ PROJECTING THE IMAGE

Immersive VR requires the use of a HMD or at least a small display that blocks out the real world. A large number of current VR projects use display devices, such as projection screens or monitors. In some cases, the reason is to provide a CAVE VR experience in which the viewer is in a room surrounded by the virtual images. But in other cases, the reason for the more traditional display device is a necessary compromise. As noted,

HMD-displays tend to have lower resolution and longer latency periods (lag times) than computer monitors or projection devices.

PROJECTION DEVICES

Projection devices are not inexpensive, but they are the only way to display a VR image onto a large wall. Most of these devices project the RGB beams directly onto the wall screen. Before buying one for your VR project, though, you should know that not all data projectors work with all graphics cards, and they require different interfaces depending on the graphics card and even how far the projector is to be from the controlling computer. A second problem is that converging the RGB on the screen requires a bit of training.

There are many data projectors on the market today including the Barcodata from Barco, Inc., in Smyrna, GA.; the Project-A-Mac II from PDS Video Technology, Inc.; the DP and the DP/GP series from NEC Technology; the VPH series from SONY Corp; and the PT-2000 from Panasonic.

Data projectors vary in how large an image they can project. The upper limit for most devices is 6 to 8 feet across if the room lights are dim. If you need a larger screen or the ability to put on a presentation in a bright room, Talaria from GE Projection Display Product uses a different technology that increases brightness dramatically. Instead of the RGB beams projected directly onto the wall, they are projected onto a plate inside the unit. A light source then projects the image from that plate onto the wall. The image can be up to 25 feet across.

COMPUTER MONITOR

Computer monitors are called CRTs because they use a cathode-ray tube to display the images. The CRT is a vacuum-sealed tube that contains an electron gun in the back. Instructed by a video card, a heated cathode shoots a stream of electrons at the screen, which is coated with phosphor.

The electrons cause the pixels or dots of phosphor to glow a color. There are three pixels per dot: red, green, and blue. By combining those colors, the screen can display any color.

The gun, in a sense, draws the screen moving left to right one line at a time. When it completes its movement from top to bottom, it returns to the top. The frequency at which it completes its vertical journey is called the *vertical scanning frequency*, or *refresh rate*. The number of frames the gun draws per second is called the *frame rate*. Of course, the gun must move horizontally many times before it completes one vertical pass. Therefore, horizontal frequency is measured in kilohertz (kHz), but vertical frequency is expressed in hertz (Hz).

The most important number on monitor specification sheets is the refresh rate. A low refresh rate will cause the screen to display shadows when the images are fast-moving. For VR applications, refresh rates should be at least 50Hz, but 100Hz is preferable.

Also, try to buy a monitor that has a variable frequency display (also called *multisynching* or *multiscanning*). Monitors that have this feature can adjust to any horizontal and vertical signal combination. Not only will this enable the monitor to be used with most video cards, it also enables it to be set to more resolution modes.

Dot Pitch

As mentioned earlier, a pixel is made up of a triad of phosphors: red, green, and blue. When electrons strike one of these triads, the eye perceives the entire three-dot pixel as one light source. The colors of the three dots combine to appear as a single hue. The dot pitch is the measured distance between two like-colored phosphors in adjacent triads. Obviously, the smaller the dot pitch, the higher the resolution and the more vivid the colors. Dot pitches of modern monitors range from 0.24mm to 0.51mm.

TRINITRON MONITORS

With non-Trinitron monitors, a shadow mask at the back of the screen helps the guns to focus on the phosphors by preventing stray electrons from igniting adjacent phosphors.

Trinitron monitors use a stripe mask or aperture grill. Instead of dots, as in non-Trinitron monitors, the Trinitron mask is divided by slots. The distance between these slots is often called the dot pitch. Trinitron monitors tend to be sharper than non-Trinitron monitors, but still, the smaller the pitch the better. Try for at least a 0.25mm dot pitch.

DISPLAY DEVICES

BOOM

BOOM (Binocular Omni-Orientation Monitor) and BOOM2C from Fakespace Inc. is designed as an alternative to HMDs. A BOOM is a CRT-based stereoscopic viewing device that is faster and offers higher resolution than HMDs. Fake Space Inc., Menlo Park, CA.

CRYSTALEYES VR

CrystalEyes VR from StereoGraphics Corp. is lightweight, wireless, electronic eyewear. It provides high resolution, full color, and stereoscopic viewing of virtual worlds. The system includes ultrasound headtracking and six-degrees-of-freedom capability to enable rapid response and flicker-free viewing. Head movement determines position, which leaves the hands free. The company's CrystalEyes Video System is a self-contained 3-D stereo video system with controls for record and playback. CrystalEyes Projection System is a large-screen 3-D stereo projection system provides imagery on screens from 5-25 feet. StereoGraphics Corporation, San Rafael, CA.

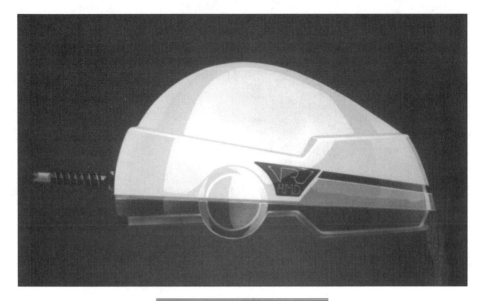

Figure 6.2 Flight Helmet HMD.

CYBERFACE2

Cyberface2 from LEEP Systems Inc. is an HMD with a very wide field of view. It accepts RGB color with NTSC or PAL synch. The company also makes the Photographic Virtual Reality Demonstrator, a hand held viewing device that demonstrates the immersion of very wide field video. LEEP Systems Inc., Waltham, MA.

CYBERSCOPE

CyberScope from 3-D ImageTek Corp. dual cathode ray tube or liquid crystal display 3-D display system which does not require glasses. 3-D ImageTek Corporation, Laguna Hills, CA.

DATAVISOR 9C

Datavisor 9c from n-Vision Inc. is a full color HMD with a wide angle optical system. It provides resolutions up to 1,280 X 1,024 pixels per inch. According to the company, by focusing the virtual world image at infinity, the HMD reduces eye strain. For applications involving extended periods of time, Datavisor 9c is integrated into a molded hard plastic shell. The company's Datavisor 10m is similar to the 9c model except that it uses monochrome CRT image sources. Another HMD from n-Vision is its Quarterwave, which is aimed at medical imaging applications. n-Vision Inc., Vienna, VA.

FLIGHT HELMET

Flight Helmet from Virtual Research is a HMD with dual NTSC inputs and stereo headphones. The company's EyeGen3 uses monochrome GRTs with color wheels instead of LCDs. Virtual Research, Santa Clara, CA.

MRG 2

MRG 2 from Liquid Image uses an active matrix LCD display, and is known for its high resolution as well as its ruggedness, which makes it suitable for public use. (The company says it drop tested the device from six feet). It's image is on a single screen and provides 240 degrees by 240 degrees field of view. It accommodates Ascension Technology's Bird or Polhemus' FASTRAK position-tracking systems. Liquid Image, Winnipeg, Manitoba, Canada.

THE SPACEHELMET

The SpaceHelmet from 3-D TV Corporation features dual LCD displays for 3-D video or 3-D graphics for less than $1,500. 3-D TV Corporation, San Rafael, CA.

TIER 1 VISOR

Tier 1 Visor from VRontier Worlds of Stoughton, Inc., is an HMD with two 4-inch LCD screens, one for each eye, that can be switched between stereoscopic and monoscopic modes. Tier 1 is lightweight and has an open-head design. It comes with stereo headphones. VRontier Worlds of Stoughton Inc., Sloughton, WI.

VIRTUAL VISION SPORT

Virtual Vision Sport from Virtual Vision Inc., is lightweight eyewear that accepts full-color NTSC signals. The image is presented to only one eye and is set below the user's normal field of vision enabling the user to transfer his or her gaze to the real world at any time. It comes with high-fidelity earphones. To keep the unit light, the power controls are on a one-pound belt pack, which includes a VHF/UHF tuner. Virtual Vision Inc., Redmond, WA.

Virtual Sound

Most VR systems include an audio component. As a matter of fact, it can be argued that a VR system without sound lacks the verisimilitude to qualify it as true VR. However, allowances have to be made for the fact that the technology to produce realistic sound has not yet been perfected. Even in those cases in which the technology is available, including sound along with graphics generally increases the load on the processor, thus raising the cost of the system.

For the sake of economy, some VR systems use monophonic sound; others use stereophonic sound. For a system to sound like the real thing, however, it needs 3-D audio, the goal of which is not only to locate sound in the horizontal plane (as in stereo) but also in the vertical plane.

There are a number of problems with programming 3-D audio. For one thing, head and ear shape affect how we locate sound, so each of us may actually use different cues to locate sound. In other words, we each may hear sounds a bit differently. In order to take each individual's physical attributes into account, scientists can use a complex mathematical function called a Head Related Transfer Function or HRTF. However, the HRTF is a very individualistic function based primarily on the subject's ear shape.

So systems developed for one subject would not necessarily provide the same effect for a second subject.

Measuring an individual's HRTF can take two to three hours. Doing so for each new VR user would be impractical. One solution, proposed by Frederic L. Wightman of the University of Wisconsin at Madison is to adopt an average "spatial filter" that would be close enough to the way most people sense the location of sound. In addition, the equipment would allow some fine tuning so that it can be effective with a large number of users.

Another solution, suggested by Nathaniel Durlach of Massachusetts Institute of Technology's Sensory Communication Group is to exaggerate the location cues to make up for any differences in the listener's anatomy. In this approach, the intensity and timing differences of the sound waves are intensified. The downside of this approach is that, although the subject may be able to identify sound location, he or she gets a distorted acoustical signal. In other words, the sound does not appear natural. So the VR experience does not seem real.

In any case, current HRTF-based systems have some problems, such as sounds occurring behind the head are often perceived by the subject to be in front. Several companies offer systems that attempt to create 3-D sound. These are used to create sounds that correspond to the action taking place in a virtual world. Typically, these systems take advantage of a human's ability to consider even subtle time and amplitude differences of sound patterns as they reach the two sides of the head at different intervals. Sound travels at 1,100 feet per second. If a sound is coming from the left side, it reaches the left ear about a millisecond faster than it reaches the right ear. Also, the sound will be a bit quieter when it reaches the right ear because the head has shadowed it. The result is that the subject knows the sound has come from the left.

The Convolvotron, from Crystal River Engineering, Inc. (Groveland, CA) enables the user to experience up to four different sound sources positioned in space, reflections from six surfaces with programmable acoustical characteristics, and Doppler shift effects.

In order to develop the Convolvotron, Crystal River scientists placed microphones in the ear canal of test subjects and recorded sound patterns both before and after they were altered by the head and pinnae (the fleshy, outer-ear appendages). Next, they devised mathematical functions, which have become part of the algorithm used to shape sound played through the Convolvotron's headphones.

Similar work has been conducted by Wightman. For the last few years, he has been recording what the inner ears hear after a sound has been altered by the outer ears. To accomplish the tests, tiny microphones are placed in the ear canals of subjects, who are then asked to sit in echo-less chambers. As sounds from different locations fill the room, they are captured by the microphone. Computers then use that data to determine the timing and intensity of the sounds. Those numbers are in turn used to determine the filtering effects of the outer ears.

The next step in the research process is to use the data gained to create an illusion of position of sounds. The computer modifies the signal going to each earphone, and the subject tries to pinpoint the direction of the sound.

The Convolvotron, which was co-developed with NASA Ames Research Center, plugs into the HMD and provides a means of coordinating sound with graphics. The primary problem with the Convolvotron is that sounds appear to come from fixed locations and they maintain those locations even if the subjects turn.

But continuing research might solve the remaining problems with the Convolvotron. New mathematical functions developed by Crystal River are getting better at simulating the way the head and outer ears scatter sounds, thus increasing the capability to pinpoint sound. In fact, by exaggerating the effect, the system may even enable the subject to have a increased awareness of the location of the sound, much as he or she would in the real world.

One daunting challenge, according to Crystal River, is simulating reflected sounds. Sound waves bounce off surfaces quite differently based on the shape and material of the surface. Predicting how sound will be affected by an object requires an extremely complex computation.

Even if systems had the computational power to handle sound reflections, there would still be the problem of understanding how humans pinpoint sound. Without that understanding, no program can replicate the process. Certainly, knowing that sound coming from the left reaches the left ear a little earlier is one step to understanding human perception of sound. But there are many more complex considerations.

Although one important application for 3-D sound will be traditional HMD-based VR systems, there are other uses for the technology, such as directing air traffic controllers and pilots, or as a navigational aid for the blind.

Air traffic controllers and pilots have a difficult task relating the voice coming over their headphone to the tower or plane on the radar screen. If each voice coming over the headset was given a directional dimension that matched the actual location in space of the person transmitting the voice, response time could increase. In a related application, pilots could be given a system in which they hear the word "traffic" coming from the direction of an oncoming plane. In tests, this system sped up pilots' response time by 1 to 2 seconds when compared to conventional collision-avoidance systems. Accordingly, the Federal Aviation Administration is planning to test virtual sound.

According to Jack Loomis, a psychologist at the University of California, Santa Barbara, a navigational aid for the blind can be developed using virtual sound and radio signals from a global positioning system (GPS), a network of navigation satellites that can pinpoint positions on Earth's surface to within a few meters. The user would carry a small hand-held computer that contained a map of each neighborhood in which he or she planned to walk. When the user wanted to reach a street, building, or other landmark, he or she would tell the computer. The computer would then transmit sounds that appeared to come from the landmark the user was trying to attain.

RESOURCES

Acoustetron from Crystal River Engineering, Inc. is a 3-D audio workstation to create high-end VR systems. The company's Convolvotron is a high-speed, digital-signal processing system that can present eight binaural sound sources. Beachtron is a digital-signal processing system for producing 3-D sound at a modest cost. The sound sources may be live, sampled, or generated from the on-board Proteus synthesizer. Crystal River Engineering Inc., Groveland, CA.

Barnaby 2000 3-D Microphone from A Lasting Impression Music Corporation is 3-D microphone for recordings that can be used in VR systems. A Lasting Impression Music Corporation, San Francisco, CA.

Focal Point from Focal Point 3-D Audio is a CD-quality convolved binaural-sound system for VR audio displays. Focal Point 3-D Audio, Niagara Falls, NY.

SoundMaster II from Covox Inc. is a music and voice-recognition system for interactive voice input/output for DOS-based PCs. Covox Inc., Eugene, OR.

Virtual Touch

Force feedback devices provide a sense of touch or feel by relaying to the user the force exerted by a virtual object. (In the case of telepresence systems, discussed elsewhere, the system relays forces exerted on actual, real-world objects.)

At the University of North Carolina at Chapel Hill, Frederick P. Brooks, Jr., a professor of computer science, developed the concept for an early VR-type project called GROPE in the early 1970s. Force feedback not only provides virtual worlds with verisimilitude, it may be essential for safety reasons. Using a computer simulation, a robot can walk though walls and destroy equipment without the user feeling anything. If the simulation is used to control a real robot in a remote location, the consequences of the lack of force feedback can be devastating, even tragic. But force feedback can be important even for applications that remain in the virtual domain and don't impinge on the real world.

Vivian Coddy, a crystallographer at the Medical Foundation in Buffalo, NY, for example, is using a force feedback system to learn how anticancer drugs and enzymes bind together. Viewing a virtual world though an eyepiece, she uses a large mechanical arm to move a simulated drug molecule into active contact with an enzyme. As she does so, the arm provides resistance providing tactile clues that the particular molecule can't combine with the enzyme.

Frederick P. Brooks is now working on a similar fore feedback system that enables a chemist to experiment with drug molecules. This system uses a servo manipulator, a force feedback robotic arm that had been used by Argonne National Laboratory to control a robot that handled radioactive materials. The system's display, on a computer monitor, shows the relative positions of the drug and the enzyme. A numeric table shows the "energy thermometers," the level of binding energy. The software that controls the force feedback was developed by a model created by Peter A. Kollman of the University of California at San Francisco. The model represents both force and torque in three dimensions. According to chemists using the system, the capability to see and feel the size and the direction of various forces makes their experiments work more efficiently. In fact, a study by Ming Ouh-Young, now working at AT&T Bell Laboratories, showed that using the system, biochemists were twice as fast in determining how to dock the drug than those working from numeric tables.

Other force feedback applications are in the works:

◇ The Atari video game Hard Drivin' transmits the forces on a race car through the steering wheel. The wheel turns in the user's hands and even conveys the bumpiness of the ride though up and down movements.

◇ AT&T plans to really enable us to reach out and touch someone. It is experimenting with a telecommunications game that works over the phone lines. Users try to navigate though a maze using a force feedback joystick. If successful, the company may allow users to receive a sense of touch over the phone. This would be useful, for example, for inspectors to feel component parts to determine whether they are sound.

◇ In an experiment in computer-aided instruction, first-year physics students at the University of North Carolina used a force feedback system to study the electromagnetic forces inside a vacuum tube.

◇ At Bell Labs, researchers are working on a project that connects a surgeon and surgical student using force feedback. Both of them wear a data glove, which gives the surgeon a feeling of the actions of the surgical student as he operates on a cadaver. The surgeon will be better able to critique the student's performance and will even be able to guide his hand.

◇ At the Institute of Engineering Mechanics at Japan's University of Tsukuba researchers have developed a CAD system with a sense of feel. Using a data glove attached to a graphics workstation, designers are able to judge how a camera will feel to the user.

Many different types of mechanisms have been used to provide force feedback information to users. Joysticks, steering wheels, or robot arms have been programmed to simulate gross force feedback to the user's hands. Low-end devices present the sum of forces acting upon them by pushing back on the user's palm or fingertips. (This shouldn't be too unfamiliar to most of us. Automatic steering devices in modern cars provide a feel of the road through force feedback technology.) Many popular VR systems use the gross force feedback method as the most economical and least processor-intensive method for providing the user with a sense of touch.

The PER-Force hand controller from Cypernet Systems Corporation (Ann Arbor, MI) was originally developed to use onboard the space station Freedom. This is a joystick-type device that controls robots as well as other objects in multidimensional space (or virtual space). The operator can use the motorized handle for precise positioning of objects. The feel of multi-dimensional objects is accomplished though a host computer that reads the hand controlling position velocity and force. The device then simulates force in six directions using motors. The system also can convey a rudimentary sense of touch. For example, it can provide a bumpy ride as the operator moves the computer pointing device over a bumpy surface.

A number of researchers, including Margaret Minsky, daughter of Marvin Minsky, the artificial intelligence pioneer, are attempting to develop force feedback joysticks that provide a more realistic sense of touch. Minsky, who is a doctoral candidate at MIT's Media Lab, has been able to get a motor-controlled joystick to create a feel of the texture of objects displayed on a computer screen. A rugged surface causes the joystick to vibrate.

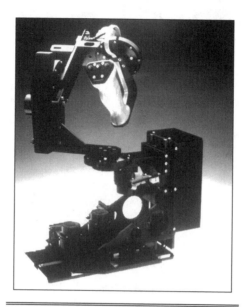

Figure 8.1 The PER-Force hand controller.

Her initial project was called Sandpaper, which enables users to arrange several pieces of sandpaper by coarseness grade using information gained from the force feedback device. As the on-screen pointer moves across the surface of the simulated sandpaper, the joystick bumps up and down in proportion to the size of the sand on the paper. Next, Minsky plans to simulate soft and sticky substances as well. If the system moves over a sticky substance, the joystick becomes more difficult to move back and forth.

Although it is possible to simulate spatial patterns of forces to the user's skin, current systems are still far from actually providing the feel, say, of sandpaper or slate. There are difficulties with developing such a system. For one thing, the sense organs of our skin need to have the pattern constantly changing (such as when we run our hand over an irregular rock).

One solution is to utilize tiny nickel-titanium switches contained in data gloves. The switching effect results from the fact that this alloy flexes when heated and returns to its original size when cooled. When the VR system needs to signal pressure on the finger tips, it sends an electrical current to the switch. The resulting heat causes the switch to flex and press against the fingertips. That type of switch, called a *tactor*, can be configured so that each fingertip has four or five, each with different degree of flex. By selectively controlling which tactor is flexed, the VR system can signal the shape of an object. For example, an edge would result in a switch that presses heavily against the fingertip; a smooth side would create a much lighter touch. As a result, the user would be able to move his or her hand around an object and find the edges through touch.

Most current tactors aren't as sophisticated as the one just described. The majority use a simple buzzing mechanism to signal the user that he or she is touching an object. The buzzing only loosely resembles the feeling of touch as you run your fingers over an object. Other prototype systems have used air jets, vibrators, and electrical currents. But so far, no virtual sense of touch that even comes close to the real sense of touch has been developed. Even if systems could be developed that accurately replicate the sense of touch, the next challenge would be to miniaturize it to the extent that it could fit in a lightweight glove.

HOT AND COLD

Although a sense of touch still eludes us, a few systems have been developed that provide a sense of temperature. Not all VR systems will need to provide users with a sense of temperature. But for those in which the temperature of objects or room temperature is an essential part of the world, there needs to be a way to create it. Temperature is also necessary to provide clues to the type of object or material being touched. Sometimes temperature may be the only way to provide a clue to the type of material. For example, it would be very difficult to create a force feedback system to simulate the feel of sanded wood and metal so that the user could distinguish between the two. But most people can easily tell the difference between metal and wood because the former feels colder because of the difference in the thermal conductivity.

Besides allowing VR to provide clues to users, temperature also simply makes the virtual world seem right. A world without a sense of temperature may appear as if something is missing. One thing that helps VR developers create a sense of temperature is that people are in general very sensitive to temperature change. On average, someone can feel a change of about 1 or 2 degrees F at their fingertips.

One commercial product offering a sense of temperature is the Displaced Temperature Sensing System (DTSS) from CM Research (League City, TX). A thermode is made up of a thermoelectric heat pump, a temperature sensor, and a heat sink. The heat pump pours heat into or out of the heat sinks to produce a temperature at the surface of the thermode. Using feedback from the sensor, the DTSS regulates the temperature of the thermode.

One use of the DTSS is to provide temperature feedback to accompany force feedback on telepresence applications. A thermode also can serve as an input device by sending temperature and surface thermal conductivity data to a computer. In a telepresence application, both the robot and the user's fingertip can be outfitted with a thermode. Temperature signals would be sent from the robot through the computer to the thermodes on the fingers of the operator.

In a more conventional VR application, the thermode would accept digital commands from the computer, which controls the temperature simulation. To accomplish this, a temperature value would have to be assigned to objects or locations in the virtual world. As the virtual hand moved close to any object, commands would be sent to the thermode ordering it to change its temperature setting.

Manipulation and Control Devices

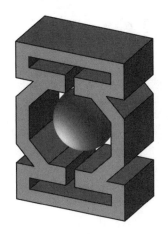

Input into a VR system can be ordinary or quite exotic. Many low-end system use input devices which can be found siting next to virtually any desktop computer or video game. Keyboards, digitizers, joysticks, mice, trackballs, and light pens are often used on the simpler VR systems. But the problem with all these devices for VR systems is that they track position in only two dimensions. A virtual world, of course, is a 3-D world—or at least pretends to be one.

To track objects in a virtual world, there has to be means of 3-D control. Perhaps a more accurate way of putting it is 6-D; virtual objects have to be tracked in three positional coordinates (X, Y, Z) and three orientation measures (roll, pitch, yaw).

Accordingly, some manufacturers have developed mice, trackballs, and joysticks that work in a 6-D mode.

⬡ MOUSE INPUT

In 1991, Logitech Corporation, Fremont, CA, announced its Logitech 3-D Mouse, the first 3-D mouse. It is a five-button pointing device. The device is meant for applications and hardware supporting multi-dimensional, spatial graphics, such as CAD/CAM and virtual reality workstations. The mouse can operate as a standard mouse on a 2-D plane (such as a desktop), or it can be used in multiple dimensions by raising it (by hand or in a head-tracker unit) off of the 2-D plane. The mouse technology is further being incorporated into virtual reality "head trackers," allowing a user to point in multi-dimensional directions by moving his or her head.

The Logitech 3-D Mouse consists of several components:

◇ An ultrasonic position reference array, which is a tripod consisting of three ultrasonic speakers set in a triangular position.

◇ The mouse, with five buttons and a triangular set of three microphones that face the speaker array and receive sound from it.

◇ A power supply.

◇ A standard RS-232-C connector.

◇ A control unit through which the mouse, speaker array, power supply, and computer are connected. The control unit controls the speaker triangle, and the mouse provides the serial communications link to the host computer. Multiple control units can be "daisy-chained" so that up to four mice can be tracked with a single speaker triangle within a single operating space.

◇ Connection to speech/sound recognition systems through a built-in microphone.

◇ A "suspend" button on both the right and left sides of the mouse (for right- and left-handed users) to suspend, or stop, all cursor movement on-screen when pressed.

Another mouse of this type is the Multipoint 3-D Mouse from Multipoint Technology Corporation (Westford, MA).

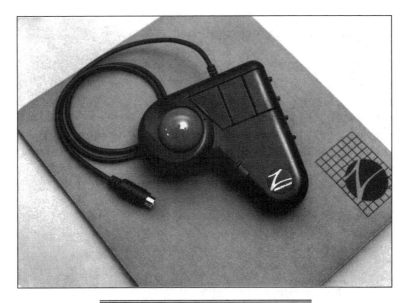

Figure 9-1 The Multipoint 3-D mouse.

⬚ HAND-BASED INPUT

By far, at present the best way to manipulate virtual objects is through the use of a glove that tracks gestures, position, and movement of the operator's hand. The hand movement can control a cursor or manipulate virtual objects on a computer screen, HMD, or other viewing device. Often, the objects may be tools that manipulate other virtual objects. For example, the DataGlove (currently being marketed by Greenleaf Medical Systems, Inc., Palo Alto, CA) can be used to manipulate a virtual steering wheel that, in turn, manipulates a real steering wheel.

The glove's gesture-sensing mechanism enables it to detect movements of the hand (gestures), such as flexing of the fingers. It also can sense the hand position relative to the display. The gesture sensing is accomplished through the use of flex sensors (contained on a flexible printed circuit

73

board sandwiched between an inner and an outer glove) that determine the degree of flex of the fingers of the operator's hand.

Hand-position sensing is accomplished though ultrasonic transmitters, a stationary receiver containing three ultrasonic receiving units, and a control circuit that measures the time delay of pulsed ultrasonic signals from the transmitter to the three receivers.

Once the gesture and position is sensed, the data has to be transmitted to the CPU. That's the job of the glove's signal processing unit. This unit includes interface circuitry for connecting the glove to the host computer. The result may be the positioning of a hand-shaped cursor on the display screen, a response to output signals from the flex sensors, or the manipulation of virtual objects defined by the computer according to commands represented by the gestures and movement of the operator's hand.

The glove can be programmed using pictorial or symbolic programming language that enables you to control a cursor shaped like the glove. This dynamic cursor corresponds in shape to the glove the user wears and moves on-screen in response to movement of the user's glove. The glove provides a basis for use of a symbolic programming language in which movements of the operator's hand are used to implement functions or operations on virtual objects displayed on-screen.

THE POWERGLOVE

For a low-cost glove, consider Mattel's PowerGlove, manufactured for use with the Nintendo game system. This device provides some limited data on hand and finger position. It uses strain gauges to track finger bends, along with ultrasonic position sensors. Unfortunately, the PowerGlove is no longer manufactured, but a growing underground market in used PowerGloves exists among some VR enthusiasts.

If you can find the PowerGlove, operating systems do exist that enable them to control a personal computer. The Glove Operating System (GOS), for example, transmits PowerGlove data to the PC via the AGE Power Glove Serial Adapter. In keyboard emulation mode, GOS enables you to send keystrokes to PC applications by making signs with your hand. If you're interested in programming the glove for more sophisticated functions, GOS comes with the Application Programming Interface.

PROBLEMS WITH HAND-BASED INPUT

The main problem with hand-based input is that it doesn't provide tactile or force feedback. You can watch the on-screen representation of your hand pick up an on-screen object, but you will not feel the action. This limits the experience and creates problems with manipulation. As a result, although a glove is adequate for gross motor activities, fine motor activities, such as manipulation of small VR objects, are out of the question. Future versions of gloves may include some kind of force feedback, although it would be difficult to provide the kind of tactile feel needed for precision.

Another problem with glove systems, according to David A. Smith, Director of Research and Development of Virtus Corporation (Cary, NC) is that to use a glove, you have to keep your hand and arm in the air. Because all the muscles of the upper arm are used, he contends that you're working harder than you would if you were manipulating a real world object. When you lift real objects, one muscle group is at rest. Smith adds that because there is no stable surface for the arm to rest against, controlling objects in mid-air requires more muscle use. For that reason, he contends that no user could comfortably manipulate objects using the data glove for more than five minutes at a time.

From Smith's perspective, a virtual world doesn't need to have an image of a hand. He says that people move objects using theirs hand in the real world simply because they have no choice and not because hand movement is the most comfortable or the most precise means of manipulating objects. Anyone who uses a mouse for controlling a cursor quickly finds out how easy it is to find position using a mouse rather than using the more traditional means of positioning pointing.

BIOCONTROLLERS

Biocontrollers, which use biological factors as input, offer VR developers a wide range of possibilities. In its most extreme form, a biocontroller may be able to "read" thoughts and act on mental commands. Of course, this would require a capability to analyze brain waves that is far beyond what any machine is capable of today.

BioMuse biocontrollers from Bio Control Systems, Inc. (Palo Alto, CA), however, do enable users to control VR systems using biometric patterns other than brain waves.

Figure 9-2 The BioMuse biocontroller.

BioMuse works though a three-stage process. First, it acquires a signal, such as muscle tension or eye movement. Next, it looks for recognizable patterns in those signals. Finally, it outputs the appropriate code to control some computer function. The device can accept as input virtually any bioelectrical signal. Currently, the company is focusing on three types of bioelectrical signals: myoelectrical (muscle), eye movement, and cerebroelectircl (brain).

MYOELECTRICAL

A myoelectrical system maps muscle electrical activity. It can be programmed to recognize a large range of muscle signal intensities and durations. One application of this system is to control MIDI (Musical Instrument Digital

Interface) devices. The amount of muscle exertion, for example, can be used to determine volume. The speed at which the muscle moves can control beat. Using this method, entire musical sequences can be played on an "air guitar" causing real music to be played on the synthesizer.

Some researchers are adapting myoelectrical systems to help people in rehabilitation programs. It has been shown that people are more willing to extend the range of their movements when the reward is hearing music. Myoelectrical systems also can be used to enable physically disabled people control devices using simple arm movements.

EYE MOVEMENT

Eye movement systems make use of vertical and horizontal eye movement to create a virtual joystick. Systems already have been developed that enable users to control video games using just their eyes. But it may have more serious impact on the lives of physically disabled people or those who need their hands free while controlling a computer or other machine.

An eye controller also is being developed to assist surgeons performing endoscopic surgery. This type of operation makes use of tiny cameras placed inside the patient's body. The surgeon's hands are usually occupied and cannot be used to control the camera. Using an eye control system, the surgeon can move the camera position using eye movements. In a sense, it would give the surgeon the same type of control as if he or she were really peering into the body and looking around.

Finally, in an immersive VR system, the eye controller can control the graphical display, the user's view. Most current systems require that the user turn his or her head to the left in order for the left image to be displayed. A system that incorporates eye tracking would provide a more natural means of viewing the virtual world since, in the real world, you can change the view merely by glancing to one side or the other.

CEREBROELECTRICAL SIGNALS

The goal a system that tracks cerebroelectrical signals is to enable users to visualize actions, which are then turned into code that controls a computer process. The user might be able to think a word that would then be typed or used as a command, such as "Print." So far, Bio Control Systems has not been able to develop a machine that can detect subvocalized words. The company has, however, been able to use cerebroelectrical signals to control some very basic MIDI output.

BRAINWAVE CONTROL

Certainly the most direct computer input device would be one that could be controlled by human thought. No computer can yet be controlled with thoughts to the same extent that it can be controlled with a mouse or voice. And because thoughts are much less controllable (they run away) than hand movement or voice, few people would want a computer that did whatever they thought. However, Colorado-based Advanced Neurotechnologies, Inc. (ANI) recently has developed a brainwave-to-computer interface system that can be used for rudimentary computer control.

"Brainlink" uses proprietary hardware and software to detect, measure, and then analyze human brain waves. The hardware part of the system is a series of sensors attached to a headband. The headband is similar to a electroencephalogram (EEG) in that it captures signals, which are amplified and converted to the digital form that the computer understands. The software analyzes the digitized signals to create an interface between the brain and the computer.

However, brain control is not easy. To use the system you have to take a two-week Brainlink training program (currently priced at $6,000). Users are taught to create graphical results on the computer screen by thinking certain types of thoughts. But although speed and accuracy does increase as the user practices, it is never nearly as high as even voice input, a technology that suffers from relatively low accuracy rates.

A few other companies are working on brainwave control of computers. But because it uses advanced digital signal processing (DSP) and proprietary protocols, Brainlink is, in theory anyway, able to offer more precise control than other systems that use general-purpose processors.

Despite this, Brainlink isn't effective or efficient as a computer control device yet. Anyone who tries to use it to control programs would quickly become frustrated at its lack of accuracy and the kind of mental control it requires. Therefore, at present, those who take the training program primarily do so to improve concentration, performance, and creativity.

▣ WEARABLE COMPUTERS

Input to VR systems will be greatly assisted if the progress in wearable computers continues apace. Researchers at the Design for Manufacturing Laboratory at Carnegie-Mellon University's Engineering Design Research Center in Pittsburgh are working on input/output devices you can wear. The project is backed by the National Science Foundation.

One of the first projects was the Vu-Man 1, a two-pound PC-compatible wearable computer. It has a three-button input device in its housing, and users watch the screen though a Private Eye HMD display. In the second version of the system, the weight was reduced to a half pound.

The third version of the wearable computer is called the Navigator. It uses a 25 MHz Intel 386 processor with 16M of memory. It contains four modules: display, speech recognition, position tracking, and telecommunications. The Navigator also contains an 85M hard drive. The computer runs on a UNIX operating system with an X Window interface.

Aside from providing input to VR systems, wearable computers may have other uses as well. They could be used for computer directed tours. Using augmented reality (see-through) HMDs and position sensors in the belt computer, users can be lead to any area they want to travel. Using a speech recognition systems, a user may say he wants to see a particular building. The see-though display would then show arrows leading the visitor in the correct direction. The system also can change from augmented to virtual reality. In that mode, the see-through display would be replaced with a map or other navigational device that could help the visitor locate something that has no direct relationship to the present reality. If, for example, the site the visitor wants to see requires driving, it wouldn't be practical to use arrows on a see-through display device. Therefore, an auto icon can appear, signifying that the site in question is not within walking distance. After the visitor enters the car, a voice command displays the appropriate maps. After the user finishes studying the maps and determines the best route, the display image disappears and the HMD can be removed.

The system also could be used for blueprint reading. By superimposing a blueprint on, for example, a wall to be wired, technicians are relieved of the difficult task of transposing paper notes onto reality.

Other input and control devices include the following:

◇ CyberGlove is an 18-sensor instrumented glove. It contains one abduction sensor and two bend sensors on each finger. It also has sensors to measure thumb and pinkie rotation as well as wrist pitch and yaw. It comes with VirtualHand display software, which can be used to calibrate the CyberGlove and display a graphical on-screen image of hand and finger motions.

◇ CyberForce provides gripforce feedback to the CyberGlove.

◇ The CyberWear series contains several wearable sensing devices, including CyberArm, CyberVest, and CyberSuit (a full-body sensing device) All Cyberwear models measure body motions and create an on-screen image.

◇ GestureGlove enables user to control a computer using the CyberGlove. It recognizes over 30 different hand formations and learns any additional hand formations. The user can program it to translate any hand formation into text output.

◇ CyberCAD is a VR CAD system that enables the use to create and manipulate 3-D virtual objects.

◇ Virtual Hand display software.

All of the above are from Virtual Technologies, Stanford, CA.

◇ The Cricket by Digital Image Design, Inc., is a 3-D interactive joystick. It contains trigger, grip, thumb, and suspend buttons. The device measures pressure on the trigger and grip buttons, and it measures both pressure and direction on the thumb button. This is both an input and feedback device (a variable vibration provides tactile feedback). The Cricket works with various 6-D trackers by companies such as Ascension, Logitech, and Polhemus. Digital Image Design, Inc., New York, NY.

◈ Global 3-D Controller by Global Devices is a 3-D graphics controller. It includes six-degrees-of-freedom function and can translate all possible combinations of linear and rotational vectors to a virtual environment. The controller also can be used as a feedback device because it offers 32 levels of vibrations in the handle. Global Devices, Granite Bay, CA.

Position Tracking

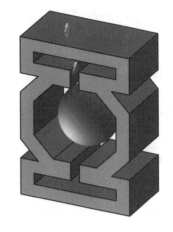

Most HMDs provide for head position tracking, a process that lets the VR system know the position and orientation of the head in order to display the appropriate image. Sometimes, movement in a VR world is accomplished by pointing a finger gloved in a sensor glove, manipulating a joystick, or moving a mouse. Although all those methods are effective in allowing the user to control the VR image, none are natural. A more realistic means of navigating through a VR world would be to move one's entire body.

For users to navigate using the movement of body parts other than the head, VR systems must incorporate some kind of tracking system.

There are several available technologies for tracking:

◇   Mechanical tracking
◇   Ultrasonic sensors
◇   Optical sensors
◇   Magnetic sensors
◇   Magnetic trackers

⊡ MECHANICAL TRACKING

The earliest tracking systems, and many in use today, use either flexible metal armatures or exoskeletal devices. The former provides data only on general location and orientation. The latter can be very exact and very fast. But it also can be very heavy and uncomfortable. The biggest advantage of the ADL-1, a mechanical tracking device from Shooting Star Technology, Inc., Rosedale, B.C., Canada, is its low cost. For $150 you can have a fast, accurate, six-degrees-of-movement tracking system.

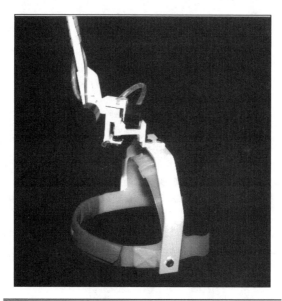

Figure 10.1 The ADL-1 mechanical tracking device.

⊡ ULTRASONIC SENSORS

Ultrasonic sensors use emitters and receivers with a known relationship to each other. The emitters are pulsed in sequence. By calculating the time lag, the distance to each receiver is measured, and by using triangulation, the location and orientation are determined. The problem with ultrasonic sensors is lack of accuracy (resulting partly from interference from extraneous noise and echoes) and long lag times.

OPTICAL SENSORS

Optical sensor tracking systems use a grid of light-emitting diodes (LED) mounted on the ceiling and a camera normally mounted on the user's helmet. The LEDs are pulsed in a specific sequence and the image from the camera is processed to determine the camera's position relative to the ceiling grid. This system is limited by the size of the grid and doesn't provide full 360 degree coverage.

Another optical technology uses several video cameras to capture simultaneous images of the object or objects being tracks. This eliminates the need to wear the camera on the helmet. However, it requires image processing, which is relatively slow and needs a very powerful and expensive processor.

There are very few commercially available optical trackers adequate for VR applications. One experimental system has been developed by the University of North Carolina at Chapel Hill. In this system, optical sensors mounted on the head unit view panels of infrared beacons in the ceiling above the user.

There are several advantages to this system for experimental use. For one thing, it can be used in rooms of any size since it is limited only by the size of the grid, which can be extended. (The current size is 16 x 30 feet, a much larger area than can be tracked by any other type of system). A second advantage of optical trackers is accuracy. The system can resolve head motions of under 2 mm in position and 0.2 degrees in orientation. Lag time also is relatively short.

Optical trackers do have several problems, however. Grid size may be a limiting factor in commercial or industrial applications because of the expense of large grids and the difficulty of moving or expanding them. Installing the grid requires a major modification to the room in which the system is used. The helmet is relatively heavy, and line-of-sight constraints also limit tracking capability.

▣ MAGNETIC TRACKERS

Currently, magnetic trackers represent the most promising tracking technology for VR systems. In these systems, coils are pulsed to produce magnetic fields. Magnetic sensors measure the strength and angles of the fields to determine location and orientation.

Magnetic trackers require users to attach small receivers to different parts of their body. These receivers are tethered to an electronic chassis using long wires (for comfort, the wires can be bundled and suspended from bungee-like cords). To track complete movement, as many as 25 or 30 transmitters should be used. For most VR applications, however, three or four usually are adequate.

One of the first commercially available magnetic trackers, The Ascension Bird, from Ascension Technology, allowed for only a single receiver and could track motion in an area of only 2 feet. That original product has been scrapped in favor of the Flock of Birds series, which allows up to 30 receivers (by putting together multiple units) and allows for a range of eight feet.

According to Jack Scully, vice president of Ascension Technology, the company is working on solving five problems that afflict the current state of tracking technology:

◇ Lag
◇ Range
◇ Metallic distortion
◇ Multi-target tracking
◇ Compatibility

LAG

Lag, which Scully calls "the single greatest problem" afflicting VR systems, results in images that are a beat or two slower than the user's movement. Too much lag reduces the realism and can even cause dizziness or disorientation in some users. In most VR systems, lag isn't entirely, or even primarily, the fault of the motion tracker. Graphics processing, image generation, and transmission rates all play a part. In order for trackers to improve their performance and help reduce lag time, they have to incorporate multi-processors. They also need to be able to adjust filters.

RANGE

Early tracking systems had such limited ranges that they were useless for most VR applications. Ascension has developed an Extended Range Transmitter, which increases the range of its products from 3 to 8 feet. (The range can be extended by using multiple transmitters). FASTRAK from Pothemus Inc. (Colchester, VT) Ascension's primary competitor has a range of 10 feet.

When comparing products, however, it's important to note that "range" is a somewhat subjective measurement. Noise normally increases at the edge of the tracker's range. Although filters can be used to eliminate or reduce the noise, that process slows transmission time. The point at which a user determines that the noise level is unacceptable is the limit of the range for that application. Vendor specification sheets can be similarly subjective. One vendor may state its product has a range of, say, five feet because it has decided that beyond that range the noise level is unacceptable. Another vendor with a product having the exact same range may rate it at seven feet, deeming the noise level in the additional two feet acceptable. It is, therefore, very difficult to compare apples to apples in this area.

METALLIC DISTORTION

Nearby conductive metals and, to a lesser extent, stainless steel can produce large, random distortion in accuracy. Scully says that using pulsed DC field trackers can reduce distortion by a factor of 4 to 12 over AC electro-magnetic field trackers.

MULTI-TARGET TRACKING

Many VR systems require some way of tracking multiple targets (either more than one participant or multiple body parts). Tracking systems not only need to provide the capability to capture multiple targets, but to avoid degradation in speed while doing so. One solution is to use multiple processors.

COMPATIBILITY

So far, there is no standard technology accepted by a standards granting organization that governs tracking systems. Accordingly, it is important that any tracker be supported by vendors of VR software, VR hardware, graphics software, and workstations.

UNENCUMBERED TRACKING

The one disadvantage of all theses tracking systems is that the user must wear wires or sensors. A true virtual world would not require such attachments. The best fictional example of an unencumbered VR system is the Holodeck on the TV show *Star Trek: The Next Generation.*

Myron Krueger is one of the first, if not the first, engineer to conceive of and build prototype VR systems. For over two decades he has maintained that true VR systems would not force users to wear bulky HMDs, uncomfortable gloves, or use artificial devices, such as joysticks or mice. Instead, they would enable the user to walk through the virtual world perceiving all it has to offer using only their five senses. In 1971, at the University of Wisconsin, Krueger created Psychic Space, a VR environment that users moved though using their own foot power. Special sensors detected the users' locations at every instant. As a participant reached different locations in the room, different images were displayed or musical pieces sounded. Psychic Space contained a virtual maze in which virtual walls would turn into real walls if participants tried to cheat by crossing a boundary. Since that time, Krueger says he has developed or helped develop over 20 different scenarios in which unencumbered users were tracked. The tracking mechanisms used in these scenarios fall into four general categories:

1. Sensors in the floor
2. TV with image-recognition software
3. A sensory floor
4. Hand gestures

Whatever technology Krueger used, the goal was complete freedom of movement and no encumbrances. Despite the best efforts of Krueger and others, tracking devices remain clumsy, slow, and restrictive. But technology is moving ahead at a rapid pace. Still, few think Krueger's dream of an unencumbered VR environment will be reached any time soon.

TRACKING DEVICES

ADL-1

ADL-1 from Shooting Star Technology is a six-degrees-of-freedom head position/orientation mechanical tracker. It uses joint angles to compute the head's geometry.

Shooting Star Technology
Burnaby, B.C.
Canada V5B 3W4

A Flock of Birds

A Flock of Birds from Ascension Technology Corporation is a six-degrees-of-freedom tracker. It can simultaneously track the position and orientation of 1 to 30 receivers over a range of three feet. Precision is rated at 0.5 degrees and 0.1 inches. The product uses DC fields, which reduce the distorting effects of nearby conductive metals and eliminate the distorting effects of stainless steel.

Ascension Technology Corporation
Burlington, VT

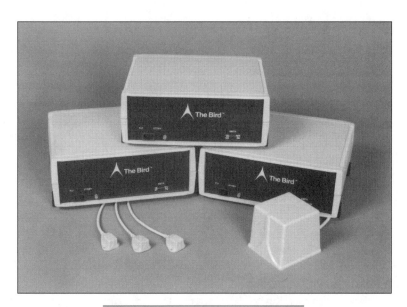

Figure 10.2 A Flock of Birds tracker.

Extended Range Transmitter (ERT)

To extend the range over three feet, Ascension Technology offers an Extended Range Transmitter (ERT). This is a long-range transmitter which boosts the range to eight feet. Multiple ERTs may be linked together to further extend the range.

ISOTRAK II

ISOTRAK II is a six-degrees-of-freedom position sensor that supports up to two receivers with a single transmitter and has an accuracy of 0.1 inches. Combined with an optional stylus, it also can be used as a digitizer.

> Pothemus Inc.
> Colchester, VT

FASTRAK

FASTRAK is an electromagnetic six-degrees-of-freedom tracking system with a range of 10 feet. FASTRAK tracks the position and orientation of 1 to 32 receivers (it accepts data from up to 4 receivers and up to 8 systems can be multiplexed).

INSIDE**TRAK**

InsideTRAK is a PC installable version of FASTRAK.

Voice Input

A perfect immersive VR system—one in which users communicate as naturally as they would in a real world—would incorporate voice input and control. Controlling the system though pointing one's finger, or worse, though a joystick or mouse, is extremely unnatural.

Fortunately, voice input and control systems are increasing in functionality and power. In fact, within the next few years, we may very well see voice systems that are fully capable of handling many types of VR applications.

The main goal of speech recognition software developers has been to create a system with functionally unlimited vocabulary and complete speaker-independence, and that allows for continuous speech and that offers very high accuracy rates.

At present, though, there is no system that gives you all those features. "Continuous speech" refers to the capability of the computer to understand words spoken in a normal cadence. Because recognition of continuous speech requires complex algorithms, current voice systems that use continuous speech have limited vocabularies. Vocabularies of two to three thousand words are much too small for many VR applications. The systems do allow you, however, to switch active vocabularies. So as the VR system changes the scene, the vocabulary the computer expects to hear can change. In this way, VR systems can greatly broaden the number of words that can be used throughout the VR session.

The opposite of continuous speech is discrete speech. Systems that employ this technology require users to pause very briefly between words. This pause can be very short, however. In fact, users have demonstrated the ability to input seventy words a minute using a sort of machine gun cadence.

Although you can get used to speaking quickly to discrete systems, few people will ever feel comfortable with it. Users report that they become fatigued after an hour or so of speaking in the robot-like discrete speech cadence.

Discrete speech systems have the advantage of offering very large vocabularies. DragonDictate Power Edition, for example, the top-of-the line software from Dragon Systems, Inc. (Newton, MA) comes with a 60,000 word vocabulary.

Large vocabularies, of course, demand more computing power. Listen for Window's from Verbex Voice Systems, Inc. (Edison, NJ), for example, allows for continuous speech in the limited domain of Windows commands. When it is used for data entry, it has to be customized to limit the responses the system expects to receive at any time. The reason for these limitations is its relatively small 2,290-word maximum active vocabulary. But it only uses 4 to 5M of disk space and 4M of RAM. And you can buy the software for about $100.

By contrast, DragonDictate Power Edition (with 60,000 words) requires 46M of disk space and 16M of RAM. It costs around $2,000. (Dragon Systems has two other versions of its Dictate product: Starter and Classic. They have a 5,000 and 30,000 word vocabulary, respectively, and use fewer computer resources than the Power edition.)

Besides making heavy use of resources, another problem of current voice systems is that their accuracy rate makes them uncomfortable for many users. Some systems require that they be trained for each use. Others, which work out of the box, are called "speaker independent." Those that require training tend to be more accurate, but many speaker independent systems now have the capability to adapt to each user's voice. So over time, they improve in the accuracy.

Although accuracy may improve, no system today boasts an accuracy rate of over 98 or 99 percent (and many are as low as 96 or 97 percent. Even a system capable of offering 99.5 percent accuracy means that it would interpret one out of every 200 words incorrectly. When compared with the capability humans have of understanding each other, this level is extremely low.

Accordingly, all current voice recognition systems require some means of allowing the user to constantly check accuracy and make changes as needed. With DragonDictate, for example, each time a word is spoken, a box appears on the screen with a list of words the system thinks you said. If the correct word is on top of the list, you go on to the next word. Words further down the list can be selected by voice or keyboard. If your word doesn't appear on the list, you must either type or spell it out.

In a VR system without a keyboard, such error checking would be extremely difficult. And if a user is interpreted incorrectly too many times, the system would quickly move from fascinating to frustrating.

Efforts to improve accuracy are stymied in some cases by the requirements inherent in the creation of a natural-feeling virtual world. One way to improve accuracy is to have the system analyze the context of the sentence for each word. To do that, however, the system needs to analyze the words that follow. In a dictation system this would mean that the screen would show one word, an initial guess, but might change its mind a few seconds later. Putting aside the question of whether this is acceptable for dictation, it can hardly be thought of as usable for VR systems, in which immediacy is essential.

Virtual Presence

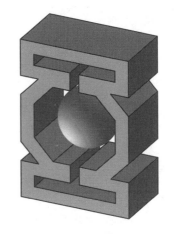

Telepresence, or virtual presence, applications enable people to operate equipment, often robots, from remote locations. By using VR technology to provide an immersive experience, the operators may be better able to control the machine for precision activities.

One of the most ambitious telepresence projects is Virtual Environment Vehicle Interface (VEVI), being considered by NASA to control robots exploring Mars.

The exploration of Mars provides several daunting challenges. For one thing, the terrain is rocky and sandy. Several Russian institutes designed a vehicle that can actually dig itself out of the sand. The vehicle, which was developed for a 1996 Mars exploration to be launched in cooperation with France and Germany, was demonstrated for NASA and McDonnell Douglas in 1993. Navigating around an airplane hangar, the vehicle's six titanium wheels were able to move around the man-made obstacle course of rocks and loose sand.

But the difficult terrain is only one challenge. The second challenge was finding a means of controlling the vehicle from tens of millions of miles away. One consequence of the immense distance is that visual images from the vehicle won't reach Earth and commands sent from Earth won't reach the vehicle for 20 to 40 minutes after they are sent. Accordingly, the Earth-bound operator may see a looming boulder after the vehicle has already collided with it. Applying a brake after the image of the boulder appears may be useless.

One non-VR solution is called the "move and wait" strategy. The vehicle moves one or two meters. Then it stops, senses the environment, and transmits the images to the earth station. Half an hour later, the remote operator receives the images, determines where the vehicle should move to next, and sends the command for it to move two meters in the appropriate direction. The problem with this method is obvious. The robot vehicle's speed would rarely reach more than four meters an hour.

Besides being frustrating and slow, there is another problem with this method. The remote vehicle would necessarily be powered at least partly by a battery pack with limited power. It would have to complete its work as quickly as possible before it ran out of energy. At four meters an hour, the system would only be able to explore a tiny area of the planet's surface.

A VR solution to the problem is being developed. Called Virtual Environment Vehicle Interface (VEVI), the system enables an operator to plan out and transmit one or two hours worth of activity at one time. The system uses a Silicon Graphics workstation and a stereoscopic viewing goggles.

After the image of the landscape is transmitted to Earth, VEVI models the digitized images. Image interpretation software determines what the images in the distance are and stores that information in the database. As the Earth-bound pilot navigates the vehicle, he or see sees a VR world that approximates what the real vehicle is seeing at that very moment.

Of course, the distance the operator is able to travel in this virtual world without having to have the data refreshed depends on factors, such as the vehicle's line of sight and the speed at which the vehicle is commanded to travel. But in all cases, the pilot in the virtual world should be at least somewhat ahead of the vehicle, thus dramatically reducing the lag time involved.

VEVI was developed by NASA Ames engineers in about six months using a combination of C, the Task Control Architecture (TCA) from Carnegie Mellon University, and the WorldToolKit by Sense8 Corporation of Sausalito, CA. Its first test was on a standard electric wheelchair.

VEVI has also been used in multi-user VR systems. The underlying communications protocol is TCP/IP. So users all over the world can share control of any VEVI robot or vehicle using the Internet. VEVI has been successfully tested with up to five network users controlling two vehicles. NASA's goal is to permit a team of scientists, geologists, and biologists to work together on a joint mission. At any time, for example, a geologist can stop the vehicle and ask the it to pick up a rock sample.

Because VEVI was designed using building block modules, the interface easily can be reconfigured to control new vehicles, according to NASA. In fact, it was adapted to the Russian vehicle in just three days.

VEVI and Interactions

In the telepresence mode, the remote camera's position and orientation are determined by the position of the operator's head. In this mode, the remote camera is required to keep up with the operator's movement like in standard VR systems. This mode normally is used when the communications bandwidth between the vehicle and operator is large and the lag time is short.

In a pure virtual environment, such VEVI, the operator does not have a direct view of the real world. Instead, he or she sees a computer-generated world. In the case of the Mars experiment, this computer-generated virtual world may be, at the time the operator views it, 30 minutes in the future. This advance notice gives the operator time to send a command to the robot based on images he or she sees at the moment. This mode of telepresence is more useful when communications bandwidth is small or the lag time is large.

A third telepresence mode is a combination of the other two modes. Ames is hoping to use this mixed mode in its future VEVI applications. In this mode, the remote operator can choose at any time to view the live video, computer-generated imagery, or a combination of the two. The advantage of this flexible mode is that it enables the remote pilot to determine the best way of sensing the environment based on the particular time delays and the type of landscape.

HEAD TRACKING

For the image to correspond to the direction in which the viewer is looking, VEVI had to incorporate some form of head tracking device. For the experiment, it used the head tracking function in the CrystalEyes HMD, which contains an ultrasonic head tracking device that tracks six degrees-of-freedom.

STEREOSCOPIC VIEWING

Stereoscopic viewing systems, whether on an eyepiece or a computer screen, create virtual worlds that look more realistic. For games and simulations, these systems help create an environment in which the viewer can suspend disbelief in the virtual world. There also are advantages in efficiency and effectiveness in stereo viewing for those using VR as a tool for telepresence.

Stereo viewing provides a sense of perspective. This is important when attempting to use a robotic arm to perform an operation on another object. Even with stereo viewing, coordinating the arm to pick up an object is usually a trial and error affair: the user moves the arm forward, misses the object, and tries again, this time moving the arm closer. But without stereo, it is extremely difficult to see whether you're moving closer or further away. (Try touching a point with a pencil while you have one eye closed to see how important stereo viewing is to fine motor activities.)

In fact, manipulating several robotic arms in motion is almost impossible. Most users find that without depth perception they crash the arms into each other. To create a stereo view of a digitized image, you have to program a series of stereo pairs from the three-dimensional terrain database. Each member of the stereo pairs display the same terrain as the other but from a slightly different perspective.

Although stereo viewing can be achieved with the eye piece, a more efficient, if also more cumbersome, method is to use a graphics workstation. In one version of the VEVI experiment, users watched a monitor on a stereo-ready workstation. Each image of the stereo pair was displayed alternately at 120 frames per second, twice the usual frequency. To see the image as stereo, viewers wore CrystalEyes eye wear. Synchronized with the monitor using an infrared emitter, the eye wear acts as a high-speed shutter, allowing each eye to see a different image. When the left image is displayed on the video screen, the shutter on the left eye opens and the one on the right eye closes. When the right image is displayed, the opposite occurs.

OTHER TELEPRESENCE EXPERIMENTS

Another telepresence system related to VEVI is NASA's glove box. Operators place their hands into gloves in a box. Each hand movement is replicated on Mars by the robot's hands. The goal is to enable the remote scientist to perform experiments with plant and animal specimens.

Yet another telepresence application was demonstrated to the Monterey Bay Aquarium Research Institute (MBARI) in Monterey, CA. The system was used to remotely operate a vehicle whose task was to create a detailed record of the underwater Monterey Canyon. Operators used a 3 x 5-foot simulated undersea terrain to perform undersea operations with a robotic arm.

Military
Applications

As weapons become more sophisticated, the cost of war games on a real battlefield and of firing live ammunition has increased over the years. Accordingly, all branches of the military have been furthering efforts to incorporate more simulations into training. Many of those new simulations include immersive VR technologies.

VIRTUAL TRAINING FOR WAR

One of the most advanced working simulations is the mission rehearsal simulator being built for the special operations forces. It not only simulates weapon and aircraft systems, it also incorporates some intelligence data. Another VR simulator is made by Montreal-based CAE Electronics Ltd. The company has long been a major manufacturer of flight simulators. Recently the company bean developing HMD-based VR simulators.

Much of the early work and experimentation with CAE Electronics' simulators has occurred at the U.S. Army Research Institute in Fort Rucker,

AL. Pilots wearing HMDs sit in a model of an Apache attack helicopter cockpit. Visual images come though the HMD. The pilot simulates flying by manipulating control rods. Evans & Sutherland Computer Corporation, Salt Lake City, UT, produces the image generator.

The advantage of HMD simulators over older simulators in which an image was shown on a screen in front of the pilot is that now the trainee can actually look outside the virtual cockpit canopy and see the missile pods and rockets.

SIMNET

Possibly the most well-known, and certainly the most ambitious simulation is the Defense Simulation Internet(SIMNET). The purpose of this project is to provide training for soldiers who may be dispersed at locations throughout the world. This project enables diverse simulators (mostly cab-type simulators but immersive VR can be used as well) to be connected into a single network. SIMNET consists of over 200 tank and armored fighting vehicle simulators in several different locations.

CCTT

The Close Combat Tactics Trainer (CCTT) program extends the capabilities of SIMNET by adding a large number of tanks and other vehicles and squads of soldiers called Dismounted Infantry. These squads are controlled by the squad leaders. Semi-Automated Forces (SAFOR) provides the opposing forces for CCTT. SAFOR contains an array of engagement rules monitored by the system computer.

STINGER MISSILE SIMULATION

Division Limited (Bristol, UK) and TNO Physics and Electronics Laboratory (the Netherlands) are developing prototypes to asses how VR can be used in military training and simulations.

One of the first prototypes is a Stinger portable missile system. Trainees carry a replica of the hand-held missile launcher, which acts as input to the system similar to that offered by a joystick. The user also wears an HMD. From the user's perspective, he or she is standing on an actual terrain with real targets. The simulation is used in such areas as target identification, operating procedures, and missile firing.

Division Limited and TNO Physics and Electronics Laboratory claim that their stinger simulation is cheaper than the traditional dome-display simulations. It also is much less cumbersome. And because it is portable, it can be shipped to users rather than having trainees fly to a central training site. Despite its small size, the companies insist that the VR system provides at least the same level of training available from large-scale simulation systems.

SPACE WALK SIMULATION

TNO has also developed a prototype of a space walk system that enables two trainees to work together. They can both access the simulation simultaneously and assemble a space experiment. The simulation simulates zero gravity by replicating the conditions of working in weightless condition and in a vacuum.

DISTRIBUTED INTERACTIVE SIMULATION

Military simulations are beginning to replace traditional war games. The Department of Defense (DoD) plans to develop Distributed Interactive Simulation (DIS) and VR simulations of weapons, vehicles, and aircraft. The next generation of SIMNET will be based on the Distributed Interactive Simulation (DIS) protocol, which has been defined by the Orlando Institute for Simulation & Training.

According to some DoD officials, the advantage of using VR for simulations is that it is can be changed at much lower cost than traditional simulations. The Department spends millions each year on simulators that can be used for only one type of training. By contrast, a VR system can be programmed, stored in memory, and activated at the touch of a switch. To change the simulation, only the software has to be altered. One VR unit can be used to simulate any number of training situations. Trainees can enter the DIS battlefield at any time. They can change locations, change sides, and replay events. Already systems, such as The Advanced Research Project Agency's (ARPA) SIMNET program links discrete weapon system trainers over wide area networks (WANs) enabling trainees in different locations to train interactively. Similar VR projects include the Air Force's JETNET and the U.S. Navy's WARNET programs.

In 1992, the U.S. Army contracted with a number of companies, including IBM, Dynamics Research Corporation, and ECC International, to develop the first operational DIS-based simulation system: the Close Combat Tactical Trainer (CCTT) program. The $400 million project will result in a simulation of combat vehicles, weapon systems, and infantry.

The CCTT will also simulate upper command and control functions, such as combat support, combat services, logistics, and engineering. It will, for example, allow trainees to send in additional forces.

When complete, CCTT will include a number of terrain databases, including one for desert terrain and a second for forested terrain. Each of the terrains will include all the features normally found there. The simulation also will display the effects of weapons, weather, and light conditions.

In the first version of DIS, 500 entities could communicate. Currently, the system can handle from 1,000 to 1,500 entities. According to developers, that number is the maximum that can be accomplished using a Local Area Network. The ultimate goal is to reach 100,000 entities.

◙ ELECTRONIC WARFARE, COMMUNICATIONS, AND INTELLIGENCE

The next step for the U.S. military is simulations that support electronic warfare, communications, and intelligence. The Army has determined that to configure current VR systems to incorporate those function would require processors not yet available. To cite just one problem, electronic warfare in air and naval applications involve vast amounts of space and exceptionally large number of electromagnetic emitters.

ADVANCED DISTRIBUTION SIMULATION TECHNOLOGY

An army project related to DIS is the Advanced Distribution Simulation Technology (ADST), which has been contracted to the Loral Corporation. It will provide an electronic virtual battlefield accessible to users throughout the world. Besides providing training, this project will allow weapon systems to be evaluated before development.

I-PORT

One of the most advanced war simulators, the I-Port simulator, is being developed by the Advanced Research Projects Agency. The first U.S. military simulator aimed at foot solders, it would project combatants into realistic combat simulations that include sound, three-dimensional graphics, tactile responses, and even physical exertion. At present, there are several design concepts for the I-Port simulator. In the most advanced form, a soldier would wear an HMD as well as a full-body data suit with exoskeletal interfaces.

The soldier will see full-color, 3-D optical array, hear through stereoscopic sound devices, and experience touch through the data suit. Physical activity will be programmed into the combat scenarios. For instance, if the mission involves scrambling down a mountain or carrying a 40-pound pack 10 miles in the hot desert, the system will ensure that the environment as well as the level of exertion will be exactly right. The soldier, or course, would face virtual enemies. He or she could shoot and communicate, be seen and heard, and interact with all other objects within sight, hearing, or range of the weapon.

One goal of I-Port is that it be more realistic than any current VR system. With most of today's VR systems, the user has to be willing to accept things in the virtual world that do not appear real. In a combat simulation such as I-Port, if a soldier does not feel he or she is in real combat, much of its usefulness will be lost. The soldier will have to experience realistic kinesthesia, which is perception of movement and touch. Vision, too, will have to be more realistic than that afforded by present HMDs.

After an intensive feasibility study, ARPA concluded that a large part of I-Port could be built using existing technology. The study stated that military and civilian agencies, corporations, and universities have already developed many of the components that I-Port simulators will need. NASA, for example, has on its drawing boards and in prototype form powerful HMDs and tactile interfaces that meet I-Port standards. The Navy's Dexterous Arm Mechanism and other robotic projects will help in the design of I-Port's exoskeletal framework.

ARPA predicts a I-Port system capable of training 2,000 soldiers simultaneously would cost about $50,000. The agency hopes to begin fabricating and evaluating prototypes in 1995 and begin limited production the following year. After the project begins, ARPA hopes to extent its use beyond training foot soldiers. The technology might be able to be adapted for the training of medical officers, who would use the simulation to practice triage operations. Eventually, it might be expanded to other branches of service as well as special operations forces and intelligence organizations. It might also be used for local and federal law enforcement agencies.

NASA is also experimenting with VR for training applications. Following are some three examples of NASA projects:

◇ At Wright-Patterson Air Force Base, the Super Cockpit project uses high-resolution HMDs to teach pilots how to fly F-16 fighter jets.

◇ At the NASA Ames Research Center, Dr. Elizabeth Wenzel, a research psychologist, is researching "virtual acoustic display" for VR systems. This includes 3-D sound to assist air traffic controllers.

◇ At the George C. Marshall Space Flight Center in Huntsville, AL, engineer Joseph P. Hale has been using HMDs and a data glove system coupled to a Macintosh computer and Silicon Graphics polygon engine to do computationally intensive ergonomic analysis. He is creating VR prototypes to test design elements. He is developing, for example, a system to evaluate a furnace for growing crystals, which is being designed for NASA's Space Station. Users can enter the VR world that contains different designs for the furnace. Users can move around, reach up, stretch, all with the goal of determining the best design. There are problems with the current version of the system, however: objects don't behave completely as they would in the real world. For example, if you grab, and then drop a crystal (used for fuel), it doesn't fall from your hand as it would in a real world.

VIRTUAL REALITY GOES TO WAR

Although military uses of VR are primarily in the training arena, some hope to be able to put it to use in combat as well. The U.S. Navy is studying ways to use immersive VR to help officers orchestrate the complex scenarios that occur in naval battles.

The problem that VR boosters in the Navy hope to solve is that it is extremely difficult to visualize the action based on the numeric data generated from the various sensing devices. The issue is a result of modern technological warfare. In years past, a naval battle consisted of a number of ships facing off against each other in the high seas. Torpedoes and ramming constituted the crude, but easy-to-follow action.

By contrast, modern naval engagements involve hundreds of weapons platforms, both sea- and air-based, spread out over hundreds or even thousands of miles of open sea. The events are tracked by spy planes and satellites as well as reports sent in by participants. The data eventually appears on a computer screen in either numeric, text, or chart form. But no matter how the data appears, it is a two-dimensional representation of a three-dimensional event.

To create a mental image of this three-dimensional action, users have to make use of data from numerous locations, and then correlate that data in their mind. Of course, there is nothing exotic about this requirement. Managers have been making the mental 2-D to 3-D transformation for years. Gaining an understanding of the financial condition of a company by studying its annual report is one example of this process. But while managers may have weeks to make sense of reports and may employ dozens of advisors, naval commanders often have to accomplish the mental transition quickly, sometimes in a matter of seconds.

Accordingly, researchers at the Tactical Electronic Warfare Division (TEW) of the Naval Research Laboratory and The George Washington

University are developing VR systems to assist in this interpretation process. The system uses a Silicon Graphics workstation and a BOOM2 head-coupled display from Fake Space Laboratories, Menlo Park, CA. Unlike standard HMDs, which the user wears, the BOOM2 is a bit like a periscope: the user peers into it.

According to officials at TEW, the BOOM2 was chosen over HMDs for three reasons:

1. It offers higher resolutions. It incorporates a pair of video CRT monitors to present the user with an extremely high-resolution, wide-field image in binocular stereo.

2. The response time is faster. As noted earlier in the book, response time is important since the image has to correspond to the position of the user's head. The BOOM tracks the user though a direct-connect mechanism. The weight of the monitors is supported by a counterweighted, six degrees-of-freedom (X, Y, Z, roll, pitch, and yaw) armature. The BOOM2 mechanical tracking devices, located at the joints, are faster than magnetic or ultrasonic tracking devices on most HMDs. Although mechanical tracking is a much older technology, it eliminates the problem with noise and interference that often plague magnetic or ultrasonic devices.

3. It is more convenient and comfortable than standard HMDs. Because it doesn't require adjustment or cleaning and it doesn't actually touch the user's head, it can be transferred from one viewer to another without having to clean it or readjust straps.

To use the system, data from the battlefield is converted to VR images by the central processor and sent to a Silicon Graphics workstation. The image is displayed on a standard computer monitor as well as in the BOOM2. Using buttons on the BOOM2, the user can choose to view the battle from any viewpoint. For example, the user can get a broad perspective by viewing the battle from the air, and then he can zoom down on any aspect of it. Or the viewer can transport himself to the deck of one of the warships, even the deck of an enemy ship.

The main difficulty with the current prototype lies not in the algorithms, but in the computational hardware system. The processor cannot keep up with the task of processing large amounts of data from so many different sources, and then generating intuitive three-dimensional images. Accordingly, the system does not currently process real-time views of the battlefield. Instead there is a delay of a few seconds to several minutes.

After the problem with real-time computation is solved, researchers hope to allow users not only to watch events but experiment by creating virtual events and viewing the consequences. A user may, for example, request a bombing run from a specific position. The user can then watch the event from the point of view of the target's radar. In that way, the commander can determine the exact amount of time that will elapse between the initiation of the action and its appearance on hostile radar. Or the commander can initiate a number of virtual operations simultaneously to help in coordinating the various actions. It would be very easy, for example, to watch a theater of operation to see whether friendly forces cross each other's path.

NON-MILITARY APPLICATIONS

The simulation industry has been in a bit of a slump recently. The end of the cold war has reduced military spending in general, and although simulations are less expensive than training with real weapons and ammo, they are costly. The fact that the military has fewer new recruits also is taking its toll on the need for training programs in general and simulations in particular.

But what's bad for the simulation industry might offer some side benefits to virtual reality technology. Simulation companies are now looking for ways to parlay their experience and products into new industries. As a result, VR technology, which got its initial funding from the military, is having a wider appeal.

One reason that military simulation companies are able to move some of their products into other areas is that simulation technology has matured to the point where products are much less expensive than the earliest versions. The cost of software has dropped and, more important, the cost of computing power has also fallen.

REDIFFUSION SIMULATION'S VENTURER

Rediffusion Simulation, Ltd. (Dorset, UK) was one of the companies to move from being a strictly military supplier to serving other industries. Back in 1985, it entered the entertainment market by developing motion-based cockpit systems as well as VR computing systems for use in theme parks, including Disney's parks.

From 1985 to 1990, entertainment-related sales represented only a tiny portion of Rediffusion's total profits. But things changed in 1990, when it acquired UK-based Super X, the maker of 14-seater entertainment simulator called Venturer.

Rediffusion improved the Venturer. Then it decided to place both feet in the entertainment market. It formed the Leisure Products division, which is dedicated to manufacturing and marketing the new VR fun line. At first, the division merely bought and sold subsystems. Next, it developed VR software and finally was able to develop complete turnkey simulation projects. By 1993, Rediffusion began to install simulation theaters that used four-axis motion systems. According to the company, 15 percent of Rediffusion's 1993 revenue results from the entertainment business. By the end of the decade, the company expects that percentage to grow to 50 percent.

EVANS & SUTHERLAND'S VIRTUAL ADVENTURES

Evans & Sutherland (Salt Lake City, UT) made its living during the 1980s selling image germination software for military simulations and other applications. Like Hughes Rediffusion, E&S also had a period during which it prepared to move into the entertainment market. In the early 1990s, it released the ESIG-2000, a low-cost image generator. It had called the previous flagship product the ESIG-3000. The ESIG-2000 is a down-scaled version. It is less expensive and smaller, but it's able to produce photographic quality images.

E&S recently joined Iwerks Entertainment, Inc. (Burbank, CA). In 1993, the two firms released its Virtual Adventures, a virtual reality entertainment experience. E&S is also actively exploring the possibilities of merging its computer graphics with game machines developed by Namco, a Japanese creator of electronic amusement-arcade games. E&S hopes the partnership will enable the company to move from specialized expensive equipment to selling more high-volume applications.

Figure 13.1 A scene from Virtual Adventures.

MARTIN MARIETTA AND SEGA

GE Aerospace, including its Simulation and Control Systems (Daytona Beach, FL)—which was recently acquired by Martin Marietta—penned an agreement with Sega Enterprises of Tokyo to share technologies and licenses in order to create VR entertainment systems. The agreement is an extension of the one originally signed by Sega and GE, in which GE's photo-texture technology was to be incorporated into low-cost graphics boards for Sega's arcade game products. In addition to continuing the GE-Sega deal, the new agreement enables Sega to adapt and use Martin Marietta's visual-database generation system, which is designed for modeling large areas of real-world terrain and creating 3-D models of that terrain.

REFLECTONE

Reflectone, Inc. (Miami, FL) recently joined forces with Landmark Entertainment (Hollywood, CA) to create four 60-passenger dome simulators for South Korea's Expo. The total contract was worth $35 million. Reflectone's entertainment division, Leisure Products Group, is currently responsible for 11 percent of Reflectone's revenues. The division has started taking orders for its new 30-seat simulators for museums and shopping malls and its 2-seat interactive "pods." As a result of these new products, it expects to expand its entertainment division rapidly over the next few years.

LORAL WESTERN DEVELOPMENT LABORATORY, INC.

Loral Western Development Laboratory, Inc., has one primary customer: the U.S. Department of Defense. But recently, it formed a long-term partnership with Entertainment Systems, Inc., to develop interactive simulation games for amusement centers and homes. The two companies plan to develop a series of games based on 3-D graphics systems, which Loral originally developed for use in military simulators. According to the company, like its military simulations, the games will enable a large number of users to participate at the same time.

HUGHES TRAINING

Hughes Training, Inc., (Arlington, TX) recently signed an agreement with the U.S. IIT Research Institute (IITRI) to market computer generated imagery for locomotive simulation. Hughes Training supplies the graphics products and services. IITRI supplies the simulators.

The partners' first customer was the Burlington Northern Railroad. It ordered two train simulators. The simulation should enable instructors to provide a better training program.

The simulation's visual database, created by Hughes, combines static and moving models. Among the models are signal flags and a large variety of locomotives as well as flagmen. Users can select day, dusk, or night conditions and different weather situations, including snow, ice, or rain. Hughes Training has also developed simulators to assist in the repair of robots and training simulators for various factory machines.

CAE ELECTRONICS

CAE Electronics, Ltd. (Montreal, PQ, Canada) is well-known as a maker of simulators for the civil and military aerospace market. Although these markets still account for around 75 percent of their business, the company now sells its goods and services to other business customers, such as simulators for air traffic controllers, factory workers, and medical clinicians.

CAE Electronics has a marketing agreement with BellSouth, Inc., to sell medical diagnosis equipment, which enables doctors to make diagnoses over the phone. The system uses teleradiology, which is the process of sending X-rays or other images over telephone lines. The system employs high-resolution monitors and scanners.

Virtual TV

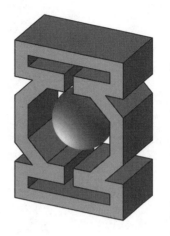

Virtual reality may become one major application of interactive TV (ITV). One of the most interesting interactive TV projects comes from British Telecom. The company is planning to allow home viewers to watch sports events, such as tennis at Wimbledon, using HMD.

According to the plan, high-resolution video cameras with wide-angle lenses will be situated at various positions around the court. These cameras will capture the entire field of view. Images from the cameras will then be sent over telephone lines to viewers sitting at home.

Wearing HMDs that include a head-tracker and stereo earphones, users will be able to see and hear the action in 3-D. As the user turns his or her head, the display will alter correspondingly. This chapter discusses what some other firms are doing to bring virtual entertainment to home television.

KAISER ELECTRO-OPTICS INC.

The most promising business deal in this regard was signed by Kaiser Electro-Optics (Carlsbad, CA) and VR1 Entertainment Inc (Boulder, CO). The agreement allows VR1 to offer Kaiser virtual reality headsets for people receiving virtual programming over television cable. Kaiser has given VR1 exclusive rights to its Vision Immersion Module (VIM) Personal Viewer for use in the home-cable market.

The VIM Personal Viewer is a high-resolution, lightweight, HMD. VR1 plans to create its own premium cable television channel, which will offer VR games and experiences. VR1 is also planning to license its software to other companies interested in developing VR software that will run on the VR1 premium service. It will also license its software to existing cable TV programmers.

In the first phase of the project, VR1 will download three-dimensional VR games to the customer's home television set. In the second step, a true interactive TV system will allow viewers at home to interact with the programming channel.

MICROSOFT CORPORATION

Microsoft is planning to create a software interface that will control the viewer display and selection mechanisms. The company stresses that its ITV interface will be nothing like Windows. Instead, it plans to develop the interface for people who have never seen a computer screen close up. The company is still tight-lipped about the exact nature of the interface.

Although the look of Microsoft's ITV operating system software may not appear like Windows, its marketing will be similar to its marketing of Windows. Microsoft will, for example, develop its own authoring tools, but it will also release the source code of the operating system to enable third-party developers to create other authoring tools. Microsoft has said that it would participate with standards bodies, but it also said it prefers to work with market-driven standards rather than those imposed by formal organizations.

HEWLETT-PACKARD COMPANY

If Microsoft contributes its software expertise to its operating system, Hewlett-Packard hopes to do the same for ITV hardware. At the National Cable Show in the summer of 1993, HP revealed its plans to create hardware standards through the development of a set-top box.

HP's first ITV customer is TV Answer, which can reach the 40 percent of U.S. homes that are not connected to cable, and businesses, which usually don't have cable. But the main advantage of the TV Answer system as a test bed for HP's set-top is that it represents less sophisticated technology than that of a fully switched digital network. Currently, HP is demonstrating its prototype set-top boxes.

HP has taken a modular approach to its set-top. The box has removable cartridges that allow cable companies to upgrade services without replacing the entire box. The modular approach also enables cable operators to provide different kinds of programming based on what type of options the viewer selects (and is willing to pay for). If, for example, a viewer wants VR programming, he or she would rent a graphics board, which could be placed in the HP box.

HP plans to produce basic set-top units that will retail for under $300. Although $300 seems a minuscule price when viewed in terms of computer equipment, many observers feel that this is too steep for the consumer market. This is especially true when you consider that the initial HP units won't have the 3-D processor board needed to display VR experiences. Later versions of the product, less expensive and more functional, will likely attract more buyers.

⊚ KALEIDA LABORATORIES AND SCIENTIFIC ATLANTA

Kaleida Laboratories and Scientific Atlanta (a manufacturer of cable set-top boxes) signed an agreement in which Kaleida will provide its platform scripting language, called ScriptX, to the set-top maker. If accepted by a number of set-top manufacturers, this development platform would enable ITV program developers to spread out their development work over many different boxes.

To encourage standardization on ScriptX, Kaleida and Scientific Atlanta (along with Motorola) are also developing terminals, servers, and networks using ScriptX. Several hardware manufacturers, including Hitachi, Creative Labs, and Mitsubishi, also are developing set-top boxes that incorporate ScriptX. To allow true interaction between viewer and the program source, distributed ScriptX will support the sharing of objects over the network and across ITV platforms. Objects would reside partially on a server and partially on the set-top. These shared objects would be synchronized in real time.

⊚ APPLE COMPUTER COMPANY

Financially, Kaleida Labs is heavily supported by Apple Computer. In fact, the computer maker supplies over 50 percent of Kaleida's budget. But in the intense rivalry to capture market share in the ITV industry, friendship goes only so far. Apple Computer is developing EZTV system, which may or may not use distributed ScriptX as its scripting language.

EZTV uses a remote control device that has a built-in microphone and speaker. The remote enables you to speak on the telephone, but more significantly for ITV, it enables you to use voice recognition systems, such as Apple's Casper, to control TV functions.

EZTV includes a large cursor on the screen and a trackball-like mechanism on the remote. The device enables you to control TV functions, such as channel selection, access to on-line services, or to move to telephone mode.

One reason Apple has delayed its decision to support ScriptX is that Apple and Kaleida may very well end up competing in the ITV market. Apple reportedly hopes to use front-end software it developed for its Newton palm-top computer as a front end to ITV. Also Apple has been making overtures to other companies that may well be strong players in the ITV market. Many of these companies, such as the Bell operating companies, are important for Apple in its quest to turn the Newton into a personal communicator.

Virtual Sports

Athletic endeavor often attracts high-tech training techniques. Current sports training programs do not neglect VR as a means of supplementing real world training.

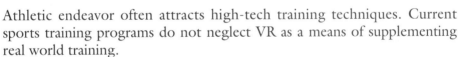 SKIING

NEC Corporation of Tokyo, for example, has developed a prototype ski training system. Skiers wear HMDs and ski boots and stand on piston-actuated metal plates. The plates provide the simulated bumps, slopes, and turns of a downhill course. A graphics workstation generates the images, which are displayed in the HMD eyepiece.

The NEC system can even be set to work with the skiers' psychological state. It includes a finger sensor that measures the flow of blood through the body. When blood flow is increased above a certain point, the system assumes that the skier is in a state of heightened stress. It can then adjust the slope to make the run gentler. On the other hand, if the skier seems relaxed with the current slope, the system increases the slope. Using this measurement, the machine always pushes the skier to reach new levels of skill but stops before the skier is in a slope too far beyond his or her skills.

⊚ Bobsledding

Before the Winter Olympics in Albertville, France, American bobsledder Brian Shimer used VR training developed by Silicon Graphics, Inc. (Mountain View, CA). The virtual course was a replica of the Albertville bobsled course. While the image was displayed on a six-foot-by-eight-foot screen, Shimer steered a four-man bobsled connected to the system.

⊚ Golf Design

The United States Golf Association (USGA) is using simulations to help establish guidelines defining legal golf equipment. The USGA high-tech center is called the Research and Test Center (Far Hill, NJ). One of its testing machines is a robot that simulates the golf swing of Byron Nelson, a leading professional golfer from the 1930s and 1940s. The "Iron Byron," as it is called, is used to test clubs and balls. The advantage is that, unlike a real golfer, this virtual sports person always makes the same swing (for example, the same speed and angle). The standards developed using Iron Byron and other simulations help assure that older courses are not made obsolete by high-tech golf equipment.

Iron Byron isn't VR, but it led to the next step: a VR-based Mannequin software package (by Human-CAD Corporation). This system uses computer aided design (CAD) to custom-create equipment for individual golfers. Currently, most golf club sets vary very little from each other. Typically, the variances are limited to weight and club head and shaft material. Although a few companies already make individualized equipment, the design and manufacturing process takes a long time and so the resulting equipment is very expensive. Mannequin uses tracking devices and body data suits to track the way a person swings. The CAD part of the program then automatically generates the perfect golf set for that individual.

VR will also be brought to bear in golf course design. Using VR systems, architects and designers will be able to try out each hole in the course many times before the earth-moving equipment begins work. All the input data for this VR system already exists. Basically, it would require three databases. One would contain information about the movement of the human body and about golf swings. Another database would require information about the design of golf courses. And a third database would contain data about the geography of the area in which the course is to be built.

The information for this last database is available through geologic maps and geologic information systems (GIS). GIS includes data about the geography of the area and about water tables, geologic formations, and property lines. With this database, the architect can choose to alter the area being designed, changing the flow of a stream or moving small hills, for example. The VR system also will allow architects and others to "see" how the course looks at different times of the day and experience the effects of prevailing winds.

▣ GOLF TRAINING

Currently, computer programs are available to critique golf swings. Golfer's swings are videotaped and the result is sent to image-processing software. The program creates a wire-frame of the golfer's actions and compares that wire-frame to its database of correct stances and swings. The result is an on-screen description of any problems with the golfer's stance and swing and suggestions for remedying the situation.

The problem with current systems is that they don't provide real-time coaching as a real coach could provide. First the golfer performs his or her swing. Next, the computer must process the information, which can take several minutes. Finally, the computer displays its critique. The golfer then tries again, and again waits for the result. Without real-time coaching, the session loses a good deal of its effectiveness.

On the other hand, VR systems that use body suits to capture data about swings will be able to provide the golfer with immediate feedback. The second a golfer makes a wrong move, the system can send an alarm and vocalize a description of the problem enabling the golfer to make changes immediately.

VR systems also will enable golfers to practice their sport in a more efficient (if less pleasurable) way than on a golf course. The advantage of VR golf is that it eliminates the need to travel to a course, giving the golfer much more time to practice. A golfer who has a few minutes before a meeting, for example, can don the helmet and play one or two holes. The simulations also will eliminate the need to walk from hole to hole, or to wait for other golfers. Finally, it will enable golfers to practice a problem area of a course until he or she is proficient at it.

At present, all golf-simulation games are screen-based games. The user manipulates an on-screen image of a golfer. Nintendo Entertainment System and Sega have golf games for PCs and TVs.

A new game, Par T Golf, by Optronics, Ltd. improves on the home-based games by using a computer, a film projector, infrared light beams, and a special enclosure to provide more of a feel for the game. The film projector displays the hole as it would look from the tee. A player places a virtual ball on a real tee and swings. Infrared lamps track the movement of the club to measure things like club-head speed and the angle of impact. The computer calculates the flight path for the ball. A video display shows how the ball would travel based on the projected flight path. (Currently the system is limited to only a few scenes, such as ball curving to the left or right or high or low.) Next, the projector displays the new location for the ball. The program continues until the player completes the course. Optronics has programs for several different courses.

The first "Virtual Reality Putting Green" was not sponsored or developed at a golf course but at the Pacific Science Center in the fall of 1993 in Seattle, WA. Designed and donated to Pacific Science Center by graduating electronic engineers at ITT Technical Institute in Seattle, the project provided users an opportunity to play a relatively realistic indoor game of golf.

Participants stand on a short, wooden platform. In front of them is a computer screen. They hold a real putting iron and use a real golf ball. After the putt, the ball goes under a platform where sensors record its movement and project where it would go if it were on a real green. The on-screen ball moves to where it would have had this been a real game. A mechanical arm retrieves the ball and sends it back for the second shot. After each putt, the ball on the screen moves from where it landed after the last putt.

How close does virtual sport come to the real thing? At present, no athlete, professional or amateur, would be wise to discontinue training on real courses or ski slopes. Certainly, the image, as vivid as it may be, is not the same as experiencing the action in the real world. The movement of the plates to simulate a ski slope or a bobsled connected to a VR system may approximate reality, but it isn't the same as the real thing.

Still, even in its current nascent form, virtual training provides benefits to the athlete. It is excellent for strength training, for example. It enables the athlete to develop those specific muscles needed to perform well in his or her sport. It also increases agility. And, although the training offered by VR systems may be imperfect, it makes up for that imperfection somewhat by providing an opportunity for more practice than is often available in the real world. Virtual worlds can always have the perfect snow conditions for skiers and bobsledders and the perfectly weather for golfer. Portable systems will enable users to train without leaving their homes or offices. And VR systems will enable athletes to get used to the kinds of conditions they will have to contend with in a far-off setting without boarding a plane.

Virtual Help
for the Disabled

Several different VR systems are being developed as a means of helping the disabled get around and to help designers develop real-world structures to assist the disabled.

A virtual world can be created to show the perspective of a person in a wheel chair. The architect's plan is entered into the VR application. Then, the architect sits in a virtual wheel chair, dons the HMD, and moves around the virtual world of his or her design. The architect navigates the chair around every nook and cranny of the structure, discovering which sections are difficult to move in, which are impossible, and which are ideal. The architect can try to turn faucets in the washrooms, open and close doors, and move up and down ramps to ensure that they are not too steep and that visibility at the top and bottom is sufficient.

As the architects explores the virtual world, he or she records any areas that need work. After the experience, the needed changes are made to the CAD drawing, and the data is sent to the VR system. The architect checks the corrections by re-entering the virtual world.

Harry Murphy is the founder and director of the Center on Disabilities of California State University-Northridge. In June 1988 the center held a conference called "Virtual Reality and Persons with Disabilities." Mr.

Murphy believes that "individual pieces of virtual reality" also can help people with disabilities. A DataGlove can be used to translate finger spelling or other gestures of a non-verbal person. The output could be letters on a standard computer screen, speech, or Braille.

For patients who don't have the ability to finger spell, such as stroke patients, the system can translate gross gestures into synthetic speech. VR also can help disabled people work, according to Murphy. He points out that although two-thirds of disabled people in the U.S. are not working, one-third of those don't work because they have no way of traveling to an office or they cannot find work in an office that can accommodate their disability.

A VR system, such as a computer that accepts hand signals as input would enable many more disabled people to work. Pieces of VR systems also may help people with prosthetics. Force feedback mechanisms and temperature-sensing equipment can enable people to "feel" though the prosthetic arm or leg. The temperature or force feedback would signal another part of the body, which the user would have to translate as coming from the prophetic. Other VR demonstrations and papers at the Virtual Reality and Persons with Disabilities conference included several very interesting and promising prototypes.

⊡ PROTOTYPE SYSTEMS

Some prototypes include the following:

◇ **BioMuse.** BioMuse is a series of biocontrollers including Eye Con, an eye controller word processor, and EMG, which enables muscle control of music and data display. BioControl Systems (Palo Alto, CA).

◇ **Brain Response.** This system uses electrical responses in the visual cortex of the brain to control keyboard functions though eye gaze. Interface Smith Kettlewell Eye Research Institute (San Francisco, CA).

◇ **Eyegaze Computer System.** This system allows the user to control the computer through eye gaze. The user also can see the position of his or her eye though an on-screen locator. LC Technologies (Fairfax, VA).

◇ **Interactive Brainwave Visual Analyzer.** This is a wireless electroencephalograph that allows brainwaves to control certain basic functions on a Macintosh computer. Meta Sound Engineering, Tokyo, Japan.

◇ **Pointing Keyboard and Tactile Feedback System for Blind Computer Users.** This is an eight-key Braille computer keyboard. The base is movable, enabling the user to scan forward, back, right, and left in a manner similar to reading embossed Braille. The position is used by the host computer to control the cursor position, and information passing under the cursor creates tactile feedback to the keys. This enables the user to read and write text without moving his or her hands from the keyboard. TiNi Alloy (San Leandro, CA).

Several universities are working on VR systems for the handicapped:

◇ **Monash University (Caulfield, East Australia).** John Lenarcic and others at the university are experimenting with the use of an electromechanical device for gesture recognition. The goal is to enable gestures to control computer functions.

◇ **University of California (Santa Barbara).** Researchers are developing a portable computer that includes a global positioning system (GPS). This combines a detailed database of the surrounding environments and a user interface consisting of an acoustical virtual display. The system enables the user to change the mode of operation and query the database.

◇ **The Johns Hopkins University (Baltimore, MD).** Researchers are developing an HMD for low-vision individuals. The real-time display will enlarge images in front of the user, creating a clearer image than without enhancement.

◇ **University of Illinois at Chicago.** Researchers are developing a new interface device, the CAVE (see Chapter 4). The CAVE surrounds the user with projected images of a virtual environment. The rear screen projection screens make up three walls of a cube. A fourth projector display an image on the floor. The viewer can move around in the virtual environment and see his or her own image as it interacts with real and virtual objects. The CAVE will be used in several ways to help the handicapped, including the design of handicapped-friendly environments.

◈ **University Of Toronto (Ontario, Canada).** In his Ph.D. dissertation, "Direct Manipulation, Through Robots, By The Physically Disabled," Charles David Halpern-Hamu explored the possibility of using pictures rather than words to help people with severe physical disabilities control robots. The human side of the equation uses VR-like graphical interfaces to create a rehabilitation environment. Halpern-Hamu calls the environment Accessible Direct Telemanipulation (physically disabled people controlling their environment by manipulating pictures to guide robots).

The first step toward accessible direct telemanipulation is to separate the user interface (in other words the virtual world) from the rest of the system (the robot moving in the real world). In other words, the way to communicate commands, such as "put the pot in the microwave," is an entirely different problem than having the robot carry out the commands.

To create a workable system using today's technology, Halpern-Hamu opted to use flat 3-D, which falls short of true 3-D conceived of in most VR systems. The first system developed using the Halpern-Hamu method is called Doorway, which shows the promise of using pictures to control robots.

Greenleaf Medical Systems is developing a gesture control system to improve the capabilities of physically impaired individuals, such as those with cerebral palsy. The gesture control system enables individuals to control computers or other devices though simple gestures. For example, Greenleaf recently crated a prototype of a system that enables telephone receptionists to have a Macintosh computer answer the phone or route calls though hand gestures.

The GloveTalker, which works along with DataGlove, will enable users with speech problems to have the computer speak for them. The computer will recognize simple hand gestures, such as American Sign language, and then vocalize the words. The program enables the user to determine the amount of freedom the computer should have in interpreting the hand gesture. So even users who are capable of only gross hand gestures may be able to use the program.

Other applications for the handicapped include the following:

1. To measure and quantify upper extremity function and movement.

2. Creating barrier-free environments for people with disabilities.

3. Help cognitively impaired and brain injured people control processes that otherwise would be too complex for them.

4. Enable disabled people to remain at home while their "virtual being" goes to work at another locations.

5. Enable blind people to navigate though a building using 3-D sounds transmitted to their headsets.

Virtual Manufacture and Design

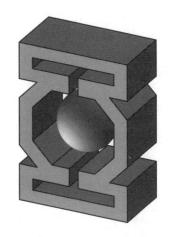

Virtual reality will assist in the development of products by enhancing computer-aided design (CAD) systems. CAD software enables users to manipulate a database that holds all the essential information about the product. In this database, the product being developed is represented mathematically. The CAD software uses the numbers in that database to generate a 2-D on-screen image. When that screen image is manipulated, the underlying numeric database also is altered to reflect the changes. if the product dimension is changed in the database, the corresponding image also is changed.

The reason CAD software is so helpful is that few designers have the skills needed to visualize a product based on its dimensions. A CAD program does that work for the designer. It enables the product to be visualized in the way humans normally visualize: though pictures, not raw data.

CAD has helped designers bring products to market more quickly. Before the advent of CAD systems, designers struggled with the numbers, drew rough drafts, and then finally created a model. The single goal of all the steps involved in the process from numeric data to real-world model is to provide a way to make sense of the numeric data. CAD programs automatically create 2-D screen images.

Still, for some users and some applications, a 2-D image is not enough. A middle road between building prototypes by hand and eliminating them through VR simulations are machines that can automatically generate models. New technologies exist that, using various materials, can build any model created by the CAD system. These machines are in essence VR made real.

In operation, these systems take a CAD representation and "cut" it into thin slices. A laser beam draws the outlines of those thin slices in a special cement-type powder. The heat from the laser fuses the powder particles together. The next layer is thrown on top, and the laser repeats the actions.

Laser sintering, as this technology is called, can produce models in wax, nylon, or some forms of metal. Currently, there are about 500 such machines in operation in America. Although these machines solve the time problem in developing prototypes, they are expensive and use expensive materials. They also cannot be used for many types of materials, a fatal drawback for some industries.

Still, the next step in automating prototyping may increase its usage, and as we shall see, enable it to be used in conjunction with VR systems. Called free-form fabrication (FFF), this technology enables automatic prototyping machines to create a metal FFF part that can work as a tool on an existing machine.

Fumihiko Kimura, professor of manufacturing technologies at Tokyo University, suggests how VR can assist in the manufacturing design process. The goal, he says, is to simulate, using immersive VR, not only the product but the manufacturing process that creates the product.

One example of this process is about to be instituted at Satra Footwear in London. The company is using WorldToolkit VR software to develop 3-D models of shoe-making operations. By moving machines around the virtual floor and experimenting with different sequences, the company should be able to make its operations more efficient. The company has decided to use a computer screen, rather than a HMD to enable faster response time and higher resolution.

Kimura says the creation of a car would include systems to test the production line, enable engineers to "crash" the car to see how stress points hold up, and even permit focus groups to "test drive" the car before it goes into real-world manufacturing.

Arlan Andrews of Sandia National Laboratories has developed a multi-user VR design system for auto design. Additionally, Sandia is working with FFF systems to fill in the details that cannot be programmed into the VR system.

Another VR experiment is taking place at Mercedez-Benz. The company is developing an auto interior planning program using VR. Working with Art + Com in Berlin, it hopes to create a system that will give test subjects the feeling of the car's interior. Then, they can give opinions on whether the interior is roomy enough.

FIRE MODELING

A British VR design project has been developed to learn about crowd behavior during a major fire in buildings. Siftware Colt Ventilation, Inc. is developing a system that imports the architectural layout of the building. Then, it asks for information about the types of people who are likely to be in the building at the time of a conflagration. (Based on research carried out at the University of Surrey, the system has a library of types of people and has coded their behavior).

To check on the safety of a building design, the architect dons an HMD, and then specifies certain features about the fire, such as its visibility and temperature, the presence or absence of an alarm, and the amount of smoke. The operator can walk though the building watching how people react to the fire and seeing whether they are all able to find exists and escape.

ENVIRONMENTAL SIMULATION

Environmental simulations enable customers or designers to test environments such as interiors of buildings or even golf courses. The Living Environment Systems Laboratory (LEL) at Matsushita Electric Works Ltd. (Osaka) has developed a system to simulate living environments using VR.

Using Provision development software from Division, Inc. (Redwood City, CA), the company has developed a way to eliminate the prototype phase.

In the past, scale models of building interiors were built to ensure that environment conditions, such as lighting, heating, air conditioning, and furniture layout were maximized. But building models for design purposes is not only costly but inflexible because any major change may require a new model to be built.

Using VR system, the designer can "walk" around the room, interacting with all aspects of it to gain a feel for its design. Any change takes less than seconds. The company has gone a step further in that consumers also are being invited to experience the virtual world. In its Kitchen World, customers can use an HMD and glove linked to a Silicon Graphics-based RB2 workstation to fly around a simulated kitchens containing cabinets and appliances they have selected. They can open drawers and doors, even remove dishes, to test the placement of equipment. They can even rotate the faucet spigot and hear the sound of running water, which becomes louder as they approach the sink.

The system is far from perfect. The display is somewhat cartoonish. It's purpose isn't to sell the actual cabinet types, but rather to enable customers to experience the general color and height of cabinets and appliances and the overall kitchen layout.

In future versions of Kitchen World, two visitors will be able to don separate VR outfits and walk though the environment as a couple. The VR system does enable customers to make minor changes to the kitchen in the VR world. They can, for example, rearrange some appliances or cabinets. If, however, the customer requires a major change, he or she works along with a designer on a CAD system. The new design is then downloaded to the SGI workstation that controls the VR application. The customer reenters the VR world to test the new design.

Because of the cost, the company only has one VR system at present. So the application is by appointment only, and it is used primarily for those who plan major changes to their kitchen or who are building a house.

Besides the Kitchen World system, several other applications enable architects to "tour" yet to be completed environments. Real estate developers can use VR systems to visualize interior and exterior environments. VR software can help with site selection to determine environmental impact and to provide the best view for houses. One company that makes real estate development planning VR systems is Environmental Systems Research Institute (ESRI) (Redlands, CA).

Architects and designers, people who have to conceive real world objects on a computer screen, will find their job much easier when using VR technology. Instead of handing a client a set of drawings or creating a set of stills to display on a computer screen, the client can don an HMD and glove and fly though the yet-to-be built structure.

A number of such walk-though product already exist and help architects visualize and their clients see the final result before breaking ground. Most of these programs enable clients to walk though houses, flick lights on and off, draw and open shades, open and close doors, move furniture, and rearrange partitions. All this can be accomplished with a few mouse clicks. Using software from companies like Virtus Corporation (Cary, NC) or Micron Green (Gainesville, FL), architects can help clients visualize their dream houses much easier than using standard artist renderings and blue prints.

Those who want to design their home without an architect can use products like MyHouse on their PCs.

All of these programs are displayed on computer screens. Immersive VR for architectural purposes has not as yet caught on. For one thing the lower resolution offered by HMDs when compared to VDTs create poorer, if stereoscopic, images. Even the lowest resolution computer monitors currently being sold have a resolution of 480 by 640 pixels, and many support resolutions of 1,152 X 870. HMDs, by contrast, are typically about 360 by 240 pixels.

Even very high-end VR systems fall short when compared with more traditional means of representing buildings. For example, the Pixel-Planes 5 computer at the University of North Carolina recently was able to display 2 million triangles per second (a world record) but only 500 to 1,000 polygons per second. The system used Sense8 VR software. According to some experts, humans can perceive 80 million polygons per second. Accordingly, the images from the UNC computer seemed flat and lacking texture compared with artist renderings on paper or computer screen.

VR systems that can handle the demands of design are still very expensive. And most architectural operations are relatively small with limited budgets. There have been, however, experiments with use of immersive VR in design. UNC has used a VR approach for part of the design work on their new research facility, Sitterson Hall. Using the architect's CAD files, VR researchers at the University created a virtual model of the facility. Using walk-though techniques, they moved around the "building." They finally decided that one area of the lobby would be too cramped and, using the walk-though, convinced the architect to move one wall to rectify the problem.

Four graduate students at UNC went on to develop an architectural modular program, an easy means of creating a virtual world. The program, called 3D Modular, or 3DM, enables you to create virtual images using tool palettes, such as those that line the screen in computer drawing programs.

The next step in using VR in architecture is to create virtual worlds made up of materials that act like materials in the real world. Currently, VR images are merely one step beyond traditional computer or paper images. A red roof is a series of shapes colored red. They don't have any of the attributes of the roofing material. The architect cannot analyze the structure by testing the properties of the components.

After systems are developed that include data about the properties of components, VR systems will enable designers to specify the exact components they need, cost out jobs, create bills of materials, and even do automatic code checks in their virtual structures.

◩ THE BUILDING INDUSTRY

Virtual design is being taking seriously by the building industry as well. The Building Industry Show (called A/E/C Systems 94) had, as its centerpiece, a VR exhibit created by Worldesign Inc., a virtual worlds design studio and product development company. The exhibit allowed designers to try out new VR technologies for rapid design and implementation of industrial, commercial, and residential construction.

One part of the exhibit was a Super Virtual Environment Theater (SuperVET), an enhanced version of the VET currently located in the Worldesign's Seattle studio. The theater included video projection and surround-sound technology. The theater was controlled by networked workstations, in which virtual worlds–called Worldspaces–are created.

The VR system was of the CAVE type. Viewers entered a 10 x 10 foot booth where they were surrounded by giant screens that displayed several virtual worlds including, the Port of Seattle's central waterfront, complete with a new port headquarters, cruise ship berths, a pleasure craft marina, hotels and office building, and the Odyssey Maritime Museum.

To show how the system can be used to facilitate design, participants were able to change the view to see current and future renditions. If a system were used in a real building application, users might compare similar buildings or experiment by placing different buildings on the building site.

In the Central Waterfront development project, visitors were allowed to walk though some buildings, change surface traffic patterns, and then see the effects of expansion on marine life. The system was financially supported by ARPA and Sun Microsystems, which also provided the workstations. Evans and Sutherland provided the "Freedom" accelerator boards.

▤ AUGMENTED REALITY IN MANUFACTURING

Boeing (Seattle, WA) is using augmented reality to design everything from complex wiring harnesses to simple rivets. The Boeing prototype was built by David Mizell. Its HMD is actually two tiny monitors mounted on an ordinary bicycle helmet. The entire assembly weighs about 1 1/2 pounds. The monitors project their images onto partially reflective lenses, enabling the user to see a blueprint or diagram superimposed on the component he or she is working on. The image changes whenever the worker moves or switches to another aspect of his or her job. The system uses either a magnetic or ultrasonic tracking mechanism.

The prototype, which has not yet been used in actual assembly process, will one day replace the arduous process of using papers diagrams. Today, workers assembling wire bundles, for example, are forced to lay strands across pegs on plywood boards. It can take more than 1,000 such boards to wire one plane. Not only is the process of laying strands of wire painstaking, but the boards take up a good deal of storage space. Using the augmented reality system, the computer would generate the image of the blueprint, thus replacing the boards.

Boeing realizes several hurdles will have to be crossed before the system can be put to general use at the company. For one thing, head-mounted tracking systems have to be perfected, providing immediate response to every turn of the worker's head. And there is the issue of cost. Although the system will eventually save the aircraft company millions, the initial layout will be around $10,000 per worker.

Virtual
Research

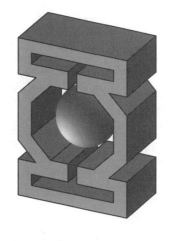

The advantage of using VR for research is that in many cases it is much easier to create graphical representation of things than actually visiting the thing itself. For example, we know much about far-off galaxies. The data we have is numeric, but from that numeric data, scientists can create a graphical representation of the galaxy. The same holds true for molecules.

Anything that can be drawn can be created in a virtual reality system. Given data about stars or about molecules, today's computers easily can generate the graphics. Create those graphics in 3-D and display them in the eyepieces of an HMD, and you have the makings of a immersive VR system. Add a sense of touch though a DataGlove or a body suit, and the VR experience is complete. This system enables you to "visit" the inaccessible.

⌾ MOLECULAR MODELING

VR can be used to make counter-intuitive processes more familiar. Take, for example, the study of molecular structure. Scientists are forced to study the atomic details using data resulting from measurements and sensors, not visual images.

To help in the study of molecules, to make it more familiar to our human experience, VR systems are being developed that create computer-generated pictures out of the abstract data. The on-screen images are not real but representations of measurements. The data from those images may be derived from X ray crystallography, in which a researcher irradiates a crystal composed of the molecule under consideration. The X ray beam scatters into a distinctive pattern, which can then be mathematically analyzed. The result is an understanding of the spatial distribution of electrons and the location of atoms.

Figure 18.1 An example of molecular modeling using VR from Division, Inc.

Another means of receiving data for the computer image is nuclear magnetic resonance (NMR) spectroscopy. A solution containing the molecule being studied is placed into a powerful magnetic field and exposed to pulses of radio waves. The nuclei of certain atoms in the molecule respond by emitting their own radio waves at predictable frequencies. These frequencies can then be used to determine the approximate distances between the atoms in the molecule.

A final method for determining the location of atoms in a molecule is scanning probe microscopy. In this procedure, a tiny needle, only a few atoms wide, is scanned across the surface of a molecule. A feedback loop providing information to the tip of the needle enables it to follow the contour of the atom. Each pass over the atom creates a different 2-D view. Multiple passes create a 3-D image of the atom.

After the coordinates of the atoms are determined, the computer generates molecular graphics, which can be flexible enough to enable them to be studied one piece at a time. For example, researchers can zoom in and out, or they can simplify the image to show only certain atoms. Jane S. Richardson of Duke University created a graphical representation of a molecule. It displayed the overall folding of the protein but eliminated the tangle of individual atoms.

B. K. Lee, now at the National Institutes of Health and Frederic M. Richards of Yale University depicted what a molecule might look like to a water molecule. The virtual water molecule was rolled around all sides of the molecule being studied. By noting where the water touched, the researchers were able to create a picture that showed the molecule's surface but eliminated those areas that were sequestered from the water molecules. This helps to determine how different molecules interact with water, which makes up most of the human and animal body.

Peter J. Goodford of Oxford University has developed a graphical means of visualizing how a biological molecule chemically interacts with atoms in other molecules. He positions a computer-simulated atom at various locations around the molecule. The computer calculates the chemical interaction between the atom and molecule at each point. Using this method, he is creating a catalog of favorable and unfavorable places of the atom. The computer-generated images depict the spots where an atom is likely to bind.

As scientists improve their understanding of biological molecules, they are able to modify molecules, a process that enables them to custom-design drugs, such as antibiotics.

Without VR, the data is collected in strip charts, oscilloscopes, or computer data analysis software. Then, a plastic model is built. But the problem with creating plastic models is that it takes such a long time to create each model. As a result, the number of molecules that can be studied is severely limited. Because of the difficulty of creating real-world models, few scientists were able to study complex atoms containing fifty or more atoms. Computer-generated molecules have been helpful in the development of drugs to treat hypertension, emphysema, glaucoma, and some forms of cancer.

Not only can computer-generated images of molecules help in the designing of drugs, they also assist in the process of testing them. Medical researchers have identified several proteins from the human immunodeficiency virus (HIV). By testing the interaction of different molecules with that virus, researchers eliminated the need to culture and test the virus in the laboratory.

Richard A. Lerner at the Research Institute of Scripps Clinic is designing customized enzymes to facilitate certain beneficial chemical reactions. Antibodies have the capability to recognize various molecules. When antibodies are modified to act as a catalyst, they might be able to attack a virus or break up a blood clot.

Together with John A. Tainer and Elizabeth D. Getzoff at Scripps, Lerner used computer graphics to help create a chemical site where metal atoms will bind. Binding a metal to an antibody is the first step toward designing catalysts, because many catalytic reactions depend on metal atoms.

The use of imaging pre-dated VR. In 1947 Raymond Pipinsky of Pennsylvania State University developed an analog machine, XRAC, to transform his X ray crystallographic data into a pictures. Today, scientists use two different methods to create pictures of molecules. In one method, the image is created out of sets of lines drawn from each collected point to an adjacent point. The advantage of this method is that vector-based displays take up less memory and can be redrawn quickly. This makes them perfect for immersive VR, where the image has to be redrawn based on the position of the viewer's head.

In the second method, the image is generated from a pixel map, a dense cluster of dots. Pixel-based drawings require much more computational power because each dot has to be assigned a number representing its color. The advantage is that the output is more realistic, allowing for realistic-looking shading and shadowing, and the colors have greater clarity. Parts of the molecule having high values of electron density, for example, can be rendered opaque and regions of low density can be rendered transparent. Volume rendering enables the software to simulates how light would travel through an object possessing those optical properties. At present, volume-rendered images require far too much computational power to be used in HMD systems. Therefore, pixel-based images are often used in "windows on the world" (WoW) or monitor-based VR systems.

The first use of immersive VR for the study of molecules took place at the University of Illinois and the University of North Carolina.

At the University of Illinois, researchers are using parallel processing supercomputers to model 24,000 atoms. These simulations enable scientists to determine how proposed drugs would affect biological cells. The result might be the development of drugs to combat diseases that originate in cell walls, such as arthritis.

At the University of North Carolina at Chapel Hill researchers can "shrink" themselves and enter molecules to study their structure. Using an HMD and a force feedback mechanical arm, they can navigate around the molecule and dock at any point to study the molecular structure. The force feedback arm lets the researchers feel the resistance and push of molecular forces as receptor and drug compounds interact. Plastic models don't enable scientists to feel the forces between two different sites.

To create this molecular application, scientists enter data about the bonding energies of different atoms. The program knows how to calculate the combination of intra- and intermolecular forces. The program then uses that data to control the force feedback arm.

The first chemical application of VR molecule visualization resulted in a pair of anticancer agents, which are now in clinical trials. They are the work of researchers at Agouron Pharmaceuticals (San Diego, CA). The drugs block the action of a key enzyme responsible for the rapid multiplication of cells. For the enzyme to work, it must open its submicroscopic cavity. Wearing stereoscopic glasses, Agouron's chemists guided images of molecules to plug the submicroscopic cavity until they found the molecules that fit snugly.

This initial work was performed on high-powered workstations. However, now programs working on PCs, such as HyperChem by Autodesk (Sausalito, CA), can perform the same function. One reason the drug industry is latching on to VR research is that for every drug that reaches the market, an average of 10,000 compounds are synthesized and screened. The process often takes 10 years and costs over $100 million.

Accordingly, Eli Lilly & Co. has determined that it can justify purchasing its own supercomputer to model complex proteins and enzymes and then use VR modeling to see how they interact in human environments.

Researchers at the Electronic Visualization Laboratory at the University of Illinois in Chicago are using VR to study the AT molecule used in the treatment of AIDS. The system enables researchers to seemingly hold a receptor molecule in one hand and the hormone candidate in the other. He or she can then see and feel how the two bind.

Besides being able to visualize atoms and molecules, VR systems, both WoW and immersive will help scientists communicate with each other. Using high-speed data networks, such as the Internet, researchers working in different parts of the world will be able to enter the same virtual world and see the same images.

Other research applications include space exploration and ecology.

▣ SPACE EXPLORATION

NASA has used VR technology to explore distant space, including Miranda (one of Uranus's moons) and Mars. The data for the system came from Voyager II. Currently, NASA is developing what it calls "telerobotic" technology. This will enable an astronaut within a space stations (or even one stationed on Earth to use VR to "spacewalk."

▣ ECOLOGY

Ecologists have already collected millions of atmospheric and oceanic samples around the world. VR researchers are now exploring ways to collect that data and use it to created animated images of the ocean. Using those animated displays to zoom in, researchers can watch how pollutants spread through the waters.

In a similar manner, researchers can see in a visual manner the spread of crop disease or how the ozone changes when in contact with various chemicals. At some point, researchers hope to create complete virtual forests. These can then be experimented with to show, for example the effects of clear-cut logging or of forest fires. They may even be able to "walk" though a forest devastated by toxic-waste dumping or deforestation.

Virtual
Medicine

Clinical medicine and biomedical research is second only to military applications in its use of virtual reality systems. Relatively simple systems have been developed to let doctors rehearse operations. Greenleaf Medical Systems (Palo Alto, CA) is using the DataGlove and data suits, both of which have sensors to track movement to obtain range-of-motion and strength measurements of rehabilitation patients.

Patients also are encouraged using the system. Mathematical data from the sensors in the glove and suit are transmitted to a Macintosh workstation, which displays impairment ratings in graphical format and also shows the patient how he or she is progressing. A similar application is used for gait analysis. Orthopedic surgery patients walk down a ramp wearing a data suit that measures motion. After surgery, the computer can display a composite before and after image.

Researchers at the Dartmouth Medical School (Hanover, NH) are working on a more complex project. Dr. Joseph M. Rosen, an associate professor of surgery at Dartmouth, along with Steve Pieper and Scott Delp (both programmers) is developing computational models of the human face and the lower extremities to examine the effects of surgical procedures. For example, the program contains data about the effects on various tissue and blood when a muscle is severed, when you stretch a muscle, or cut a bone. This data will be the basis of a surgical simulation that will enable surgeons to rehearse intricate and rare operations using a VR system.

⊚ X-Ray Vision

Henry Fuchs, a professor of computer science at the University of North Carolina at Chapel Hill is also working on "X-ray vision" glasses for physicians. To be precise, the experiment involves not X-rays, but ultrasound. Researchers use an HMD containing LCD screens to display superimposed ultrasonic images of a fetus onto a live video image of a pregnant woman's abdomen. In essence, the doctor seems to be peering into the patient's body through a window.

The main advantage of the system is that it might allow doctors to gain an accurate perspective of the position of a probe inside the body. In a traditional amniocentesis, for example, the physician has to make a visual correlation between the sonogram display, usually projected on a video monitor at bedside, and the position of a needle as it enters the uterine cavity and the amniotic sac. Using the VR system, the needle as well as the ultrasound image would be displayed on the same LCD screen, making the correlation automatic.

In the first test of the system, a researcher viewed the women's abdomen though the HMD while a technician moved an ultrasonic scanning instrument over her abdomen. The two-dimensional ultrasonic images were projected onto the HMD display in the correct spatial orientation. To coordinate the images, researchers used a head-tracking mechanism on the ceiling, which tracked the position of the surgeon's head. The two images were coordinated using a graphics-processing computer.

Although the system showed promise, the prototype also revealed some of the problems with using VR for ultrasound or X-ray applications. For example:

◇ The ultrasound imaged appeared pasted on top of the abdomen rather than appearing to show an interior of the abdomen. One solution was to create a graphical hole in the abdomen using graphics software. Then the image would appear to come from a recess or pit.

◇ Current processing power of the graphics computer allows only one eye of the HMD to be operational. Besides increased computing power, in order to gain a stereoscopic perspective, a three-dimensional ultrasound (not yet available) has to be developed.

◇ The resolution in the HMD is relatively poor and the head-tracking mechanism is still relatively slow.

VR also can be used to synthesize diagnostic images of a patient's body received from ultrasound, magnetic resonance imaging (MRI), and X-ray. This combined digital model provides much more complete diagnosis than any of the separate imaging techniques.

For cancer patients, electronic representations of the body can be used as input for a VR systems to allow a radiation therapist to travel around a tumor, viewing it from every angle. This should permit the radiation therapist to target the tumor more easily and accurately. By providing visualization of the relationships of various viewpoints rather than viewing numbers on a workstation may help the therapist to design more effective treatment methods.

Researchers in the Neurology Research Center at the Loma Linda University Medical Center (Loma Linda, CA) are using a DataGlove from Greenleaf Medical Systems to analyze hand motion in patients with Parkinson's disease. The DataGlove is a thin lycra glove with fiber optic cables running over its surface. The glove, along with an attached sensor, records the motion of the joints and the angular motion of the hand. It enables researchers to sample 10 joints simultaneously at 30 Hz to 60 Hz.

The initial purpose of the test is to provide objective data about the performance of the patients, whose disease results in muscular tremor and slowed movement. Without the glove, testing methods are relatively subjective. Examiners watch the patient perform some tests, and then estimate the level of performance. The DataGlove, on the other hand, provides objective numbers. The data collected from the glove is displayed as a representation of actual hand movement on a computer with the Advanced Visualization System (AVS) sold by Stardent Co. (Concord, MA).

Researchers are able to time studies to show objectively the effects of certain drugs over time on patients' motor performance. In one series, the patients arrive in the morning, begin some performance tests, then take their medications, and continue testing throughout the afternoon. The program displays subtle changes throughout the day.

In a more direct use of VR, the DataGlove and Stardent's visualization system are being used for rehabilitation work. The patient dons the glove, and then sees a representation of his or her hand on the screen. They then use the on-screen hand to play with virtual objects. According to researchers, the motivation in this type of exercise is higher than that when the patient is merely asked to do twisting and turning motions. Another advantage is that, because virtual objects don't weight anything, patients are able to manipulate them easier than manipulating real objects. For rehab patients, it becomes a mid-step in the process of regaining hand motion.

The Neurology Research Center is also experimenting with an eye-tracking system. In one application, an 18-month-old baby with a spinal injury was able to move a graphical element around the screen by moving her eyes.

▣ VR Surgery

At Ipswitch (England) Hospital, surgeons have performed operations using VR technology. Gastroenterologist Dr. Duncan Bell, for example, performed a colonoscopy with the help of a computer screen that displayed the precise position and shape of the colonoscope in three dimensions. He was also able to see 3-D views of the patient as the operation progressed.

The basis of the system is an sensor operating in a low-level magnetic field. The magnetic field allows a computer to track the precise location of the sensor relative to the colon. Images from the sensor are sent to the computer, which then produces three-dimensional color images. In the present version, the sensor must be slid along the length of the colonoscope's biopsy channel in order for the screen to show the full colon. In future versions, multiple sensors will continuously send data to the processor about their location. This will allow the computer to display the changing shape and location of the colonoscope as it penetrates the patient's body.

In the future, the system might be used to allow surgeons to perform operations remotely. They will wear HMDs, which will display true 3-D images of the interior of the patient's body. The surgeons will wear VR gloves to transmit the movements of the hands and fingers to robotic arms, which will replicate the surgeon's actions. Feedback of forces and pressures of the robotics hands will be transmitted back to the surgeons gloves, allowing them to get the feel of the movements.

The U.S. government is also interested in funding research in medical procedures. The National Competitiveness Act of 1993 allots $210 million over the next five years to develop "visualization technology" and "databases of remote-sensing images" over computer networks. These images might be transmitted on the data superhighway.

STROKE VICTIMS

VR can help stoke victims relearn impaired functions. The VR world can be set to a slower pace than the real world (objects can dropped or thrown at slower speeds.) After the patient becomes comfortable with catching or manipulating the slow-motion objects, the action can increase in speed gradually. As the patient progresses, the speed increases to the point where it is close to real-world speeds. Finally, the patient is ready to practice the same skills in the real world.

PSYCHOLOGICAL APPLICATIONS

Patients suffering from phobias often find relief if they are able to experience the thing that frightens them while they simultaneously relax their muscles. The ideal way to accomplish this is to allow the patient to practice on a slightly less threatening situation than that which exists in the real world. A VR system might, for example, allow a person who is afraid of heights or afraid to fly to experience the thing he or she fears in the virtual world. Because the person knows the experience is not real, he or she may be able to practice relaxation exercises during the experience. After a few VR sessions, the person may be able to experience the situation in the real world.

▣ MEDICAL TRAINING

Virtual reality may also be used for medical training. Dr. Richard Satava, a surgeon at the Silas B. Hayes Army Hospital in Fort Ord, CA, conducted a practice gall bladder operation on a computer-generated image of a human torso. Satava had developed a computer program to generate images of the human torso and internal organs onto an HMD. Using current technology, the images were portrayed in what Dr. Satava describes as "cartoon-level graphics." However, future versions will be more realistic, he expects.

Besides the HMD, Dr. Satava wore a DataGlove during the simulated operation. As Satava moved his hand and DataGlove, the hand in the computer-generated scene moved in a corresponding manner. Each action of the computer-generated hand, such as an incision, resulted in an appropriate effect on the VR torso.

Other VR cadavers, some built from scanned images of bone and soft tissue, are able to perfectly represent an injured patient. The system enables orthopedic surgeons to experiment with various means of corrective strategies, such as transplanting a tendon. The VR patient can then get up and "walk," allowing the surgeon to test the transplant under conditions of stress.

High Techsplanation, Inc. (Baltimore, MD) created a 3-D system to teach surgical skills. Rather than viewing slides or photos in a book, surgical students use stereoscopic lenses to view 3-D images of the interior of the human body. In this way they avoid the problems with the standard method of studying organs in isolation. When studying the prostate, for example, they can see the anatomy surrounding the prostate, such as the bladder. They also have a realistic view of blood vessels, nerves, bones, and muscles.

But the doctor not only sees the 3-D image in the High Techsplanation simulations, he or she also can operate using virtual instruments. If the doctor makes a mistake, cutting a blood vessel, for example, text appears explaining the mistake. But more importantly, the display shows the bleeding or other consequences of the error.

Recently, the National Institute of Health and Merck and Co. contributed funds to High Techsplanation to help the company develop a simulation for primary-care physicians. The first such system is meant to teach doctors how to perform rectal exams in order to distinguish between prostate cancer and benign prostatic hyperplasia. The system uses a data glove to give the doctor a sense of touch. (Touch is important in this type of exam). The doctor views a display showing what he or she is "touching." As a result, doctors later examining a real patient should be in a better position to visualize the organ as he or she feels it.

A number of orders for this simulation system have already been placed, including orders from Duke University Medical Center in Durham, NC, and George Washington University Medical Center in Washington, D.C.

Ixion Co. (Seattle, WA) recently developed simulations for various laparoscopic procedures. Dr. Joel Childers, an assistant professor in the division of Gynecological Oncology at the University of Arizona in Tucson, pointed out that the simulations are important because they help surgeons practice fine motor skills needed to perform laparoscopic surgery.

Michael Sinclair, a senior research engineer of the Office of Interdisciplinary Programs at the Georgia Institute of Technology in Atlanta, and other researchers from Georgia Tech along with doctors from the Medical College of Georgia have developed an eye surgery simulator. This machine looks like an operating microscope. Users peer at the eye through the microscope lens and use special instruments to "feel" such things as the contact of the eye structure and cutting. In the past, surgeons practiced on donor eyes. But donor eyes don't feel much like living eyes. The simulation provides a more realistic sense of touch and vision.

Researchers at Stanford University have developed a leg simulator. Doctors use it to try to predict what will happen if a muscle or tendon is moved from one place to another. This helps doctors learn the effects of transferring a tendon to a different spot after an injury.

Besides teaching medicine, another advantage of medical simulations is that they provide an objective and standardized way to evaluate a resident's surgical skills. Normally, an evaluation has to be done by another doctor who has limited ability to see what the operating surgeon is doing. Using a simulation, the computer can score the doctor on very objective parameters. The result will be not only an objective rating of surgeons that can apply nationwide, but also can result in more uniform and objective medical training. No matter what school you go to, if you use the same simulation machine, you will be trained at the same level using the same grading requirements.

Because the National Institutes of Health recognizes the value of these simulations, it will soon develop a computerized description of the human anatomy, called the Visible Human program. The 40 gigabyte program will be available via the Internet.

◉ TELEMEDICINE

Telemedicine is a technology that combines telecommunications, video conferencing, and medical technologies to allow doctors to treat patients in remote locations. Although telemedicine does not at present use immersive VR (and sometimes doesn't use VR at all), this technology is a strong candidate for the use of VR in the near future.

Telemedicine in general is growing in popularity. Since 1991, some 25 telemedicine projects have been implemented all over the U.S. Many of them connect rural hospitals with urban health facilities. A 1992 study estimates that the United States could save $132 million by making extensive use of telemedicine.

Telemedicine traces its roots to 1967, when Dr. Jay Sanders, now Director of Telemedicine at the Medical College of Georgia in Augusta helped develop a telemedicine system aimed at reducing the time doctors at Massachusetts General Hospital had to fight traffic en route to Boston's

Logan Airport Medical Center. The system, which connected the airport and the hospital, involved a television monitor and microwave unit.

Telemedicine projects being planned at Massachusetts General Hospital enable physicians to monitor patients remotely. As a result, the home may become the center of health care as it was 50 years ago. Many see a future health care system in which the center of patient care will be a "black box" computer. It will sit on top of the TV and provide two-way communication between patient and doctor. Several remote monitoring devices already exist. One example is the MDphone, which uses a portable defibrillator to restart a heart by remote control over a standard or cellular phone line.

One of the most ambitious telemedicine projects to date was initiated by the Medical College of Georgia (MCG) in 1991. A 130-mile telecommunications link was set up between the medical center in Augusta and Dodge County Hospital in Eastman. This project includes a diagnostic camera with a 16-power zoom lens that enables the doctor in Augusta to either pan the entire examining room or to zoom in on a tiny skin blemish, and another camera to which a variety of medical scopes can be attached. Using the equipment, an examination performed in Eastman can be simultaneously viewed by specialists in Augusta.

Physicians at MCG using the system are at present satisfied with the visual display and there are no plans to replace it with an HMD or screen-based 3-D display. However, the first implementation of VR technology in the project may be the use of a sensing glove. The one problem with the current version of the system is that specialists in remote areas are unable to touch the patients. A physician at MCG is presently working with several developers and universities to develop a VR glove for this purpose.

COMMUNICATION PROBLEMS

The main difficulty with telemedicine in general is communication bottlenecks and costs. Researchers worry that as more data has to be transmitted to incorporate 3-D images and sensory data for VR, telecommunications will be even more of an issue. It wasn't until the 1990s that the crisis in health care costs got people in the medical community interested in finding ways to cut costs. At the same time, a number of new technologies that could assist in telepresence arrived on the scene.

New compression and decompression algorithms were developed. Called *codecs*, the algorithms could be implemented on special DSP chips, in the case of Intel's Indeo codec, in software. More powerful and cheaper DSP chips that were needed to compress multimedia and to change analog signals to digital were developed by companies such as AT&T and Texas Instruments. In 1982, hardware codecs were the size of a chest of drawers, cost a quarter of a million dollars, and could compress a picture to 1/300th of its original size. Current codecs are the size of a computer chip, cost from $20,000 to $100,000, and they compress video to 1/800th its original size.

Communication costs also are dropping as throughput speed is increasing. Digital communication and networking, including ISDN, is becoming available to more people. The availability of Integrated Services Digital Network (ISDN) service, although still rare in rural areas, is expanding. The cost of leased lines, which are needed to transmit multimedia, also is dropping. Two years ago, for example, Jim Reid, the project director of the Eastern Montana Telemedicine Project in Billings, had to choose between a dedicated T-1 network from the regional Bell operating company or a dedicated T-3 network from a regional telephone cooperative. Both were very expensive and they also gave him more bandwidth than he needed for the video conferencing system he bought from VTEL (Austin, TX). He finally opted for a $8,000 a month T-1 line. But a more recent telemedicine project in Kansas was able to lease surplus T-1 line usage from the state at $35 an hour during the day and $10 per hour during evenings and weekends. And in Iowa, the state hospital association has proposed legislation that would allow hospitals to use a fiber optic network owned by the state government for telepresence projects.

Asynchronous Transfer Mode (ATM) will eventually provide the fastest bandwidth and make all these delivery technologies obsolete. ATM switches are in use at a VR telemedicine test project at the University of North Carolina. The project connects a Cray Y-MP 8/432 supercomputer, an image processing system, and a medical workstation to a remote site. The Cray is used for radiation therapy planning.

One alternative for telemedicine is to use current cable lines in place of telephone company lines. Digital Equipment Corporation (Maynard, MA) recently released a system that makes use of existing coax cable television lines for the transmission of high-speed multimedia data networking. Cable operators are expected to charge less than $500 per month for their lines, which can carry about six times the traffic that T-1 lines can carry. In the first implementation of this system, the Scripps-Howard cable company of northwest Georgia provided physicians at three different sites in the state access to magnetic resonance images and full-motion video from remote areas.

The cost of video conferencing systems have also dropped. A decade ago, when systems had to be customized, a typical price would range from about $250,000 to $500,000 per room. Current off-the-shelf systems can go for as low as $15,000 per room. In fact, several desktop video conferencing systems have been developed that enable users to see others on their 386, 486, or Pentium PC. PCS 100 from PictureTel (Danvers, MA) turns a personal computer into a videophone. It costs about $6,000. Compression Labs makes the Cameo personal video system (about $3,000) that runs on a Macintosh.

▣ MEDICAL WARNING

Although most doctors and medical researchers applaud the introduction of VR techniques into medical research and clinical practice, many also are a bit cautious. They see potential dangers, ethical and material, to using this technology, especially in clinical practice.

In 1991, an editorial in the British medical journal *The Lancet* speculated that VR may eventually be used to provide patients with illusory cures. The editorial suggested that a whole body DataSuit may allow the neurologist to restore virtual motor power to a brain-injured patient. Or VR psychotherapy may be used to transport phobic patients away from the thing that frightens them. Or VR might be used to distract and cheer up those with pathological grief. Although the editorial suggested that such attempts would be well-meaning, it was concerned with the "capacity of

VR to distort reality-testing in patients whose judgment is already impaired, the loss of freedom of choice of experience when in VR, and the dangers of medical paternalism."

It suggests a scenario in which a doctor enables a physically handicapped patient to "escape" from the confines of a bed or a wheelchair. The VR system has a menu of experiences, the details of which are necessarily based on the real life experience of others. The patient can go for a walk or climb the Himalayas. He or she can ride a horse or compete in the Indianapolis 500.

The editorial suggested that given this VR opportunity, the patient might choose to live most of his or time in the VR world, cutting off ties with real people and real things. In one sense, such a scenario may be positive, allowing the patient experiences which may be impossible in the real world. But the problem is that VR experiences lack one important aspect integral to events in our lives: no effort had to be made in order to achieve the experience. The editorial asserts that experiences contribute to our individuality because of the effort expended to acquire those experiences. Experiences also allow us to modify our views about the nature of reality.

Although real-world experiences provide many levels of purpose, VR experiences are unidimensional. Their only purpose is sensory, a distraction. Accordingly, the editorial warns against exposing vulnerable patients to VR until the full extent of its impact has been determined. A second danger is that the menu of VR-experiences will be limited by factors such as the capabilities of the computer system, the creativity of the designer, and the preferences of the supervising clinician. The patient's choices are therefore much more limited than the choices presented to the average person in the real world. Being able to restrict choices gives the clinician the same level of control as a jailer or a medieval emperor. The VR experience can be used to educate the patient in a way that the clinician deems important or even to torture the patient.

The editorial also worries that by restricting the patient to experiences that can be constructed on computers, it presents an artificial barrier to life. People living in the real world comprehend life based partly on freedom and restrictions (for example the inability to live forever, the inability to fly); VR-enhanced patients, however, will be forced to contemplate life based on the abilities afforded by the current state of technology at any given time.

The editorial states, "For patients seeking to understand, as many do, the purpose of their suffering, VR is as unlikely as hallucinogenic drug use to provide access to a deeper reality in their search for meaning." The result may be what the editorial calls "medical paternalism", which might lead to premature clinical applications of VR. The editorial calls for professional self-regulation to avoid abuses by experimenters and inept therapists. It concludes that VR may be developed for clinically justifiable purposes, but the medical community should examine the responsibilities that arise from the clinical use of VR.

STRIP
IN
SINGLE
PAGE
NEGS

Virtual
Exploration

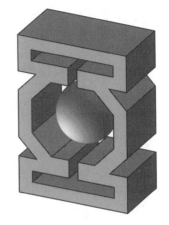

VR visualization technologies are helping in oil field exploration. VR has enabled geologists to view fault block models of complex geologic settings to determine yield calculations. For geologists to decide whether a fault block has reached its economic limit, they have to calculate the structural interpretation of each fault bounding the block and the horizons between the blocks. Next, calculations of reservoir shape, size, and volume are performed. The process of creating three-dimensional models of a fault block is relatively straightforward but extremely time-consuming. The interpretation part of the job normally takes geoscientists and engineers months.

In some highly faulted and heavily developed fields, the task is complicated by the wellbores that penetrate the area. A fault block may have sufficient reserves to warrant another wellbore. But when the engineers consider the task of drilling in the downhole area, heavily congested with old wellbores, they may determine that the process is too financially risky or even dangerous. One solution is to evaluate the wellbore traffic in three-dimensions using graphical representations.

The first attempt to use 3-D graphics to depict wellbore traffic took place at California's Wilmington oil field. Discovered in 1934, the Wilmington field has produced 2.4 billion barrels of oil. In the system, raw horizon data about the fault was turned into color-coded horizon points. The result was a 3-D fault model, which made the process of analysis much easier.

As the graphs became more interactive, closer to window-on-the-world VR, the analytical work became even more intuitive. For example, second and third versions of the system enabled users to return to an individual fault file, and view it from different angles. The user chooses which wells, or portions of wells, such as a sidetrack, to display. Those wells or portions not selected remain thin wellbore lines. In the Wilmington experiment, the interpreter displayed all of the more than 1,500 wellbores penetrating the target horizon.

Besides being more efficient, calculating volumes from a 3-D model is much more precise than doing so from 2-D maps. When economic margins for a field are narrow, precise reservoir volumetrics are extremely important. Besides determining reservoir size, the system enables engineers to plan well trajectories and to place new steam injectors. The system is also being used to determine whether a small target can be reached economically.

Wilmington field geologists and reservoir engineers found that, using 3-D modeling, they were able to verify and edit 50 years of interpreted data, which included many geologic horizons and faults. Previously, many of the field's structural relationships were not well understood. As a result, not all drilling operations resulted in optimal economic recovery.

In the future, geologists hope 3-D modeling will enable them to answer new questions, such as the proximity of the well to the nearest fault. They also hope to use completely immersive VR techniques to view the inside of a well as an astronomer may view the sky.

Information Navigation

Not all VR systems will be used to create a world that looks and feels like the real world we live in. Some systems will make it easier to visualize information by representing that data in virtual world images. This process is called *information navigation*. Systems allow you to navigate around data–in other words, find the information you want–similar to the way you would navigate around a city or a universe.

Metaphor Mixer, for example, is a PC program from Maxus Systems International (New York, NY) that uses a virtual world to let users visualize what's happening to stocks and other securities in many markets simultaneously. It begins with standard data from financial wire services. But instead of the data being represented in the traditional way as columns of numbers, it is shown as figures on a large chess board-like playing surface. When a stock's value rises, the image that represents it begins to rise above the board. If the value falls, its image sinks below the surface of the board. The image offers other visual clues as well. If the stock is volatile, for example, it spins rapidly.

The program can be user-programmed to provide visual buy and sell tips. If, for example, a user is interested in a company and its stock slips below the surface, indicating that the stock's value is falling, the stock's image can change color. So, for example, a trader can merely look for blue spinning stocks that are below the surface to find securities to purchase.

Information Visualizer, under development by Xerox, displays a variety of rooms, each of which represents a different project. You can furnish your room with tools that sit on a desk, such as a word processor or a calculator. Clicking on a tool brings up the corresponding program. You also can have bulletin boards or calendars on the wall. You can circle deadline dates on the wall calendar or leave messages for colleagues on the bulletin board. A fax machine in the corner allows you to send and receive faxes. Books on the desk enables you to open lists of data. The program also enables you to created sophisticated 3-D charts.

Virtual
Thrill Rides

The hottest new items in theme parks and amusement centers are VR movie rides. These rides offer a moving visual image along with motion. The motion simulates the physical experience of the visual action, which may be a roller coaster or a race car.

Simulator rides can be considered VR only in the broadest meaning of the word. The reason they fall short of being true VR is their lack of interactivity. But simulator rides quickly gave birth to those that include VR interactions.

When compared to real rides–roller coasters, for example–simulators fall short. Although a roller coaster ride may be created to replicate the physical feelings of riding in a real roller coaster, it lacks the danger element from actually being hundreds of feet in the air. However, simulator rides offer the advantage of providing a variety of entertainment without taking up the space requirements of real-world amusement parks. Simulators also can provide experiences, such as race car driving, not available to those who visit amusement parks.

Still, some observers believe that motion-based rides are becoming boring to many people. The story line is the same. The viewer is almost always in some vehicle, a car, a jet, a roller coaster. The vehicle takes off, picking up speed. It banks and rolls in conjunction with the theater movement base. And finally it lands or parks. The most conflict or true adventure may be something going wrong, a crash, or an enemy showing up and shooting. For many observers, once you have experienced this kind of ride three or four times, you have had enough. That can be a serious problem for ride developers and amusement park owners who have to spend hundreds of thousands of dollars for the simulators.

Accordingly, many observers feel the next step will be a move to more of a story-line type of experience. One step, although a tiny one, in this direction is Peter Gabriel's "motion storybook" video for his song *Mind-blender*. Although the video doesn't actually have much of a story line–certainly nothing like a traditional movie–it does offer scene cuts and varying camera angles and points of view. The video synchronizes live action, 2-D illustration, and 3-D animation to the presentation theater's motion base.

Still, longer feature-length films with serious plot lines may not show well in these special format theaters. In fact, having the system create motion after a period of non-motion (as would be necessary in a feature-length movie) may be distracting from the plot.

One of the first VR location-based games that include interactivity is BattleTech, from Virtual World Entertainment. The experience is realistic in a number of ways, even those things outside of the virtual world. For example, assistants are in correct space-age costumes. And yellow-and-black caution tape is affixed around the Ready Area. The VR experience includes warring feudal families, advanced technology, and the ability to control a gigantic robot. Each player has a control stick and a hand throttle. Those are the only two controls needed to play, but the instrument panel has dozens more controls for the advanced player.

When the game begins, the virtual sky turns a dark hue and you see your robot on your screen. Enemies, other robots and other craft appear on the landscape. You move your robot into the open, and begin shooting. Suddenly the sky becomes alight with missiles. Then a second robot appears; it's two against one. You turn from one to the other, and then decide to make your escape. You turn and push the throttle forward at full speed. Suddenly you're in a different landscape. It's time to explore. Taking one more look at the landscape to ensure that it's safe, you move around the new rocky area.

Some games were originally developed for training purposes. Hughes Training, Inc., (Arlington, TX) for example, has introduced MIRAGE, a multi-seat capsule that integrates real-time computer graphics, an advanced display system, and a digital sound system. The technology for MIRAGE is based on the simulation used in military flight simulators.

When seated in MIRAGE, players travel through a virtual world and interact with each other. Hughes is working with LucasArts Entertainment Company to develop games that can be customized to meet the requirements of movie-based fantasies, such as Star Wars.

Although simulations may never completely replace traditional thrill rides in amusement parks, several companies are opening amusement centers that feature virtual reality simulations. One example is the $30 million Cinetropolis that opened at a casino owned by the Mashantucket Pequot tribe in Connecticut. Although only slightly larger than a supermarket, it contains four different kinds of cinemas (some in motion-based cabs) surrounding a promenade of shops and restaurants. One cinema shows feature films shot on Iwerks 870mm format film (six times the size of 35mm film) and projected on a giant 60-foot-high screen. Another has a 360-degree projection and surround-sound. A third has a "turbo-tour" VR military-style flight simulations. And the fourth has VR experiences which change regularly. Despite its small size, Cinetropolis can offer its customers up to 15,000 rides a day in its 150-seat Turbo Tour theater. And unlike traditional rides, all Cinetropolis attractions are programmable. By changing the software at least three times a year, visitors will be encouraged to return again and again.

Another example of a virtual amusement park has been created by Virtual World Entertainment (VWE), which got its start creating VR thrill rides like BattleTech and Red Planet. The company recently has opened its Virtual World theme park in Walnut Creek, CA. This park has VR thrill rides plus a complex fantasy environment. According to the fantasy, Virtual World is the current home base of the Virtual Geographic League. This secret society, created by Alexander Graham Bell and Nikola Tesla in 1895, has as its goal the exploration of unimagined worlds. In 1990, the League board of directors voted to open it to the public. As you walk into the lobby, the history of the League is all around. Pictures, books, and displays are included in the Victorian-era decor.

The VR experience begins with an eight-minute introductory video starring Judge Reinhold and Joan Severance. Next comes 10 minutes of game playing. Finally, a blow-by-blow review of the game is printed out and distributed to attendees. You can choose from two different rides. BattleTech or Red Planet. The latter is a hovercraft race across the surface of Mars. Each ride holds 8 players, who control their robot or hovercraft using an encapsulated pod that has more than 100 controls (although you can play the game on a basic level using just 2 controls).

The next step for the park is to develop virtual underwater exploration adventure. This game will differ from all current location-based games in that players will be allowed to start a new game where they left off the last time they played.

◎ VR Rides in Restaurants

A few restaurants are incorporating VR experiences in order to bolster business. The advantage is that VR rides are much less expensive and take up much less space than most real rides. Accordingly, restaurants are able to offer compact amusement parks not only in central locations but in dozens of neighborhoods around the country.

Still, for the present, no restaurant chain has committed to supply neighborhood Disneylands. One of the first restaurants to offer VR experiences is Dave & Buster's, which opened a 69,000-square-foot unit on the Philadelphia waterfront. The restaurant includes, among other attractions, a fighter-plane simulator.

Hollywood Trenz Video and Rock Cafe in Fort Lauderdale, FL, is two-story, 50,000-square-foot entertainment center that includes three bars, and 400 dining seats, which are divided among six theme sections: adventure, horror, science fiction, Western, comedy, and mystery. Each includes some form of VR experience, often taking place on the table tops. The center also has 36 virtual-reality games including motion simulators.

▣ TECHNICAL CONSIDERATIONS

Technologically, VR movies, played in what is called "special format theaters," are very different from traditional feature-length movies. For one thing, the visuals on the VR rides are shot with 65mm (rather than 35mm) film. This provides more realistic visuals because the image doesn't have to be enlarged as much. Also, the VR rides are recorded at and are projected at a rate of 60 frames per second rather than the 24 frames per second as are traditional movies. (Actually traditional movies show each frame twice, thus providing a projection rate of 48 frames per second.)

VR films are projected on larger screens and use longer films (up to 15 perforations vs. the traditional 4 per frame), both of which provide crisper images. Creatively, VR films are nothing like traditional movies. So far, none of these films use any plot line. Rather, they provide a brief but intense experience. Therefore, the landscape has to be crowded with objects and people. There has to be something new to look at each second.

Another consideration is that all the action has to be from one single point of view and form one type of shot. There cannot be close-up, medium, and long shots unless that is associated with the action of the viewer. In other words, the only way a close-up would make sense is if the viewer is supposed to be actually moving closer to the object. A close-up any other time would be confusing.

▣ SYNCHRONIZING MOTION

Most important to the verisimilitude of the experience is the synchronization of the movement (of the motion base) with the visual image. Developers say that doing so is not always easy. Usually the film comes first, then computer programs are used to create a program for the motion base. Then three seconds of that motion is played on the special format theater along with the movie to determine whether everything is in synch. Usually, some fine tuning is necessary.

Although there are major differences between VR films and traditional feature firms, many of the big players in VR version are traditional studios. For one thing, Hollywood studios own the rights to the movies on which the simulator movies are based. Some examples of Hollywood-owned VR attractions are *Star Wars*, *Back to the Future*, and *ET–The Extra Terrestrial*. The relationship between Hollywood and ride developers is a symbiotic one. When a ride is created based on a popular film, it extends the life span of that film. Keeping the film in people's minds continues to make money through video tape sales and television showings. On the other hand, having a ride based on a popular movie gives the ride an imprimatur that brings in the crowds. Theme parks owned by traditional studios are also big players in showing the VR attractions. MCA's new Universal City Walk in the Universal complex in Los Angeles, for example, offers Showscan (Culver City, CA) simulator theater.

⊚ OTHER VR THRILL RIDES

These rides are available at various locations around the country:

◇ **AS1.** A relatively simple game in which you enter a space capsule and fight star wars along with Star Commander Michael Jackson.

◇ **Back To The Future.** There is very little virtual reality in this ride, which emphasizes bumps and a video displayed on a giant curved screen.

◇ **BattleTech.** This is one of the most complicated games to learn to play. BattleTech originally was a board game, which was turned into a video game. It involves giant robots, called Mechs, that skulk around the terrain trying to vaporize you. You control various robots and vehicles.

◇ **Cybergate.** A space shoot-'em-up. Visitors are strapped into a space ship, wear a helmet, and tote a gun. The shoot-out, however, is not lethal to humans. Only enemy spaceships die, the participants cannot be hurt. This ride features beautiful space graphics, including a breathtaking shot of Saturn.

174

◈ **Dactyl Nightmare.** In this adventure, each participant stands by him or herself. The idea is to navigate a robot up the stairs and around obstacles as it engages the robots controlled by other players. The graphics are relatively simple, but the game has a good deal of adventure and excitement.

◈ **R360.** This space ship trip provides more movement–bumps, gyrations, and thrills–than any other VR experience. This is about as close as you can get to a real-world ride in a virtual package.

Interactive
Amusements

Virtual reality is made up of animated, make-believe worlds. VR systems also can be used to enable people standing in the real world to interact with imaged characters.

The Performance Animation System (PAS) from SimGraphics Engineering Corporation (Pasadena, CA) transforms real actors into cartoon characters in real time. Live actors stand behind a projection screen. They wear a special face mask that records gross facial movements. Sensors in the mask pick up and send to a processor data about the movement of eyebrows, cheeks, head, chin, and lips. That data then controls the facial movements of on-screen cartoon characters. Physical movements of the on-screen characters other than facial movements are controlled by the real actors using 3-D mice, joysticks, and foot pedals. During the show, the real actors watch the audience in order to interact with it. The on-screen actor may ask an audience member who is whispering to be quiet or one who dripped popcorn to be sure to clean it all up.

Future versions of PAS may do away with hand controls and facial masks. The company hopes to eventually replace them with TV cameras and object recognition software that will be able to digitize movements without the use of sensing devices.

Motion trackers, used primarily to track movement of users in a VR system, also are being used to create animation. The animation may be interactive or not. When used for non-interactive animation, the advantage of motion tracking is that it creates realistic images in a short period of time. Realistically animating actions as complex as break dancing, for example, is extremely difficult using traditional methods. Using motion capture systems, the process is virtually automatic.

Flock of Birds from Ascension Technology Corporation is one of the most popular motion tracking systems. Recently, animation packages from SoftImage–Alias and Wavefront–received interfaces that enable them to accept input from Flock of Birds trackers. Characters created in these packages can move correspondingly to human actors whose physical movements are tracked and digitized by Ascension hardware.

Using Flock of Birds, actors attach up to 29 small receivers to different parts of their bodies. The position and orientation in space of each receiver can be computed up to 144 times per second with accuracy of 0.1 inches and 0.5 degrees. The measurements are references by one or more extended range transmitters, which allow referencing of movement as long as the subject remains within an 8-foot radius. Each receiver on the body is connected through 25-foot wires to a central rack of electronics. (To allow more freedom of movement, the set of cords can be bundled and suspended from above using a bungee-type cord.)

Virtual Sex

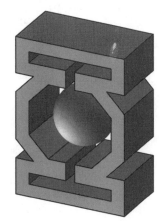

Virtual reality is a fantasy form of education similar to TV and movies. Because fantasy sex (sex in movies and TV) is such an integral part of our culture's entertainment choices, it is impossible to think of VR without at least speculating on its value to titillate. There is no doubt that when the technology is feasible, virtual pornography (hard-core and soft-core) will be a popular seller.

There are two potential scenarios for virtual sex. In one, real people separated by miles send their bumps and grinds to each other over a computer and modem. In this scenario, each user wears a data suit that tracks motions and that plays back movement through force, tactile, and temperature feedback.

In the second scenario, there is no one at the other end of the modem. The virtual reality program is programmed by the user to automate the sexual movements and feelings. Each of the scenarios may include a visual element that the user sees through an HMD. But the visual element would be more difficult to generate in the first scenario because each user would have to have a number of strategically placed video cameras to accomplish this.

There are philosophical questions as to whether virtual sex is really sex at all. If two people communicate their physical activities over a modem, are they really coupling? Or does coupling require that the two lovers actually be in the same room? The issue may seem trivial, and for many it may well be. But people will have to come to grips with the question of whether virtual sex is adultery.

What Would the System Be Like?

In most cases, an HMD with high resolution 3-D graphics and a data glove would have to be part of the system. But for a full-body experience, much more apparatus would be needed. A full-body suit that provided force feedback and that could be used for position tracking would have to be part of the picture. There would probably have to be probes and other apparatus in order to simulate penetration of any orifices that the virtual or real partner would want to enter. Additionally, the body suit would have to have exact pressure sensors which could transmit caresses. Is all this possible?

Well, to an extent it is. But the result will be little more than a sex toy. There's no danger that virtual sex will replace the real thing. One problem is the feel of another human is very difficult to replicate using body suits with sensors. Even if the temperature and pressure are right, feeling caressing through a body suit is not the same thing as doing so in the raw. But the major problem is that when all is said and done, the virtual partners are not in the same room. They are alone, and that's no way to be intimate.

One of the most advanced, if speculative, VR sexual experiences was conceived by Larry Vingelman. His paper, "SOMA, Sexual Orientation Manipulation Application," published in *Virtual Reality News*, discusses a virtual interactive environment application that uses biosystem monitors, artificial intelligence, and real-time brain wave analysis.

For someone to receive a sexual experience through VR, he or she needs to have as many senses fully immersed in the system as possible. SOMA's goal is to fool the nervous system into believing the data it is receiving comes from the real, not a virtual, world. Accordingly, SOMA uses an HMD that encompasses the user's entire sense of sight along with 3-D (Convolvotron) sound.

SOMA also includes relatively crude tactile feedback in the form of a vibration delivered to the hand via a pointer. Newer versions will include a more complete tactile feedback system that includes small tactors fitted into gloves. Experiments with tactors have proven that they give the user the ability to distinguish between virtual silk and virtual sand paper. Further in the future will be SOMA versions that include body suits containing expanding bladders that give the participant's body a complete tactile environment. Currently, SOMA's visual stimuli is not very interactive. A sexually explicit full-motion video might be played in such a way that the viewer appears to be watching the action through a window.

In some cases, the characters in the SOMA visual image are able to interact with the user. But those characters tend to be of lower resolution than the full-motion videos. In some versions of SOMA experiences as the participant moves closer to the animated screen characters, the latter respond with a word or a sound. The level of sexuality in the verbal response depends on how close the participant moved in the character's direction.

SOMA is a pretty good lover. By measuring the participant's biological responses to stimuli (blood pressure, heart rate, eye tracking, and erogenous zones), it creates a sexual preference indicator scale. On this scale, each category is assigned a sexual preference identifier (SPI). This enables SOMA to find a sexual catalyst, a sexual category which most interests the participant. In one application of SOMA, the participant is progressively relaxed until a suggestive (often called hypnotic) brain wave pattern is established. This state is enhanced though the use of light, sound, and electrical impulses, which activate the brain to a selected hertz level. The user is then asked to fantasize. SOMA controls the participant's internal visualizations by measuring heart rate and blood pressure response to sound and tactile input. Any response that appears to show that the participant is having a sexual fantasy is rated on the scale. The reward will usually be sight and sound in the direction of the sexual catalyst.

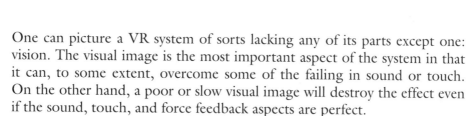

Virtual Graphics

One can picture a VR system of sorts lacking any of its parts except one: vision. The visual image is the most important aspect of the system in that it can, to some extent, overcome some of the failing in sound or touch. On the other hand, a poor or slow visual image will destroy the effect even if the sound, touch, and force feedback aspects are perfect.

Anyone who has worked with 3-D images knows that the biggest problem is speed of rendering. Accordingly, VR is being fueled in part by the graphics industry. This may be seen perhaps most dramatically by the fact that Toronto-based Alias Research, Inc., best known for developing the graphical software used to create the special effects in such movies as *Beauty and the Beast*, *Terminator 2*, and *Jurassic Park* is now heavily into VR. The company is developing systems for industrial applications of virtual reality technology.

The goal of a good virtual reality program is to enable the viewer to suspend his or her disbelief in the reality of the virtual world. But the creation of a VR world is much more mundane. Basically, it is a 3-D drawing function, not dissimilar to a basic CAD or 3-D modeling and rendering program.

Creating the 3-D image on a 2-D medium (the computer screen) involves a number of steps. It is a geometric application. The objects are expressed in terms of points, lines, and arcs. The combination of these three elements enable VR designers to describe the outline of any form. Of course, the characteristics of the elements of these line drawings also have to be described in some cases. For example, all computer drawing programs enable users to define the attributes of lines, such as the line width. But almost virtual world is made up of lines and meshes. In all cases, the objects have to be filled.

These elements make up "graphics primitives." Because graphic primitives are basically mathematical representations, they take advantage of what computers do best: math processing. They also enable the use of math accelerator cards to speed up the process of generating the image on the screen. The alternative would be creating the picture pixel by pixel, a relatively slow process. Obviously, the success of VR applications depends on speedy image generation.

Another advantage of using primitives is that most drawing systems don't impose any size or location constraints. In a few cases there may be some basic limits (such as a requirement that coordinates be stated in integers). But for the most part, the description of the drawings stored in the computer does not specify size or position. This enables the mathematical representation of the image to be sized to fit whatever viewing device the image is displayed on. By contrast, pixel-based images can be generated only at the resolution they were created.

The process of sizing these drawings is called *clipping* or *scissoring*. In a basic scissoring process, the entire contents of the drawing is rendered, but only the portion that fits on the screen is displayed. More complex scissoring processes can use a rectangle or other shape as a mask. This enables a VR program to show aspects of an image that are visible to the user.

An alternative to scissoring is to use geometrical transformation to change the relative size and position of screen images. This process enables designers to position the image in space by specifying the coordinates of all the lines, points, and arcs of which it is made. To change the location or size of an object, mathematical transformation algorithms are applied to its coordinates.

So far, this discussion of graphics generation has referred to 2-D graphics. Moving into the third dimension, of course, increases the complexity of both the drawing process and the process of creating the on-screen image. To place an object in 3-D space, its "projections" have to be defined. Projections are mathematical algorithms that define how a 3-D object can be represented in 2-D space (the display device). For example, projections have to define how a light source reflects off an object. There is nothing intrinsically high-tech about projections. One-, two-, and three-point projection techniques were developed during the Renaissance.

Although creating the illusion of 3-D from a stationary prospective may present challenges, the difficulties are small compared with the problems of doing so for a visitor to a virtual world who is in motion and so is continually changing perspective.

To create the drawing from the perspective of a moving object, the computer has to be given data on the following:

◇ Where the observer is looking. This information is determined by gauging the position of the observer's head and in some cases the position of his or her eyes.

◇ Which way is up and which way is down.

◇ The field of view, including the width and height of the field.

Of course, virtual worlds are rarely populated with only one object. Typically, there are many objects, whose edges may overlap, and which are constantly obscured by each other. Changing perspective also causes objects to change in shape and size relative to each other.

Creating 3-D forms does nothing to provide data about the relationships between object parts or between two distinct objects. To create these relationships, designers use geometric models. Not only do geometric models enable VR designers to create realistic worlds, but they also enable real-world examination of geometric shapes. Pharmaceutical developers, for example, can use geometric models to examine the interactions of substances before synthesizing them in the laboratory. And aerospace engineers can use models to stress-test the performance of aircraft components.

A type of geometrical modeling often used by VR developers is called Standard Programmer's Hierarchical Interactive Graphics System (SPHIGS). SPHIGS uses a hierarchical structure for storing information. The lowest level of the hierarchy contains information about an object's graphics primitives. The components can be composed into highly complex groupings that represent the complete object. Because each component object can be associated with its own mathematical transformation matrix, the system can use a small set of reusable virtual components that can be scaled and rotated, and translated into a variety of sizes, positions, and orientations.

A chronic problem daunting VR system developers is to find a means of creating images that look realistic but which are simple enough for the computer to generate quickly. Mesh objects created on a standard graphics workstation normally are very complex. For instance, most users of 3-D modeling tools try to specify a large number of segments for any spherical elements of objects. The more segments specified, the smoother the final rendered object will appear. On the other hand, the more segments specified, the higher the cost in memory and processing time. In fact, spheres are typically the most CPU-intensive shapes to render.

One solution is to create complex meshes only when those graphics are essential to the realism of the system and use simple polygons at other times. But determining in real time which objects should be generated in complex or simple form creates it own computational problems. The computer has to consider factors, such as the total number of vertices of all visible objects and how important each object is relative to the rest of the objects in the environment. The system would also have to determine in real time the amount of processing power and memory available in order to determine the total number of meshes to generate.

A number of researchers have been working on algorithms that enable VR systems to determine which objects are important to render in complex form and which can be more simply created. One such algorithm looks at how recently an object appeared in the VR world. The theory is that newly appearing objects will capture the user's attention. Therefore, those objects should be created in a photo-realistic manner (complex). After the user has seen the object for a few seconds, future rendering can be progressively simpler.

MODELING

The first step in image creation is modeling–creating the shapes that make up the objects that will people the virtual world. The *bete noir* of all VR systems is slow speed. An image that doesn't change quickly when the viewer's perspective changes or an image that has flicker makes it difficult for the user to believe in the virtual world. Accordingly, many systems create models considering how difficult it will be to render them. Rendering requires so much computational power that a complex figure with photo-realistic rendering can destroy a VR system by slowing down response time badly. Accordingly, many VR systems lack detail and tend to be peopled with simplistic images that are relatively easily rendered.

Of course, the most simple screen images are 2-D, and many CAD packages create data as 2-D views. And some programs can approximate a 3-D view when it is given a number of 2-D views of that object. Simple 3-D images are called *polypoints*, a collection of points in space, and *polylines*, a collection of vectors that form a single, continuous line. Many VR systems use flat polygons. A *polygon* is simply defined as a closed figure that has a number of sides. Higher end modeling packages can create concave or convex polygons; lower end ones create only convex polygons. Some systems require convex polygons. The one problem with polygons is that they create a jagged, multifaceted look even on surfaces that should be smooth. Rendering techniques can smooth out the jagged edges, but that requires computational time. Polygons can be smoothed using a technique called texture mapping, in which a picture of a an object is "pasted" onto one or more of the polygon's surfaces.

To reduce rendering speed for polygons, some systems use a polygon mesh. The objects in the mesh share a common set of points. For example, a point at the edge of a cube is only referenced once rather than three times, one for each of the sides that share that point. Some VR systems create the visual display through the use of primitives, which are cones, spheres, and cubes. They are used to create all the objects. A slightly more complex variation of this technique enables the primitives to be altered a bit in order to create more unique objects.

Solid modeling uses primitives, but applies operations to them such as addition, subtraction, and Boolean algorithms. Many engineers use solid modeling to enable them to calculate the physical characteristics of objects that don't exist in the real world. Because solid modeling is so calculation-intensive, however, it is not often used to create virtual reality images.

Another calculation-intensive modeling method uses curves and curved surfaces as a way of representing complex shapes. The calculations involved in locating each pixel, however, makes this method difficult for VR systems. One alternative is to design an object using curves, but then compute a simple polygonal representation of the object's curves.

Many VR systems include a means to enable objects to change their shape or form. Flexible objects, such as rubber balls may have to change shape. Morphing, in which objects completely change geometry, is being increasingly seen in commercials and movies. The simplest and least processor-intensive method of doing a 3-D morph is to precompute the geometry of all the shapes, and then have the program step through them.

RENDERING

One of the most photo-realistic rendering techniques, ray tracing, simulates light refractivity, shadows, transparency, and other lighting effects. The problem with ray tracing for VR is the amount of computation it requires. The technique requires that the processor calculate how each light source and the light bouncing off each reflective surface interacts with surfaces in the scene.

Additionally, it calculates light refraction in transparent surfaces. So a pencil in a glass of water will have that realistic disjointed look. Phong rendering is the most basic photo-realistic rendering. This type of rendering provides shadows, environmental reflections, basic transparency, and textures.

Of course, the more lights and the more reflective or transparent surfaces a scene contains, the more processing the rendering program has to do and the more time it takes to render the image. A complex ray tracing can take 10 hours or more, and even a Phong rendering can take 1 or 2 hours.

When you consider that film moves at 24 frames per second (FPS) and NTSC TV at 30 FPS, it's clear that such rendering techniques would be impossibly tortoise-like for VR systems. (The human eye will perceive a series of frames as a smooth animation at about 20 FPS. Below that speed, the animation begins to appear jerky.)

So visual renderers for VR systems use lower end techniques such as Z-Buffer, a basic shaded view, and Gouraud, a basic technique to smooth out the polygonal edges (the so-called "painter's algorithm." VR rendering involves more than merely creating the image. The series of sub-processes that create each frame are referred to as a *rendering pipeline*. The rendering pipeline includes a description of the world, which includes all the data needed for rendering–objects, light source, and camera location. To save processing time, VR renderers first eliminate all images that are invisible to the camera.

The next step is the lighting or shading process (pixel rendering), which can use any of a number of different algorithms. Flat shading, for example, fills in an entire area with a single color. This is the fastest pixel rendering method, but it lacks highlights and reflections. The next step up increases the brilliancy by providing variations in the color shading. When you begin to use smoothing techniques, the processing time and memory requirements begin to increase so that they strain current technology.

One way to reduce rendering time while providing a realistic image is to use texture maps, which are usually scanned real-world images that are pasted onto surfaces of a virtual world object. A picture of an orange peel, for example, can be pasted on the surface of a virtual orange to eliminate the need to create that texture from scratch. So instead of complex calculations for lighting and shading, the VR renderer only has to decide what part of the texture map is visible at any given time. Some VR systems also use a texture map in conjunction with "billboard" objects to provide the illusion of movement. By placing a series of different texture maps onto a stationary object (the billboard), the system gives the impression that the user is moving around the object.

An alternative to a texture map are procedural textures. These are algorithm-based textures that are generated by the computer. Procedural textures require some trial and error to get right, and they rarely look as realistic as texture maps. Also, because they are generated by the computer, they take longer to create.

▣ DIGITIZING OBJECTS

The most direct means of creating 3-D representations of objects for VR applications is to begin with a real-world object and digitize it. One way this is accomplished is though the use of a stylus, which touches points or traces lines on a real-world object. The stylus transmits this data to software that reconstructs the object from the entered geometry.

HyperSpace/Metrecom from Mira Imaging, Inc., (Salt Lake City, UT) combines the Metrecom coordinate measuring machine (CMM) with 3-D modeling software. The CMM's stylus, which can reach up to six feet, can be used as a camera and light source to enable you to view the model from any angle and check for completeness.

A higher end alternative is 3-D laser digitizing. This has been described as photocopying for 3-D objects. The real world object to be digitized in placed in the bed of the digitizer. The laser sensor then rides above the object taking readings of coordinates determined by scan density and user-determined pattern parameters. The coordinates are then stored in a file that can be exported to CAD software, which recreates the image in virtual form.

The Surveyor series from Laser Design, Inc., (Minneapolis, MN) uses a triangulation-based sensor that projects a small spot of laser light about 0.001 to 0.002 inches in diameter onto the surface of the object being digitized. A change coupled device (CCD) array views the spot and determines where the spot is located on the array. This information is used to compute the coordinate of the laser spot.

Figure 25.1 The Surveyor 3500 3D Laset Digitizing Sytem.

In order for the laser light to fall on the surface of the CCD array, the laser source has to be a minimum distance (called a standoff distance) from the object. The furthest distance a point can be located is called the range. The Surveyor series has models that range from a 2.4- to a 6-inch standoff. The range can be configured to from 0.32 to 0.16 inches. The shorter the range, the higher the resolution.

Many digitizer systems, including some in the Surveyor series, incorporate redundant arrays to compensate for shadowing, a situation that occurs when the reflected spot is prevented from reaching the array because of an obstruction. If the primary CCD is blocked, the second (redundant) one is queried.

There are two other ways that laser digitizers sometimes compensate for shadowing. An anti-shadow axis automatically rotates the laser sensor until a good sensor read is found. A second method is to employ an articulating laser head that changes the orientation of the beam to other than parallel to the object. Using one or all of these methods, shadowing usually can be eliminated except in very uneven surfaces.

When buying a laser digitizing system, you have to be concerned with both resolution and accuracy. Resolution is the smallest change in direction that the laser can detect. Accuracy is more a function of the optical characteristics of the object being digitized, although accuracy can be enhanced after digitization using software. If the object has a glossy surface, for example, the laser beam may shimmer, creating noise in the image. This noise can normally be filtered using software that comes with laser scanners. Another source of inaccuracies is the arm mechanism that controls the direction of the laser beam. No mechanical apparatus will be able to maintain the tight tolerances required to work with such precise measuring functions performed by laser beams. Accordingly, most digitizers use software that compensates for any variances introduced by the mechanism.

Laser digitizing is usually faster than CMM, but the speed is dependent on the color of the object. Darker objects require more exposure time and so are slower than lighter objects. Laser Design officials say their models average between 30 and 60 points per second. Besides speed, laser digitizing offers another advantage over CMM systems. Because it is non-contact, it can be used with fragile objects. The laser beam also is smaller and more precise than mechanical probes. So laser digitizing works better with objects with fine details, such as those in which crevices are too small to place a probe.

CMMs, on the other hand, are better at measuring objects with micrometer accuracy when shapes are basic, such as holes or corners. Also, although laser digitizers can be purchased with the capability to digitize objects as large as 8 feet square, the large format machines are very expensive—much more expensive than CMM devices. There is also the issue of safety. Laser digitizers are considered by the FDA to be an ocular hazard. Accordingly, special glasses or the use of video cameras are required if the beam is to be viewed at close distance.

◇ **Graphics SoftwareESIG-2000.** ESIG-2000 from Evans & Sutherland is a turnkey computer image generator specialized for the production of imagery for VR applications. It generates photo-realistic 3-D images and includes anti-aliasing and texturing. It can display images at a rate of 60 images/second. Evans & Sutherland, Salt Lake City, UT.

◇ **ImageCELs.** ImageCELs from Imagetects is a CD-ROM library of 1,150 photo-realistic images to assist in the creation of virtual worlds. It includes texture maps and backgrounds. Among the images are various examples of building materials, such as bricks and wood. There are also a number of general-purpose patterns, such as geometric designs. Finally, the collection features background objects, such as people, vehicles, trees, benches, and industrial equipment. The ImageCELs CD-ROM has 4 multi-platform file formats in 8-, 16-, and 24-bit color. Sets are available for PCs, Macs, UNIX machines, and Amiga. (The company also sells smaller sets of images.) Imagetects, Saratoga, CA.

◇ **PhotoVR.** PhotoVR from StrayLight Corporation helps you create photo-realistic VR software for DOS-based PCs. First, you create the 3-D VR environments using AutoCAD or 3-D Studio. Next, you import your images into PhotoVR. The scenes are displayed with realistic shading, including multiple lights, textures, reflections, shadows, Phong shading, and bump maps. Speed is a maximum of 10 frames per second. The system includes support for a large number of HMDs, NTSC, and VGA monitors. StrayLight Corporation, Warren, NJ.

◇ **StereoSynthesis 223D.** StereoSynthesis from Latent Image Development Corporation is a process by which VR developers can convert 2-D film, video, or still images into stereoscopic 3-D. Using this system, developers can make use of their standard desktop images in a VR environment. 223D, also from Latent Image Development, is a computer paint system that enables the creation of stereographic images in true 3-D. Latent Image Development Corporation, New York, NY.

◇ **VActors and VR Workbench.** VActors from SimGraphics Engineering Corporation enables you to create "virtual actors," computer created characters whose movements are controlled by real actors. The actors wear devices that tracks movement on their face, hands, and body. VActors can be used for real-time entertainment or for the development of animation. The company also makes VR Workbench, a collection of libraries for building user interfaces, SimGraphics Engineering Corporation, South Pasadena, CA.

◇ **VSS-1 and VSS-Workbench.** VSS-1 from Virtual Scene Systems is a graphics sub-system for creating interactive real-time rendering of 3-D environments. One major advantage of this system is that the data is stored and accessed in compressed form, and then is decompressed frame by frame as needed. VSS-Workbench is a software program for compressing 3-D texture-mapped objects and 3-D animation sequences. Virtual Scene Systems, Bourne, MA.

STRIP
IN
SINGLE
PAGE
NEGS

Creating
Virtual Worlds

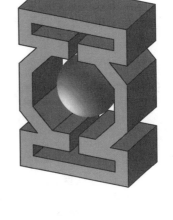

Creating a VR world is a matter of combining the skills of artist, novelist, and computer programmer. Although the means of populating the VR world is beyond the scope of this book, it is helpful to gain an understanding of the things the VR designer has to cope with.

VIRTUAL VISION

Creating a visual image on a VR system involves the creation of the 3-D images. But that is only the first step. VR is interactive, but the images are not sequential. The image also should have a much larger field of view than traditional animation. This "wraparound" view may provide as much as 240 degrees of vision horizontally.

High resolution, wraparound view, and interactivity makes very heavy use of processing power. So any VR system has to take into consideration means of lowering the computational, storage, and data transfer rate requirements. Accordingly, the program has to include ways of lowering these processing requirements whenever possible. So there may be short periods of time with high interactivity and high resolution, but at other times the resolution may be less vivid. One option is to generate in full texture and shading only those images in front of the viewer, using flatter drawing for those objects in the periphery or background.

VIRTUAL HEARING

All VR systems that include sound have at least stereophonic sound. Without stereo, it is almost impossible to pick up individual sounds from a "landscape" that contains many sounds. However, good VR software has 3-D sound. This enables the user to determine the direction the sound is coming from. VR systems that do not contain 3-D sound, and many of them do not, seem flat and unrealistic. Often, the audible cues that you get from stereo conflict with the message being sent to your eyes. This results in a disturbing disconnected feeling, one that makes the VR experience unreal.

VIRTUAL TOUCH

Currently, few VR systems use touch. The reason may be stated simply: developers have more pressing problems. Placing a user in a VR world where he or she cannot touch objects may force the creation of a somewhat limited system. But the system can be real, as far as it goes. Still, to create a fully realistic immersive VR system, at least some touch is required. Touch involves two sensory systems. Mechano-receptors are the nerves in the skin that respond to pressure. Pro-prioception is feedback from our muscles. This is also called force feedback.

Of the two, mechano-reception is much harder to simulate in VR system, so most don't include it. Pro-prioception, or force feedback, is more important, and, fortunately, easier to simulate. Pro-prioception enables you to estimate the weight of a virtual object or to determine the amount of force needed to move a remote object, such as a robot. Most VR system translate the sum of forces into a single device, such as a joystick. This is a relatively simple operation, which has already been used to convey a feel of the road to drivers of cars with automatic steering. The goal of any good VR system is to have the user suspend his disbelief in the system. He or she should think the VR world is actually real.

COORDINATE SYSTEMS

The programmer is constantly reminded that it is, after all, only a computer program which has to be limited to that which can be coded. Each object in the VR world is, at the code level, merely a set of numbers representing the location of each point. The location of each point, or *coordinates*, are expressed in length, height, depth–more often referred to as X, Y, Z coordinates or Cartesian dimensions. Some coordinate systems use decimals, (floating-point numbers). This provides for a large range of numbers, allowing more attributes about the individual pixels (dots or points on the screen) to be specified. But it slows down processing, so other systems prefer to use only whole numbers. The proliferation of floating-point processors, which sped up the processing of decimals, has increased the use of that type of coordinate system.

WORLD DATABASE

The world database contains information on all the objects that are part of the VR world–not just the objects that are currently in view, but all objects that may at any time appear. The world is a major part of the design of a VR system. The database contains physical descriptions of the objects and scripts that describe how those objects behave. A world database would also contain information on all sensory experiences caused by the behavior of VR objects. Each action on a VR object by the user may result in a reaction by the output system that controls the user's movement, sense of touch, temperature, or the force exerted on a force feedback system.

Sometimes the world database is stored as a single file. Other times, it is a collection of files. In this method, each object has a number of files, each one housing different attributes, such as geometry and behavior scripts. For simplicity and speed, only one motion script should be active for an object at any one instant. Motion scripting is a potentially powerful feature, depending on how complex you allow these scripts to become. Care must be exercised because the interpretation of these scripts will require time, which affects the frame and delay rates.

Additionally, a script might be used to attach or detach an object from a hierarchy. For example, a script might attach the user to a car object when he wishes to drive around the virtual world. Alternatively, the user might pick up or attach an object to himself. World scripting is the process in which the interactions in the virtual world are described. Scripts that define how objects move in the virtual world enable the system to modify the position and orientation of objects. These scripts also define how the light or viewpoint changes based on movement.

Lights in VR worlds can be everywhere or they may have position and orientation. Normally each user only has one viewpoint at a time. Some systems, however, require that a second viewpoint, for example, an overhead shot, be played concurrently with a frontal view.

Scripts not only determine how objects react when they are impinged upon by other virtual objects but also how they react to objects, normally humans, who live in the real world. Therefore scripts have to include information about what happens when various inputs from tracking or other devices are sensed by the system. For example, in order for a real world human to pick up a virtual world object, that object has to have a script defining how it reacts when the data from the DataGlove regarding the human's hand is received.

If the virtual world is made up of different scenes, the script may be changed for each area. The trigger to changing the script from one pertaining to one scene to the script for another scene is usually an action by the user. Often this action involves moving though a specific portal, such as a door or a gate. Sometimes it is a certain amount of movement in one direction, or it may be pointing to an on-screen control.

Normally, the script is called into play in each frame (also called "tick" or advance) of the VR program. Some scripts define reactions when some event takes place. For example, how does the object react when it collides with another object, comes in close proximity to an object, falls to the ground, or is called by the VR system user. For each motion (each tick), the scripts that determine reactions have to be implemented. For example, a collision detector has to determine for each move whether a collision has taken place.

Scripts can be textual or they actually can be compiled into the program structure. The use of visual programming languages for world design was pioneered by VPL Research with their Body Electric system. This Macintosh-based language used 2-D blocks on the screen to represent inputs, objects, and functions. The programmer would connect the boxes to indicate data flow. Sometimes the entire collection of files is loaded into memory during program launch. Other systems are more disk-based, loading files from magnetic media as they are needed.

In order for the system to be alterable, each object in the VR world usually has a list of attributes, which can be changed without re-coding the entire object data structure. When objects appear in the VR system, they have to be positioned and oriented. Most VR systems, therefore, allow objects to be modified by applying translation and rotation operations. To save on coding and processing times, some objects may be stationary in the VR world.

One shortcut is to make objects part of a "family." This is called a hierarchical structure in which there are parent, sibling, and child objects. Objects in a hierarchy usually belong to a single system. An arm, for example, is made up of hand, forearm, and upper arm. In hierarchies, any transformation that occurs to the parent (the arm) results in corresponding transformations to the children (the parts of the arm).

The description of many objects also includes a bounding volume. This lets the system know the object's boundaries in order to allow it to detect collisions. It is also used to determine how objects obscure each other or which parts of an object are off the screen. Two very simple bounding volumes are the bounding sphere, specified by a center and radius, and the bounding cube.

The most important part of creating a VR world is modeling the shapes and geometries of the objects that populate it. Many VR programs are forced to sacrifice clarity in object modeling to increase throughput and speed. Therefore, the most commonly used objects in today's VR systems are flat polygons, a planar, closed multi-sided figure. The problem with polygons is that when they are rendered, they often have a faceted look. Advanced rendering techniques, such as smooth shading and texture mapping, can smooth out some polygonal-based objects.

Another method is to create all objects using simple triangles or quadrilaterals rather than polygons, which can be of any shape. Having a limited number of shapes can simplify the rendering process. But some objects will have to be built of more triangles or quadrilaterals than it would of polygons. In fact, some programs produce only primitive objects, such as cubes and spheres. These are combined to make up all the objects in the VR world. One variation is to use a system that can slightly deform the primitives.

Solid modeling uses primitives, but it increases the capability to build objects using primitives by allowing Boolean and arithmetic operations to be performed. This is an excellent method of defining physical characteristics of objects to do analysis on them. For example, this method permits designers to see the destruction wrought on the body of a car that sustains a crash at a given speed. The downside of this method is that it requires significant calculation time.

Obviously, drawing the objects is only one part of the visual process. The second is animation. Some animation uses simple formulas for the motion of objects, for example a rotation around a specific axis. More advanced animation can include complex paths and variable speed for the object. As in all things graphical, the more complex the animation, the more realistic the system, but also the more taxing on computations resources.

Most of the interactions in a VR world occur as a result of natural user input, such as pointing to a place in which one wants to travel. However, there is also a need for a more computer-like interface. This enables users to change programs (visit a different VR world), set preferences, or provide some needed information (such as the user's name) to the program.

If the system is a window on the world type in which a computer screen, rather than HMD, is the display, a simple pull-down menu might suffice. The menu can be strung along the top of the screen, as in standard Mac and Windows software. The virtual world would be in a window below the menu. Or the menus can be placed in the virtual world itself. Although this method creates an unnatural-looking scene, it may be helpful for those who need quick access to menus and don't want to shift their gaze away from the virtual scene.

Alternatively, the options can be part of the 3-D virtual world. In this option, they are not actual menus in the standard sense. Rather, they may be disguised as tree, a flag, or a person. When the finger is pointed at or a mouse clicked on one of the objects, the option is activated.

The problem with 3-D controls is that they use up a good deal of computation power for something that adds little to the verisimilitude of the program. Having a menu option activated by a moving person or a tree swaying in the breeze is more difficult, computationally, than having the user click on a 2-D button.

2-D controls are similar to the controls found in many Windows and Mac programs. For example, a button is an on-screen shape, usually rectangular, that causes a discrete action in the VR world. A text button is a special type of button that usually is represented by a word in a sentence. The text on the screen may state, "You may now visit the space adventure or the undersea adventure." Clicking on either the word "space" or "undersea" causes the appropriate VR experience to begin.

A slider, which usually looks like a sliding control on a rail, enables you to gradually change some part of the VR experience. A slider may depict the word "sunny day" on the left side and "stormy day" on the other. By moving the control from the left to the right, the VR experience occurs in increasingly more severe weather. Sliders may sometimes look like a dial, but dials are more difficult to create and often more difficult for the user to manipulate.

A map 2-D control is similar to that used in many geography programs. Each section of the map is actually a button disguised as a geographic location. By clicking or pointing with a finger at the correct section of the map, you can navigate around the VR world.

3-D controls, placed in the VR world, may look and act very much like 2-D controls. The 3-D icons also can have gauges, sliders, and buttons. Sometimes the controls float around the VR world, appearing in each scene in a specific portion of the display. Other times, the controls are scene specific and are camouflaged as virtual objects.

Some individual virtual objects may have their own 3-D controls as well. For example, a television or radio in a virtual world may be controllable like their real counterparts. Virtual vehicles might also be controlled with virtual controls. Although some virtual objects may be controlled this way, many are controlled though hardware. Vehicles, for example, are almost always controlled though a joystick or a steering wheel. The use of a hardware control often makes the user more comfortable in the VR world. Because virtual controls, by and large, have no tactile sensation, they are often difficult to use. A real steering wheel is much easier to control that trying to grasp a virtual one.

The downside is that creating code (or including in the world database) information about input devices makes the program more complex. And data transfer rate is an issue. The result may be a slower system. Whether you use a 2-D or 3-D on-screen control, the user needs some way of knowing whether the system received his or her command. The easiest way to accomplish this is to have the selected item highlighted in some way. For example, the selected item may change color, display a marquis-type border, or merely blink a few times. Alternatively, an audible signal or some form of touch or force feedback may be used.

◎ CREATING A VIRTUAL WORLD FROM THE INSIDE

It is possible to build your virtual world so that it encompasses one of the most important aspects of the real world: the ability to create and change. Most virtual worlds are static–you visit them, you may be able to make minor alternations, such as moving on objects a few feet, but you can't build an entirely new virtual scene.

A growing number of virtual programs, however, include both an authoring mode and a playback mode. In some simpler systems, the authoring mode is merely a text editor and compiler system. But immersive authoring systems are beginning to be developed as well. These allow major changes to the virtual world. Earlier in this book, for example, we discussed systems for designing kitchens. The VR aspect of the system enables the users to view their kitchen, but not make any changes to it. An immersive VR authoring system would allow users to remove walls, move cabinets, and replace fixtures with other fixtures. After they leave the VR world, the system would automatically generate the blueprints and a bill of materials.

Virtual Reality Software

VR software differs from traditional graphics program in one primary way: it allows for interactivity between the viewer and screen animation. Of course, many non-VR computer games offer a degree of interactivity–users can select from a hierarchical of choices. By comparison, VR software allows users a wider number of options that do not have to be chosen hierarchically. So, although standard graphics game users may select different scenes to view, in a VR experience, they can actually change the scenes. They can move objects around a room, change their point of view, circle around a scene or even start a series of events, such as a fire, that results in other events occurring (the house burning down). Another way to look at VR software is to divide it into the various chores it has to perform.

The first step is to accept input from the input and control devices that are attached to the system. The most-used inputs are those familiar to any computer or video game user: keyboard, mouse, trackball, joystick, and steering wheel. VR programs, though, may use more exotic devices, such as 3-D mice, head trackers, 6-D position trackers, data gloves, temperature gauges, voice (from a voice input system), video (from an image recognition system), or network data from body suits.

The next job of VR software is to create the simulation logic (not the graphics–that comes later). The simulation engine has knowledge about the meaning of various inputs, knows about the properties of objects in the VR world, and understands the consequences of any action as the input data interacts with virtual objects. The simulation engine has to be fast, because for each time frame, the simulation process has to be repeated. The new input and new interactions have to be considered and the new result has to be generated. If the VR system has more than one user at the same time, a simulation engine that coordinates the actions of all users (in essence coordinating the simulation engines on each user's systems) has to be included.

After the simulation engine creates the logic (the scenario of the VR world), the system has to render it on the screen or HMD for visual VR. This process also is responsible for creating sound and, if the system includes them, smell, touch, temperature, and taste. The most common rendering process, as well as the most complex and most demanding of computer resources, is visual rendering. By and large, it is the quality of the visual rendering process that determines how real the VR experience feels. The three aspects of the rendering process that affect quality are lag time, resolution, and frame generation rate. Unfortunately, with current systems whose processors are straining under the weight of computing requirements, trade-offs are needed. If the visual rendering process is set to create a fast frame rate or is set at a very high resolution, the lag time (period between the user's action and the visual representation of the consequences of that action) is increased.

Still, high frame rate is extremely important if the VR experience is not to look like an old-time movie. In general, 20 frames per second (FPS) is the minimum rate at which the animation will appear smooth. For the sake of comparison, 24 FPS is the standard rate for film, 25 FPS for PAL TV (the European standard), 30 FPS for NTSC TV (the U.S. Standard), and 60 FPS for Showscan films.

Even at 20 FPS, very few high-end rendering techniques are available to VR visual systems. Anyone who has tried to use a desktop machine for ray tracing or radiosity knows that it can take hours for the rendering process to be complete. Some compromises have to be made to reduce the time to 1/20th of a second. Therefore, alternative methods, such as the "painter's algorithm," a Z-Buffer, are relatively fast and make lighter use of computer storage and buses.

The rendering process is actually not one action, but a number of actions. These actions have to take into account the physical description of the objects in the virtual world, the camera location (the user's viewpoint) and lighting. After the rendering engine has data about the world, its first job is one of elimination. It has to remove from the visual field all objects that should not be visible from the camera. This is done by first creating a viewing pyramid, a description of the area that the camera is able to see. Next, all the objects are clipped using the pyramid as a sort of mask. The remaining objects have their geometries transformed into the eye coordinate system.

Next, the lighting or shading algorithm has to be applied. More than anything else, the sophistication of these algorithms determines both the realism of the VR world and the processing power needed to render it. The least realistic but simplest method is flat shading, in which each flat surface is filled with one color. This is an extremely fast method but creates images that look like cartoons. The next step up is to include some variation in color; this adds more of a feel of realistic lighting and texture. For some VR systems it is a good middle road, but the realism is far from what one would see in even an old 8mm home movie. Higher end lighting techniques that produce smooth shading across surface boundaries and reflections require compromises in processing power or a high-end processor and have to be used sparingly.

One alternative to creating lighting effects using the VR processor is to paste texture maps onto the objects. These are actually pictures of texture (which include lighting effects) that are merely mapped onto the virtual objects. The processor is thus relieved of the need to calculate lighting, Instead, all it has to do is determine which part of the texture map should be visible. One trick some VR designers use is to have a number of larger objects, such as hills or buildings, always facing the user. As the user moves to the right or left, different texture maps are pasted on the objects. This provides an efficient way of creating the illusion that the user is moving around the object and seeing it from different angles.

◎ PARTS OF VR SOFTWARE

◈ **Object Database.** All VR systems include a database, which houses the descriptions of the virtual objects. The database may be generated using VR software, but more often an external graphics program, such as AutoCAD, is used to create the files. CAD design programs usually begin with two-dimensional shapes, such as polygons, circles, curves, and typographic elements. These shapes are then extruded into the third dimension. Other means of creating a third dimension are surfaces of resolution, formed by spinning a 2-D object.

The CAD database contains numeric data about the objects. This data is then used in the modeling and rendering of the object on the screen of HMD.

◈ **Attribute Database.** Many VR systems also have a database of object attributes. These attributes, things like motion, orientation, color, and sound, may be fixed or conditional based on an external data source.

◈ **Sensor Driver.** The job of the sensor driver is to monitor the tracking devices in order to know the user's position.

◈ **Display Driver.** This updates the display based on the sensor driver as well as the various databases. (Sometimes, the display driver resides on a graphics board, such as the Reality Engine from Silicon Graphics.)

◈ **The Simulation Manager.** This is the brains of the VR system; its job is to coordinate the activities of all the components. The manager sends instructions to the graphics generated, tracks on-screen objects to see whether they collide, and maintains the correct viewpoint.

◈ **Programming.** To program a VR system, first you create the object database. As you do so, you specify the properties and the behaviors of each of the objects. You also have to program the system's response to sensor data derived from the sensor driver.

Virtually all VR programs are written in C++, a language rarely used by beginning programmers. VR applications have several ways to help less-experienced users create VR experiences. For example, toolkits are made up of libraries of programming routines that can be combined to create the content of the VR world. They eliminate the need to write a lot of code from scratch and thus reduce errors. However, the toolkits do expect you to be able to program in C++ if you want to make changes to the agents in the libraries. For the non-programmer, VR authoring programs provide a point-and-click interface to organize building blocks, shapes, and colors, into the buildings, forests, paths, and deserts of the VR experience.

THINGS TO FIND OUT BEFORE BUYING VR SOFTWARE

Before you buy any VR software ask yourself these questions:

Does the software offer a run-time version?

Run-time versions enable users to interact with the virtual world you created but don't permit them to create virtual worlds. The advantage of a run-time version is that you don't have to buy full version of the software each time you want to distribute it. (Run-time versions typically cost less than 10 percent of the cost of the full version).

What hardware does it support?

Each vendor includes drivers that support different input and tracking devices. So far, the lack of standards in VR hardware has created problems for developers.

What platforms does the software run on?

Look for programs that run on as many platforms as possible. The best products have a Macintosh, a PC, and a UNIX version. Not only does platform independence enable you to more easily distribute your software, it enables you to use the best development platform for each of the tasks when developing the VR system.

WORLDTOOLKIT

SENSE8
1001 Bridgeway Suite 447
Sausalito, CA 94965

Currently, WorldToolKit (WTK) is the most popular general-purpose VR software. One of the best things about the software is that it works well with major VR hardware offerings from companies like Intel, StereoGraphics, and Crystal River Engineering. Accordingly, using WTK to create stereoscopic video and 3-D sound is a relatively seamless process. Currently, WTK runs on several different workstations and on MS Windows.

WTK components include the following:

⬦   Animation sequences
⬦   Graphic display devices
⬦   Input sensors
⬦   Object manager
⬦   Real-time rendering pipeline
⬦   Simulation manager

WTK has tools for anti-aliasing, geometry construction, vertex-based lighting. The WTK Network Upgrade is set of C functions for constructing shared virtual environments in which users can interact.

A demo version of WorldToolKLit for Windows is included on the disk that accompanies this book. It contains over a dozen sample files that have been created using this development tool.

PHOTOVR

StrayLight, Inc.
150 Mount Bethel Road
Warren, NJ 07059

PhotoVR was created with the purpose of building realistic looking VR worlds in mind. Accordingly, this package is heavy on graphical tools. VR worlds created using PhotoVR tend to have better looking textures, shading, lights, colors, reflections, and shadows than those created with other programs. But there is a price in terms of the high level of complexity (and the reduced use of computer resources). A typical PhotoVR scene is composed of more than 100,000 polygons compared to most other systems that achieve rendering compositions of only 10,000 or fewer polygons (and many programs only use 200 or 300 polygons).

PhotoVR works well with a CAD database, especially one created in AutoCAD, to create VR worlds. Accordingly, a primary application for PhotoVR is to create a walk-through of a space created in a CAD program. PhotoVR is used less often as an interactive VR development program. The computational power required to display the high-end graphics works against too much interaction between user and system. PhotoVR also is often used to create VR-type displays at trade show. In fact, StrayLight has recently begun to act as a service company designing corporate-specific VR environments.

VREAM

VREAM Inc.
2568 North Clark St., Suite 250
Chicago, IL 60614

Virtual Reality Development System (VRDS) is excellent for non-programmers and VR neophytes. It provides an easy-to-use point-and-click environment. Users can enter the 3-D environment and quickly build the VR world. In addition to creating objects, developers can add attributes, such as motion, sound, or weight. The program also has a simple way to enable users to develop dynamic links. For example, pulling a cord moves the curtain, or turning a key causes the automobile to start running. One nice thing about this program is that users can enter the world as it is being built in order to test it on-the-fly.

The system runs on DOS-based PCs and with either low-end interface devices (joystick or mouse) or high-end interface devices (HMD or

DataGlove). Users can even build the VR world by entering into it. For example, once they have developed the basic world, they can move objects around or activate the world by manipulating the dynamic links.

VIRTUS WALKTHROUGH

Virtus Corporation
117 Edinburgh St., Suite 204
Cary, NC 27511

Virtus WalkThrough and Virtus Voyager are drawing and visualization software that lets users navigate through 3-D designs in real-time. The product, which has versions both for Macs and Windows, is extremely easy to use. Its most-common application is to enable designers and architects to walk through their creation to get a better feel for the space. It includes pull-down menus, a complete tool palette, and design-view and walk-view window options.

VIRTUAL REALITY STUDIO, VERSION 2.0 (VRS 2.0)

Domark Software
5300 Stevens Creek Blvd
San Jose, CA

Virtual Reality Studio is low-cost basic VR software that runs on PCs and Amiga computers. Its interface is almost entirely point-and-click, which limits the types of objects that can be built. And the graphics are more cartoony than realistic. Still, this program is one of the easiest to use.

Virtual Reality Studio includes a clip-art library that can make the creation of a VR world possible even for someone who has never used a computer before. You just clip and paste the building, trees, animals, and people. This product is primarily for hobbyists, not for professional VR developers. According to the company, however, designers are using the product to visualize simple creations, such as stage designs.

CYBERSPACE DEVELOPER KIT

Autodesk Inc.
2320 Marinship Way
Sausalito, CA 94965

Cyberspace Developer Kit (CDK) is a set of C++ libraries and related routines to assist developers in the construction of VR applications. The program enables developers to model the geometry and the behavior (such as gravity and friction) of 3-D objects. One of the biggest advantages to using a system by Autodesk is that it is the company that developed AutoCAD, one of the most popular CAD programs. Accordingly, it is very easy to import into CDK any geometry created in AutoCAD.

One of the best features of CDK is its capability to provide what it calls real-time "response awareness." This enables it to simulate natural phenomena, such as gravity. The CDK also interacts with any number of VR interface devices including trackballs, mice, data gloves, desktop monitors, or head-mounted displays.

SUPERSCAPE VRT3

Dimension International
Zephyr One, Calleva Park
Aldermaston, Berkshire RG7 4QZ, England

This is a high-end VR development and editing system. Its components include the following:

◇ Superscape visualizer
◇ World editor
◇ SCL virtual object control system (which has over 500 commands)
◇ Shape editor
◇ Sound editor
◇ Texture editor

◇ Screen layout editor

◇ Keyboard editor

◇ Dialog box editor

◇ DXE import and export

◇ Virtual clip art library (200+ objects)

◇ Example virtual worlds (20+ worlds)

EXPALITY, VIRTUALITY 1000 CS, VIRTUAL CAMERA, ANIMETTE, DESETTE

> W Industries Ltd. Virtuality House
> 3 Oswin Rd. Broilsford Industrial Park
> Leicester LE3 1HR, England

W Industries is a major player in the VR marketplace. Following is a list of some of its major products:

◇ Expality is a multiprocessor computer system designed specifically to be used with W Industries software and hardware.

◇ Virtuality 1000 CS is a portable VR system that includes a space joystick controller. Virtuality 1000 4D is a sit-down system with joystick or steering wheel.

◇ Virtual Camera provides a third-person perspective on the activities taking place in an interactive virtual world.

◇ Animette is a VR operating system.

◇ Desette is a software system for virtuality-based systems.

THE PERSONAL SIMULATOR

> RPI Advanced Technology Group
> P.O. Box 14607
> San Francisco, CA 94114

The Personal Simulator is a custom-created software and hardware integrated package for PC, UNIX, or Macintosh-based systems. RPI is the systems developer and also provides hardware and drivers. The product may include the Head Mounted Sensory Interface (HMSI), which is a sensory interface to VR systems.

▣ TURNKEY (OR ALMOST TURNKEY) SYSTEMS

CYBERTRON

> CyberEvent Group Inc.
> 355 Degraw St.
> Brooklyn, NY 11231

CyberTron is an immersive VR system used primarily for promotional events. The semi-customized software enables developers to place virtual billboards in the VR world.

INTERACTIVE KIOSKS

> Immersive Technologies Inc.
> 2866 McKillop Rd.
> Oakland, CA 94602

Interactive Kiosks is a complete, turnkey VR system used for point-of-sale applications. It includes high resolution, photo-realistic images, a 135 x 20 field of view, surround sound, and 3-D joystick control. The company also has an immersive system. Laser Helmet is a wide field-of-view, high-resolution, interactive HMD that also is used for point-of-sale applications.

VIRTUAL REALITY STUDIO

Virtual 'S' Limited
The Limes
123 Mortlake High St.,
London SW14 8SN, England

Virtual 'S studio is the first and possibly the only dedicated, rentable VR facility in the world. It is fully outfitted with SGI workstations, PCs, Macintoshes, special design and audio software, Onyx RE2 and Division's Provision VR generators, 16-track 24-channel direct-to-disk recording, Roland's RSS 3-D audio processor, and VHS and Betacam video equipment. Price ranges from $110 to $425 per hour depending on the activity.

VR Companies

CHAPTER 28

▣ COMPANIES INVOLVED IN VR PRODUCTS

Abrams Gentile Entertainment, Inc.
New York, NY

This company created the PowerGlove, a low-end VR input device for Mattel and is now working with various universities on VR products.

Advanced Robotics Research, Ltd.
Salford, UK

Advanced Robotics has been looking into VR technologies as a way of controlling robots that will be working in hazardous environments. The company's Virtual Environment Robotic Division has been a major contributor to telerobotics and VR research. In one experiment, operators use HMDs, gloves, 3-D mice, and speech recognition systems as input to control robotic vehicles.

Air Muscle, Ltd.
Besford, UK

Air Muscle makes what is probably the best VR gloves for measuring tactile information as input and for replaying tactile information as output. Air Muscle gloves come in different models at different prices. The best gloves have a number of zones even on the fingertips. These gloves can create the experience that an object is slipping out of your grip. The company also is working on a force feedback DataSuit. This could provide the feeling of weight on the arms, allowing the user to feel that he or she is carrying a virtual object.

Alternate Worlds Technology
Prospect, KY

Alternate Worlds makes VR entertainment experiences. Its primary product is called the Reality Rocket. This was first displayed at the Kentucky Kingdom during the Kentucky State fair in August 1992. This arcade attraction uses position tracking and an HMD to provide an immersive VR experience.

AmusiTronix, Inc.
Flushing, NY

AmusiTronix created a 2-D VR experience based on a television screen monitor and television cameras. Users walk onto a stage that is photographed by the TV cameras, and they can see themselves on-screen performing sports, such as boxing, soccer, or tennis, or other activities, such as body painting. To use the system, the user pantomimes the activity. For example, with boxing, he or she shadow boxes. The actions of the real user affect the virtual objects on-screen. For example, if the boxer hits the virtual opponent, he may go down for the count.

Angel Studios, Inc.
Salt lake City, UT

Angel Studios makes computer animation, which it hopes to eventually use in VR systems. The company created the 3-D characters in the VR sequences of the movie *The Lawnmower Man*.

Applied Science Group, Inc.
Waltham, MA

The company makes eye tracking equipment that measures the user's gaze. The system can be used as input to a VR system. It enables the VR system to change the virtual scene as a user's eyes dart from one location to another. The system also can be used to control software programs, both VR and non-VR. It can, for example, be used to control pull-down menus, draw on the screen, or select windows.

Artificial Reality Corporation
Vernon, CT

Artificial Reality's approach is to use projection devices and TV monitors rather than HMDs for the VR output and to use TV cameras rather than tracking devices to sense body movement. The company believes that current HMDs and tracking devices are not yet capable of doing their job quickly enough and at reasonable cost.

The company is working on several VR projects. One of its first projects resulted in the Video Desk. A TV camera on top of the monitor captures an image of the user's hands and displays a silhouette onto the monitor. The fingers of the silhouette can control screen menus, highlight text and perform other functions usually accomplished with a hardware input device. The advantage of the system is that because the on-screen image is a silhouette and because it is limited to hands, the system is cheap, quick, and requires relatively small amount of computer resources compared to other VR input and output technologies. The company's next system is called Video Place which, portrays a complete body silhouette on the screen.

Video Place and Video Desk can be used to help patients in rehabilitation programs increase their range of movement. It also can be used in some forms of sports training. To see examples of Artificial Reality's technology, including Video Desk and Video Place, visit the Connecticut State Museum of Natural History.

Ascension Technology Corporation
Burlington, VT

Ascension Technology makes body tracking equipment called Flock of Birds. One use of this system is to create animation. Actions of real world actors are captured and transformed into animated characters. The animations can then be enhanced using graphics software.

AT&T Graphics Software Laboratory
Indianapolis, IN

The Lab's primary product, Topas, includes 3-D modeling and animation features. This can be used to create VR worlds. The program also includes world rendering tools.

AutoDesk, Inc.
Sausalito, CA

AutoCAD, which is AutoDesk's primary product, is the leading computer-aided drafting tool for PCs as well as work stations. AutoCAD often is used to create objects that are then imported into VR programs. The company's CyberSpace project (CyberSpace is AutoDesk's term for virtual reality) is an object oriented programming language called Trix. This is similar to C++, but it is geared specifically as a software development tool for VR programs.

BioContol Systems
Palo Alto, CA

BioControl's main product is BioMuse, which can sense bodily functions and use that data as input to VR systems. The functions that BioMuse can sense include eye movement, muscle tension, speech, and even brain waves.

Boeing Computer Services
Seattle, WA

Boeing's Virtual Reality Lab is experimenting with VR manufacturing and design process. Boeing also is working with NASA on developing VR systems to help in the planning of NASA's Neural Buoyancy Tank Tests. These are deep pools that are used to simulate zero gravity to test space-related systems.

Bolt Beramek & Newman, Inc.
Cambridge, MA

BBN's main VR activities come from its Systems and Technology division. The company is working on natural language systems, speech input, and image generation–all of which can be used in VR systems. The company also is involved in SIMNET, a VR training program used by the military. The company developed several VR battlefields for SIMNET. One SIM-NET battle included over 1,000 virtual vehicles. Participants from six different locations around the world took part in the simulated battle.

British Aerospace Defense, Ltd.
Humberside, UK

The company is working on ways to mesh real worlds with virtual worlds. The company believes that approach will create the most realistic training programs. The company believes that the cockpit of "window on the world" simulations lack visual reality and immersive VR simulations lack physical reality because there is no realistic tactile feedback. By combining the two, users get the best of both worlds. Therefore, the company has developed a cockpit that exists in both the real and the virtual world (displayed on an HMD). This provides users with a very realistic visual experience. But because it also has real world controls, users also get a realistic physical experience. The system can easily be altered by changing either the virtual or real world or both.

Cadomac
London, England

Cadomac is developing desktop VR environments for use in "window on the world" systems. This system functions as a user interface to traditional computer applications. For example, a database interface might be a library where users select books, flip through chapters, or use the index to find the data they need.

CAE Industries limited
Quebec, Canada

CAE makes a high-resolution color HMD.

Chameleon Technologies, Inc.
Alexandria, VA

The company makes cockpit VR rides. The rides vary in size up to 20 seats and use a motion base. The screen inside the cab is 38 by 52 inches.

Core Software, Inc.
Pasadena, CA

Core Software makes the HardCore program that can extract 3-D coordinates from 2-D photographs. This can be a great assist in VR development. System developers can use photographs of, say, a battle site or a planet, scan it into the system, and have 3-D objects created almost automatically.

Crystal River Engineering, Inc.
Groveland, CA

Crystal River manufactures Convoltron, the most commonly used 3-D sound system for VR application. The product enables VR participants to experience sound coming from specific directions in 3-D space. By combining Convoltron systems, several sound sources can be simulated.

Cybernet Systems Corporation
Ann Arbor, MI

Cybernet System's main product is the PER-Force hand controller. This a joystick-like instrument that provides feedback on motion and force. It was developed for NASA as a means of controlling remote robots building the space station. it is now available commercially.

Cyberware Laboratory, Inc.
Monterey, CA

Cyberware makes laser scanners that capture the shape and color of objects in the real world. The company also makes software called ECHO that can be used to control and edit the scanned image. Users can work on the software using LCD shutter glasses (from StereoGraphics), which are synchronized with the screen image to produce a 3-D view.

Digital Equipment Corporation
Maynard, MA

DEC is the world's leader in open client/server solutions from personal computing to integrated worldwide information systems. DEC's scalable Alpha AXP platforms can be used to control VR systems. The company makes graphics chips, which can be used for VR development and display. In 1994, the company introduced a high-performance PCI graphics accelerator called the DECchip 21030. According to the company, the chip was developed to support "3-D CAD applications, such as wire frame and solid modeling, virtual reality and animation, and high-end desktop publishing and drawing applications."

The DECchip 21030 graphics chip is designed to take advantage of the high-performance capabilities of microprocessors, such as Alpha and Pentium, as well as the high bandwidth capabilities of the PCI bus.

Digital Image Design, Inc.
New York, NY

The company's Scape/AVS is a VR interface for desktop VR systems used in scientific exploration. Another product, Cricket 6-D, is a joystick-type control device that can sense pressure.

Dimension International, Ltd.
Berkshire, UK

Dimension's main product is SuperScape, a desktop VR system that includes software and hardware. The hardware includes a monitor, graphics card, and a 486 PC-compatible. The company plans to include a Pentium-based system in their product line soon.

Software includes a Virtual Reality Toolkit for creating the VR world and a run-time version that enables users who don't have the software to run any program created with the Virtual Reality Toolkit.

Dimension Technologies, Inc.
Rochester, NY

The company makes autostereoscopic glasses that allow the viewing of 3-D images without the need for polarized (one color for each eye) glasses. The company has grants from various U.S. agencies to improve the resolution offered by the display.

Division, Inc.
Redwood City, CA

Division, Inc. was created by three leaders in virtual reality technology: Division, Ltd. (Bristol, UK), Crystal River Engineering (Groveland, CA), and Fake Space Labs (Menlo Park, CA). The company's purpose is to market the products of its three founding companies and provide integration services to end users.

Division, Ltd.
Bristol, UK

Division, Ltd. is working to find ways to provide the needed computing horsepower for VR systems. Accordingly, it has developed operating systems for distributed and parallel processing. It also makes several graphics work-stations for use in VR or related technologies, such as graphics or CAD.

Domark Software, Inc.
San Mateo, CA

Domark makes Virtual Reality Studio software, a set of tools for 3-D object modeling and VR world creations. The software runs on Amiga and IBM PC computers. On-screen icons and buttons enable object character-istics as well as behaviors to be defined.

Doron Precision Systems
Binghamton, NY

Doron makes a motion platform called the SR2, which can hold 12 people and can be used to create a cockpit or cab-based VR thrill ride. The system can be programmed by the user. Alternatively, the company can provide canned titles that include motion and visual on-screen effects. Before building entertainment devices, the company specialized in simulations for training pilots and for training bus drivers.

Dragon Systems, Inc.
Cambridge, MA

The company makes speech recognition software. DragonDictate Power Edition has the largest vocabulary (60,000 words) of any voice control sys-tem. Speech recognition may eventually become a primary means of inter-facing with VR worlds.

DTM Corporation
Austin, TX.

DTM makes equipment to create 3-D CAD drawings.

EEV
Essex, UK

EEV makes tiny monochrome CRTs, which are sometimes used in HMDs in place of the more common LCD screens.

Electric Eggplant Entertainment
Enselmo, CA

The company is attempting to create what it calls "surrogate travel experiences": VR games in which users can spend several hours traveling to foreign lands.

Etak, Inc.
Menlo Park, CA

Etak makes position finding software that locates vehicles based on the history of steering adjustment and the odometer reading. The company hopes the software can be put to use in VR systems. The software will control the visual display based on how far the user travels and how the steering wheel is turned. By using Etak software, the virtual display can show where the user would be, based on the movement of the controls in the virtual vehicle.

Evans & Sutherland Computer Corporation
Salt lake City, UT

The company, a major player in the VR marketplace, sells 3-D image generators. Its early products were used in military simulations. The company recently joined forces with Iwerks Entertainment, Inc. (Burbank, CA) to create Virtual Adventures, a virtual reality entertainment experience.

Exos, Inc.
Burlington, MA

Exos makes the Dexterous Hand Master, which is a glove that measures hand movement and which can be used to generate input for a VR system. The device measures all joint movement as well as side to side whole hand movement.

Fakespace, Inc.
Menlo Park, CA

Fake Space designs and manufactures products for markets requiring high-quality three-dimensional imaging. It is the leading supplier of immersive VR systems used in scientific and commercial research, development, and engineering. The company's products include hardware systems, software for integrating applications into 3-D visualization systems, and consulting services for applications development. In 1994, Fake Space announced shipments of the BOOM3C, the latest version of its field-sequential, full-color immersive display to two customer sites: the NASA Ames Research Center and the Naval Research Laboratory.

The BOOM3C is a binocular-like display, mounted on a counterbalanced and articulated arm, for viewing high-resolution 3-D scientific visualization and virtual environment graphics created on Silicon Graphics workstations. In the BOOM3C, three separate color filters are placed in front of the CRTs. The filters are synchronized to the red, green, and blue color field output of the Silicon Graphics Reality Engine graphics video output.

Fightertown
Irvine, CA

Fightertown makes simulations of various fighter planes including the F-111 and the F-4.

Focal Point 3-D Audio
Niagara Falls, NY

Focal Point makes sound cards for Macintosh and PC computers. The sound cards were used in several U.S. military VR simulations.

GEC Avionics, Ltd.
Kent, UK

The company makes augmented reality systems that overlay radar images or night vision images on the user's real world vision. For example, the company recently introduced its Knighthelm, an HMD designed for day or night flying.

Global Controller
Granite Bay, CA

The company sells tactile feedback VR input devices.

Greenleaf Medical Systems
Palo Alto, CA

The company is working on medical and disabilities-related applications for VR. Glove Talker, for example, enables people with hearing disabilities to use sign language to create text on a screen (so that people who do not know sign language can understand). It also has a system that measures upper extremity motion for patients recovering from strokes or accidents.

Haitex Resources
Charleston, SC

The company makes 3-D glasses that use LCD shutters to create stereoscopic effects. The glasses were first developed for use in Amiga system games.

Harris Corporation
Fort Lauderdale, FL

The company's Computer Systems Division and Evans & Sutherland Computer Corporation have introduced a new integrated computer/image generator for use in VR systems and simulations.

The system, the ESIG-2000 HERITAGE, combines Harris's Night Hawk host computer and Evans & Sutherland's ESIG-2000 image generator in a single cabinet. The product is the first effort resulting from a recent joint agreement between the two companies to develop and market new products that integrate state-of-the-art image generators with high-performance computers.

Helisys, Inc.
Torrance, CA

The company's Laminated Object Manufacturing System creates real-world models out of virtual worlds or CAD systems. It does so by fabricating 2-D cross sections from various materials, including plastics and paper.

Horizon Entertainment
St. Louis, MO

Horizon Entertainment is the U.S. distributor for virtuality units from W Industries. It is developing and selling VR games that are installed in theme parks and malls.

Hufnagel Software, Inc.
Clarion, PA

Hufnagel's Romer3 software for PC-compatible computers creates interiors of buildings that can be exported in AutoDesk format, a commonly used format for VR systems.

Hymarc, Ltd.
Ottawa, Ont., Canada

Hymarc's Hyscan 3-D laser digitizer can scan real objects. It has been used to create 3-D images of real-world objects for virtual experiences.

IBM
Thomas J. Watson Research Center
Yorktown Heights, NY.

The center's primary effort has resulted in an architecture for VR systems called VUE (Vertical User Environment). VUE attempts to solve the problems of supplying large amounts of computing power to VR systems by separating the VR functions. This enables different processors on a network to each work on a different piece of the task. Because the company is interested in industrial applications that can be applied in the next three to five years, it specializes in developing systems that can be run with multiple workstations–workstations that are currently available at reasonable cost.

The IBM "Rubber Rocks" project, for example, which enables two users to experience a simple VR world, runs on six IBM RISC System/6000 machines. Two of the workstations are in charge of creating the user interface; one renders the 3-D graphics; two machines support the input devices (gloves, joysticks, trackers, and so forth); and one runs the VR dialog.

Imaging and Sensing Technology Corporation
Horseheads, NY

The company makes high-resolution monochrome CRTs, which are used in some HMDs. CRTs provide better resolution and faster response times than LCDs. But the latter is lighter and less expensive and, as of this writing, the only reasonable way to fit color display into an HMD.

Incom
Southbridge, MA

The company makes a system that can deliver an image from a display, such as a monitor, and send it to another display closer to the viewer. This can be used to send images on a monitor to an HMD.

Iscan Corporation
Cambridge, MA

Iscan makes eye tracking devices. The devices, which can be mounted on the user's head, notes the exact position of the user's gaze. These devices have been used to control computer systems (using eye gaze to determine cursor locations) for rapid weapon aiming and camera guidance. For VR systems, ISCAN is being used to determine where the viewer is looking as a means of limiting the display requirements.

Iterated Systems, Inc.
Norcross, VA.

The company makes image compression systems that reduce storage and bandwidth requirements for VR programs.

Iwerks Entertainment, Inc.
Burbank, CA

Iwerks creates virtual reality experiences for theme parks. The company was founded in 1986 by two former Walt Disney employees. Recently Iwerks teamed up with several investors, including a Japanese trading company, Itochu, to develop 30 Cinetropolis centers throughout Asia. The first will open in Nagoya, Japan. Another 30 sites are planned for America and Europe. Iwerks's other shareholders include Evans & Sutherland. In April of 1994, Iwerks acquired Omni Films International, Inc., which is a vertically integrated entertainment technology company specializing in the design, manufacture, and sale of 70mm, large-screen, high-definition video-projection systems as well as 3-D and motion-simulation theater systems.

Ixion
Seattle, WA

Ixion makes several VR training systems. It has, for example, a system to train doctors in endoscopic surgery. As the surgeon inserts instruments into the dummy, a visual image is displayed showing where the instrument would be in a real person's body. As the instrument moves, the display changes accordingly. The company also makes a welding simulator. Students hold welding tools, which are actually tracking devices. The display shows the result of the welding as the student moves the welding tool over the part being worked on.

Kurzweil Applied Intelligence Corporation
Waltham, MA

The company specializes in speech recognition systems. Its primary product is VoiceMed, a voice-controlled system for medical dictation. The company is reportedly working on a general-purpose dictation system, which may eventually be used to control VR worlds.

Landmark Entertainment Group, Inc.
Hollywood, CA

Landmark Entertainment is one of the largest developers and sellers of theme park attractions, including VR rides. For example, its "Journey Into the Fourth Dimension" is a motion platform-based simulation, which was featured at the Korean Expo.

LaserDesign, Inc.
Bloomington, MN

The company's LaserScan 3-D can scan large real-world objects, creating a graphical file of the image that can then be placed in a virtual world. LaserScan can be used to scan objects as tall as eight feet.

Lateiner Dataspace Group
Upper Montclair, NJ

The company, which makes 3-D rendering packages, is a major player in the voxel-based rendering market. Most 3-D graphics work is accomplished by extracting polygons. Voxel visualization renders the data in 3-D space directly without first creating a polygon.

The disadvantage of polygons is that they are generalizations of the underlying data. Voxel visualizations exactly represent the data, so they are best for visualizing scientific data that cannot be generalized. The main problem with voxel visualization is that it requires more computational power than polygon rendering. But newer and lower cost workstations may result in more common use of voxel-based visualization. The company's first product, released in 1993 is the Vox-L Visualizer, which runs on Digital Equipment Corp.'s Alpha workstations.

LC Technologies, Inc.
Fairfax, VA

The company makes eye-tracking equipment called Eyegaze Development System.

LEEP Systems, Inc.
Waltham, MA

LEEP makes the Cyberface series of VR audio and visual display devices. Cyberface clips onto masks, which are inexpensive enough for each user to have his or her own. This solves the hygiene problem resulting from many users sharing a single HMD. The company also makes BOOM displays similar in design to those sold by Fakespace.

Logitech, Inc.
Freemont, CA

Logitech makes ultrasonic head tracking equipment and 3-D mice primarily for the low-end VR market.

Magic Edge, Inc.
Mountain View, CA

Magic Edge motion-based platforms for VR experiences. The company pioneered the method of offering greater freedom of movement by attaching the cab to the platform via a single connection in the back. Another innovation is that Magic Edge rides are programmed using industry standard SGI machines rather than using proprietary software and hardware as are most other rides. The first implementation of a Magic Edge cab was an F-18 Fighter simulation written by Paradigm Simulations, Inc. (Dallas, TX).

MaK Technologies
Cambridge, MA

The company is a major player in the distributed VR market. Its primary claim to fame is distributed interactive simulation (DIS), which it created for the U.S. military. DIS enables soldiers scattered all over the globe to participate in large-scale VR training simulations. The company is under contract to many U.S. agencies to develop DIS-based simulations and other types of VR training systems.

Matsushita Electronics Works
Japan

This company develops custom kitchens, not VR systems. But it is included here because it created what may be the first use of immersive VR to enable end users to help design interior spaces. The company's Kitchen World exhibit enables customers to test out the kitchen they purchase by entering a VR world and experimenting with the height of cabinets, the location of appliances, and so forth.

Mattel Toys, Inc.
El Segundo, CA

Mattel, which has no VR products at present, is well-known in VR circles as the company that sold the first low-cost data glove. Mattel's

PowerGlove, developed to control Nintendo games, is used in many home-brewed VR programs.

Maxus Systems International
New York, NY

Maxus makes VR-based financial analysis tools. The tools use buildings and other 3-D images to represent companies, stocks, and other items of importance to financial workers. Users can access information about any company by (using a 3-D mouse) clicking on the virtual building that represents it.

Micron/Green, Inc.
Gainesville, FL

The company is developing walk-through software that not only creates a virtual world out of CAD drawings but also enables architects to make changes in the virtual world. Any change in the virtual world is reflected in the CAD drawing.

Mira Imaging, Inc.
Salt Lake City, UT

Mira has created a relatively low-cost way of digitizing real-world objects in order to use the image as a virtual object. The company's HyperSpace (for the Macintosh) enables users to trace objects using a stylus. The result is an on-screen wire frame that can be edited or rendered.

Modacad
Los Angeles, CA

Modacad makes several graphics software products that can be used for creating virtual worlds. Modavision provides stereoscopic viewing of 3-D images; Envision and Industrial Visualizer are rendering packages.

Mouse Systems, Inc.
Freemont, CA

The company makes the PC Mouse 3-D/6-D, which is a 3-D mouse with six degrees of freedom of movement.

Multipoint Technology Corporation
Westford, MA

Multipoint makes a 3-D mouse, called the Z Mouse, which often is used for desktop VR control.

NEC Corporation
Kanagawa, Japan

NEC is working on networked VR systems. Each user sees the same virtual environment on his or her workstation. Any changes a user makes to a local workstation is automatically reflected on the screens of all the other workstations in the network.

NewTek Inc.
Topeka, KS

NewTek's Video Toaster board for Amiga computers is often used in home-brewed VR games to control video inputs.

NTT Visual Media Laboratory
Kanagawa, Japan

NTT is working on Virtual Collaborative Workspace. It uses a telephone-like handset rather than HMDs to enable distributed users to see each other's facial expressions.

Optical Imaging Systems, Inc.
Troy, MI

Optical Imaging makes most of the color, active-matrix LCD lenses that go in HMDs.

PCI Remote Sensing Corporation
Richmond Hills, Canada

The company is best known for FLY!, a program that makes the study of satellite images easier by allowing users to "fly" over the virtual image. The scene is displayed in stereoscopic 3-D (users wear 3-D glasses). The company also makes image-processing software.

Polhemus Navigation Systems
Colchester, VT

Polhemus makes FASTRAK, a tracking device used in many VR systems.

Primary Image Ltd.
Surrey, UK

Primary Image makes Stride image-generation hardware and software that often is used in the creation of VR images. The company's StrideEgan is a database generator compatible with AutoCAD files, which is the format most VR toolkits use.

Real World Graphics, Ltd.
Herts, UK

The company makes Reality and Super Reality image-generation systems. The systems provide for varying textures, which enable users to decide whether speed or complexity of graphics is more important. This makes the system good for VR programs that often use a variety of simple and complex images in the background and foreground in order to control response time.

Rediffusion Simulation Ltd.
Dorset, UK

Rediffusion is one of those that is moving from being strictly a military training vendor to one also in the entertainment market. Its first VR product was the Commander, a two-person cab on a motion base.

Reflection Technology, Inc.
Waltham, MA

The company is best known in VR circles for its Private Eyes eyepieces. These are not HMDs, but small eyepieces that clip onto the user's glasses and can be worn to one side, enabling the user to shift his or her gaze from the real to the virtual world. However, a few researchers have used Private Eyes to create completely immersive systems in which the user sees only the virtual world.

Ride & Show Engineering, Inc.
San Dimas, CA

The company makes the physical part of VR experiences found in many theme parks. Ride & Show does not make VR software.

RPI Advanced Technology Group
San Francisco, CA

The company's Personal Simulator is a goggle (not HMD) eyepiece for virtual reality applications. The goggles themselves do no head tracking, but they work with trackers from various other companies.

Sense8 Corporation
Sausalito, CA

Sense8 makes WorldToolKit, one of the most popular VR development software packages. A demo of this program is included with this book.

Showscan Corporation
Culver City, CA

Showscan's primary product, Dynamic Motion Simulator, includes a motion platform with a 70mm, 60 FPS movie. So far, the displays are not interactive. Users watch movies of car chases, roller coasters, and so on while being bounced around by the motion platform.

Shooting Star Technology, Inc.
Brunaby, BC, Canada

Shooting Star makes a head-tracking device for VR systems. Called ADL-1, the tracker has the advantage of being very fast and relatively inexpensive. But it is based on physical links between the user and computer that's controlling the VR experience. Because the user is encumbered, the system is often considered uncomfortable.

Silicon Graphics, Inc.
Mountain View, CA

SGI workstations are the most popular for graphical applications and for VR. Although most of its workstations (the Indigo series) cost over $50,000, the company recently released a low-end series called Indy, which starts at around $5,000. At the SIGGRAPH '93 conference in Anaheim, CA, SGI presented a very interactive VR game. Called "Discovery Park," it allowed viewers to approach a simulated pterodactyl and control it in real time by pulling on its reins. (The VR simulation was developed using VR software from GreyStone Technology in San Diego.)

There is, however, a problem with having VR experiences like "Discovery Park" in amusement centers. Immersive VR is basically a one person, or at most two person, experience. So far it is technologically impractical (almost impossible) to have more than two people share a VR experience. Even having two people in a single VR scene requires an immense amount of computing power. Accordingly,in an interactive movie only a few people in the audience would have the opportunity of actually interacting with the scene. The rest would have to be satisfied with watching. According to reports, thousands of people tried to ride SGI's pterodactyl. But only 20 people could enter the room at one time. And of those 20, just 1, 2, or 3 people could actually interact with the dinosaur.

> Sin Graphics Engineering Corporation
> Pasadena, CA

The company makes Performance Animation System, in which a live actor can control an animated character. The system often is used in promotional events to enable people in the audience to interact with animated characters in real time. But the product also is used as a graphics development tool. When used as a tool, the animation is captured onto film.

> Software Systems, Inc.
> San Jose, CA

The company's MultiGFen software automatically creates a photo-realistic 3-D image from a scanned photograph.

> Spaceball Technologies, Inc.
> Sunnyvale, CA

The Spaceball is a 3-D VR control device that senses movement along three axes and orientation.

> Spectrum Dynamics, Inc.
> Houston, TX

The company sells VR tools and products for low-end computers.

> SRI International
> Menlo Park, CA

SRI has several VR projects and studies on the drawing board. One of its first introductions was a simulator to train aircraft marshals (the people who guide pilots on the ground). The company also is doing studies to determine how good eyepieces have to be in order for users to be able to do their jobs with the aid of virtual reality.

StereoGraphics Corporation
San Rafael, CA

The company makes glasses that enable users to see images on computer screens or projected onto screens in stereoscopic view (3-D). In the active glasses, a shutter eliminates sight in one and then the other eye in synch with a display on the computer screen. In the passive glasses, the two halves of the stereo image are seen by alternating a clockwise and counter clockwise polarization of the glasses.

Strata, Inc.
St. George, UT

Strata makes StrataVision software for the Macintosh computer. StrataVision incorporates texture, lighting, and other effects onto CAD files.

StrayLight Corporation
Warren, NJ

StrayLight makes PhotoVR software for PC compatible computers. It enables photo-realistic rendering of objects.

Sun Microsystems, Inc.
Mountain View, CA

Sun shares with SGI the distinction of offering the most popular UNIX workstations. So far, SGI holds the lead in terms of VR applications because the company's machines are typically used in graphics applications. Sun workstations have historically been sold mostly to scientists and engineers who need high-end calculations. But the distinction between the two companies may be fading. Sun has been developing demonstration systems for VR development and display. Also, like SGI, Sun recently released a low-end workstation for around $5,000.

Tektronix, Inc.
Beaverton, OR

Tektronix makes active stereoscopic glasses that alternately obscure the left and right eye as the computer monitor displays one half of a stereoscopic image. The result is a 3-D effect.

3-D TV Corporation
San Rafael, CA

The company has complete systems that enable PC-compatibles, Macs, or Amiga computers to display stereoscopic images. The systems, which are low cost compared to similar products, include glasses, board, software, and cables.

TiNi Alloy Co.
San Leandro, CA

The company makes what are called "shape memory alloys." These are materials that take on a pre-determined shape when heated. The company uses the alloy to make tactors, devices that provide tactile sensations to the fingertips. The computer signals the tactor in the glove to press against the fingertip, simulating pressure.

Verbex Voice Systems
Edison, NJ

Verbex makes continuous voice-recognition systems. Although Verbex systems are more comfortable for users than the discrete voice recognition systems that require a pause between words, they have relatively small vocabularies. However, because the types of actions possible in VR systems are usually relatively narrow, a limited vocabulary voice system may not be much of a disadvantage.

Virtual Reality Group
Vienna, VA

The company makes a high-end HMDs similar to that available from Virtual Reality Corporation. The HMD uses CRTs rather than the more common, and lower resolution LCD technology. The CRTs are mounted next to the user's ears and the image is transmitted to the eyes using various lenses.

Virtual Reality Corporation
Pleasantville, NY

The company makes a high-end HMD similar to that available from Virtual Reality Group. The HMD uses CRTs rather than the more common, and lower resolution LCD technology. The CRTs are mounted next to the user's ears and the image is transmitted to the eyes using various lenses.

Virtual Reality Inc.
San Luis Obispo, CA

The company makes VistaPro, a three-dimensional landscape simulation program. It uses data from the United States Geological Survey. A demo of the program is included with this book.

Virtex, Inc.
Stanford, CA

Virtex makes a series of CyberGloves, which have from 18 to 22 different sensors to sense the position of fingers and hand.

Virtual World Entertainments, Inc.
Chicago, IL

The company makes location-based VR experiences for amusement parks and other locations around the world. Its most famous ride is BattleTech.

Virtus Corporation
Cary, NC

The company makes Virtus Walkthough. This walkthough product includes two windows: one is a traditional drafting 2-D window, the second is a 3-D walkthough. This approach enables designers to make changes on the 2-D drawing and see the results in near real time on the 3-D walkthough.

VREAM, Inc.
Chicago, IL

VREAM makes Virtual Reality Development Software, which is meant to assist in the creation of desktop, or window on the world, VR systems.

W Industries, Ltd.
Leicester, UK

The company makes Virtuality games, which are the most widely distributed VR arcade games in the world. These are HMD-based, immersive VR systems that can be used in either sit down or stand up adventures.

W Industries signed a strategic joint venture agreement with Sega Enterprises Ltd. of Japan to develop VR hardware and software. This joint venture will combine W Industries' pioneering VR technologies with Sega's advanced computer graphics hardware and software technology for interactive virtual reality. The joint venture products will use Sega's graphic board and original cabinet as principal hardware components. W Industries will license its operating system and will develop and license the VR software concept. Sega will retain the worldwide distribution rights for the first arcade game.

Wavefront Technologies, Inc.
Santa Barbara, CA

Wavefront makes various modeling, animation, and rendering packages.

Xtensory
Scotts Valley, CA

The company's Tactools Tactile Feedback System is a glove system that includes tactors, or metals that respond to electrical impulses. The system provides a sense of touch to VR gloves by enabling the computer to flex the metal alloy tactors, applying pressure to the fingers or other parts of the hand.

Colleges, Universities and Research Centers

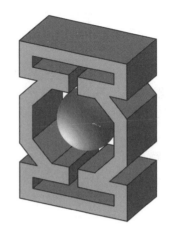

CHAPTER 29

Banff Centre for the Arts
Banff, Alberta, Canada

The Centre has an artist residency program called Bioapparatus, which is meant to foster experiments in virtual reality-related art. One of its first projects was created by artist Robert McFadden. It was called "Picture Yourself in Fiction." The project enabled viewers to touch body parts of on-screen people. Each body part triggered a different fragment of poetry to be read. Another VR project developed at the Centre was created by Lawrence Paul, a Canadian Indian. The project was named "Spint Lodge." It is a smoke lodge-VR experience created using Sense8 Toolkit. Another project, called "The Art and Virtual Environment Project" is actively seeking proposals for new VR systems.

California State University at Northridge
Northridge, CA

The university sponsors "Virtual Reality and Persons with Disabilities" conferences. The conference proceedings are available from the university.

Carnegie-Mellon University
Pittsburgh, PA

The university's Studio for Creative Inquiry is working on networked VR systems. The project looks at ways to enable users located in remote areas to work together in immersive VR environments. The project uses telecommunications hardware and VR hardware, such as HMDs and tracking devices. The first implementation resulted in students at Carnegie-Mellon and attendees at the EPEDITION92 Conference in Munich, Germany, working together in a VR world. The university also demonstrated to Ford Motor Company a VR system in which engineers in different locations can work together in a VR environment to design cars.

George Washington University
WashiÒngton, DC

The university holds occasional VR conferences.

Hines Rehabilitation and R&D Center
Hines, IL

The center is developing VR systems to help the disabled. One of its primary projects is a VR system that allows designers to test handicapped access. The designers can move around the interior of the building in a virtual wheel chair to test various spaces for accessibility.

Loma Linda University Medical Center
Loma Linda, CA

The university has an Advanced Technology Center that looks into ways to use VR in clinical applications. One of its main projects is a neuron-rehabilitation workstation.

MIT Media Lab
Cambridge, MA

The lab does research in all areas of media including high-definition TV. VR projects include an advanced DataGlove input system.

NASA/Ames Applied Research Office
Moffett Field, CA

NASA/Ames is one of the most aggressive research centers in terms of finding ways to apply VR to practical uses including scientific study.

NASA/Jet Propulsion Laboratory
Pasadena, CA

JPL is working on several VR projects, most of them related to telepresence.

National Center for Supercomputing Applications
Champaign, IL

The center has several VR projects. One of its most famous was completed in conjunction with Caterpillar Company. Called "Virtual Backhoe," the VR system enabled designers of earth-moving equipment to check visibility in their design.

David Sarnoff Research Center
Princeton, NJ

The center works on several projects that are significant to VR technology. It is trying to create HMD with resolutions similar to that on desktop monitors. It is also working on VR systems to help pilots in the debriefing process.

Syracuse University
Syracuse, NY

Syracuse is working on several projects in which high-end computing and manufacturing functions are incorporated into VR applications. The school may also soon begin work on lower end, home-based VR applications.

University of Central Florida
Orlando, FL

The university has a Institute for Simulation and Training, which is funded by the federal government, the state of Florida, and private sources. The university is the only academic site for development work on SIMNET, the military VR-based training simulation. The school is also studying ways to apply VR to other areas of training. It also has created VR walk-through programs for architects.

University of North Carolina
Chapel Hill, NC

UNC has more VR projects on its drawing board than any other university. It probably also has produced the largest number of VR engineers and scientists. University professors and students have published many VR research papers, which are available via the Internet or by mail.

Following is a partial listing of these papers:

◇ **"Geometry of a Three-Camera Headmounted System," John H. Halton TR93-022.** A three-dimensional scene, such as a proposed building, an imaginary landscape, or an organic molecule, is selected, described in abstract terms, and stored in a computer's memory. A person wears a special helmet in a laboratory whose inner walls and ceiling are dotted with "landmark" LEDs. The helmet is equipped with a location system and a projection system. As the wearer moves in the laboratory, changing the helmet's position (and orientation) in a natural manner, the location system enables the computer to keep track of the helmet's position. The computer sends appropriate information to the projection system to display the view of the selected scene (suitably scaled) that would be seen by the wearer during this motion.

The paper describes, in mathematical terms, the geometry of an arbitrarily arranged three-camera headmounted system for identifying the position and orientation of the helmet, relative to "landmark" pinpoint-LEDs distributed over the inside walls of the laboratory. The paper also presents and evaluates a fast Newton-type method for performing the required positional computations.

◇ **"Precision Normals (Beyond Phong)," T. Marc Olano, Terry S. Yoo TR93-021.** Almost all graphics architectures today support Gouraud shading, linear color interpolation between vertices. System designers aim toward a Phong shading model, linear interpolants of surface normals with a lighting model that supports both diffuse and specular components, as a superior means of rendering accurate images. The Phong model, however, still retains serious artifacts. This paper points out the shortcomings of linear interpolation of normals and presents a surface interrogation method for parametrically defined surfaces.

◇ **"Modelling and Prototyping Collaborative Software Processes," David Stotts, Richard Furuta TR93-020.**

◇ **"The X Engine Library: A C++ Library for Constructing X Pseudo-Servers," John Menges TR93-019.**

◇ **"Angiogram Simulation Software Documentation," Jannick P. Rolland, Derek T. Puff TR93-018.** They have developed software for the realistic simulation of a single vessel from an angiogram. Initially, a parametrized space curve is generated, which specifies the path of the vessel in a three-dimensional space. The position of an aneurysm or stenosis along the path of the vessel may then be specified. Finally, the volume of the vessel is constructed along the space curve, and the resultant image is acquired from projection through the vessel volume. This software enables the generation of remarkably realistic angiogram simulations for application in various medical image interpretation studies.

◇ **"Volume Reconstruction and Parallel Rendering Algorithms: A Comparative Analysis," Ulrich Neumann TR93-017.**

◈ "Open Issues in Object-Oriented Programming: Learning Methods, Object Decomposition, and Inheritance and Reuse," John Hilgedick TR93-016.

◈ "Nineteenth Annual Progress Report–Interactive Graphics for Molecular Studies," Frederick P. Brooks, Jr., William V. Wright TR93-014.

◈ "The Data Model of the ABC Distributed Graph Storage System," D.E. Shackelford, J.B. Smith TR93-012.

◈ "Interacting With Surfaces In Four Dimensions Using Computer Graphics," David Banks (Ph.D. dissertation) TR93-011. High-speed, high-quality computer graphics enables a user to interactively manipulate surfaces in four dimensions and see them on a computer screen. Surfaces in 4-space exhibit properties that are prohibited in 3-space. Can a user actually make sense of the shapes of surfaces in a larger- dimensional space than the familiar 3-D world? Experiment shows he can. A prototype system called Fourphront, running on the graphics engine Pixel-Planes 5 (developed at UNC-Chapel Hill) enables the user to perform interactive algorithms to determine some of the properties of a surface in 4-space. This dissertation describes solutions to several problems associated with manipulating surfaces in 4-space. It shows how the user in 3-space can control a surface in 4-space in an intuitive way. It describes how to extend the common illumination models to large numbers of dimensions. And it presents visualization techniques for conveying 4-D depth information, for calculating intersections, and for calculating silhouettes.

◈ "Position trackers for Head Mounted Display Systems: A Survey," Devesh Kumar Bhatnagar TR93-010. (This report is available electronically at the e-mail address netlib@cs.unc.edu. Send the request "get 93-010.ps from techreports".) The paper is a survey of existing position tracker technologies for HMD systems. The four major categories of position trackers–magnetic, acoustic, optical and mechanical–are discussed. The chief characteristics, advantages, disadvantages and examples of each category are described. A set of metrics for comparing the performance of position trackers is identified. The expected future trends in the field are also discussed.

◇ "Adaptive Perceptual Pattern Recognition by Self-Organizing Neural Networks: Context, Uncertainty, Multiplicity, and Scale," Jonathan A. Marshall TR93-009.

◇ "Unsmearing Visual Motion: Development of Long-Range Horizontal Intrinsic Connections," Kevin E. Martin, Jonathan A. Marshall TR93-008. Human vision systems integrate information nonlocally, across long spatial ranges. For example, a moving stimulus appears smeared when viewed briefly (30 ms), yet sharp when viewed for a longer exposure (100 ms) (Burr, 1980). This suggests that visual systems combine information along a trajectory that matches the motion of the stimulus. Our self-organizing neural network model shows how developmental exposure to moving stimuli can direct the formation of horizontal trajectory-specific motion integration pathways that unsmear representations of moving stimuli. These results account for Burr's data and can potentially also model other phenomena, such as visual inertia.

◇ "Working Together: Interview on Collaborative System Design," Marcy Lansman, Anne Larme TR93-007.

◇ "Patterns of Interaction in Same-Time, Same-Place Collaborative Programming," Eileen Kupstas TR93-006.

◇ "Just-In-Time Pixels," Mark Mine, Gary Bishop TR93-005. (This report is available electronically at the e-mail address netlib@cs.unc.edu. Send the request "get 93-005.ps from techreports".) This paper describes Just-In-Time Pixels, a technique for generating computer graphics images that are consistent with the sequential nature of common display devices. Motivation for Just-In-Time Pixels is given in terms of an analysis of the sampling errors that will occur if the temporal characteristics of the raster scanned display are ignored. Included in the paper is a discussion of Just-In-Time Pixels implementation issues. Also included is a discussion of approximations that enable a range of tradeoffs between sampling accuracy and computational cost. The application of Just-In-Time Pixels to real-time computer graphics in a see-through head-mounted display also is discussed.

◇ "Fast Collision Detection between Geometric Models," Dinesh Manocha, Ming C. Lin, John Canny TR93-004. This paper presents an efficient algorithm for collision detection and contact determination between geometric models described by linear or curved boundaries and undergoing rigid motion. The set of models include surfaces described by rational spline patches or piecewise algebraic functions. In contrast to previous approaches, this paper first presents a roughly constant time algorithm for collision detection between convex polytopes using coherence and local features. An extension using hierarchical representation to concave polytopes and a scheduling scheme to reduce the frequency of collision detection also is described. Finally, the paper applies these algorithms along with properties of input models, local and global algebraic methods for solving polynomial equations, and the geometric formulation of the problem to devise efficient algorithms for convex and concave curved objects.

◇ **"The Distributed Graph Storage System: A User's Manual for Application Programmers," Douglas E. Shackelford TR93-003.** As the title suggests, this is a manual for people who will be using the Distributed Graph Storage (DGS) system to write applications. Because the focus of the manual is on the Application Programming Interface (API), it does not include specific information about the implementation, nor does it give specific details about how to compile an application. This information is provided in other documentation.

◇ **"Fast Analytical Computation of Richard's Smooth Molecular Surface," Amitabh Varshney, Frederick P. Brooks, Jr. TR93-002.** (This report is available electronically at the e-mail address netlib@cs.unc.edu. Send the request "get 93-002.ps from techreports".)

◇ **"Characterization of End-to-End Delays in Head-Mounted Display Systems," Mark R. Mine TR93-001.** (This report is available electronically at the e-mail address netlib@cs.unc.edu. Send the request "get 93-001.ps from techreports".) This technical report presents the results of measurements made to characterize the end-to-end delays in HMD systems. The term "end-to-end delay" describes the total time required for the displayed image in a HMD to change in response to the movement of a user's head. Included in the total end-to-end delay is the following:

1. Tracking system delay, which is the time to measure the position and orientation of the user's head.

2. Application host delay, which is the execution time within the application host.

3. Image generation delay, which is the time for the graphics engine to generate the resulting picture.

4. Display system delay, which is the time required to display the image in the head-mounted display.

Primary motivation for this work was the desire to characterize the relative performance (in terms of measurement latency) of the various technologies currently in use at the University of North Carolina at Chapel Hill. Included in the test were four commercial magnetic trackers: two from Ascension Technology Corporation (the Ascension Bird and the newer Flock of Birds), and two from Polhemus Incorporated (the Polhemus 3Space Tracker and the 3Space Fastrak models). Also included in the test was UNC's own Optical Ceiling Tracker. Note that both the Ascension Bird and the Polhemus 3 Space Tracker are older models and no longer are in production.

Though the main variable in all of the described measurements was the tracking technology in use, the utility of these measurements was not limited to the characterization of tracker measurement delays. These experiments provided an opportunity to determine the contribution of all the components in a HMD system to the end-to-end delays.

The experiments described in this paper are a part of the overall program at UNC to reduce the end-to-end delays in head-mounted display systems. It is believed that these delays are a key detractor from the feeling of presence in a virtual world. In addition, for see-through head-mounted displays, the presence of end-to-end delays greatly complicates the critical task of registration of virtual and real world objects. Reducing these system end-to-end delays, therefore, is one of the keys to improved head-mounted display system performance.

University of Southern California
Los Angeles, CA

The university has created a VR-like system that assists in the viewing of MRI images.

University of Virginia
Charlottesville, VA

The university specializes in low-cost VR systems. Dr. Randy Pausch at the school's computer science department has produced a famous report entitled "Virtual Reality on Five Dollars a Day." The university also has a toolkit of on-screen control tools (such as sliders, gauges, and so forth) to include in VR applications.

University of Washington
Human Interface Technology Laboratory

The Lab's goal is to find the best way to couple human senses and function with complex machines. It's most startling and well-known project is the Virtual Retina Display, which projects VR images directly onto the user's retina. Although still limited and in prototype form, this is the most promising technology to date for the elimination of bulky HMDs in immersive VR systems.

University of Waterloo
Waterloo, Ontario, Canada

The university distributes free VR software called REND386, which is a library of routines for creating graphics on a 386 or 486 computer. A Pentium version should be available soon.

VR Samplers

To have a truly immersive experience, the use of goggles, gloves, and other typical accoutrements, which we have come to associate with VR, are obviously required. Even without them, however, it is still possible for us to experience the effect of a 3-D textured VR program through the limited confines of a typical 2-D PC display. In fact, the two demonstration programs that come with this book–WorldToolKit for Windows and VistaPro–clearly show that. Each of the demos also emphasizes a different type of virtual reality, illustrating the breadth of potential in this exciting field. To set them apart further, one is for Windows and the other is for DOS.

WorldToolKit for Windows Demo

The WorldToolKit for Windows Demo is designed to show some of the more general capabilities of WorldToolKit. You can "drag and drop" models and textures into the universe or simply use the dialog boxes to load models and apply textures to polygons. You can interactively fly around your models and change the color or texture of various surfaces or polygons–and all these in a program that doesn't require total immersion in the system!

You can, for example, go to the top of the recognizable San Francisco's TransAmerica tower (file name SANFRAN.NFF) and enjoy the view of the city. Or, you can explore an entire island (file name MEGURO.NFF). In all, the program provides you with more than a dozen different universes and objects, each distinct from the other, some simple and some complex, including the following:

- ◇ BALLOON.NFF
- ◇ CAR.NFF
- ◇ COIL.NFF
- ◇ CUBOSTEL.NFF
- ◇ DIE.NFF
- ◇ HILLS.NFF
- ◇ ISTBK.NFF
- ◇ KPLAMP.NFF
- ◇ KPROOM.NFF
- ◇ KPSOFA.NFF
- ◇ KPSOFA2.NFF
- ◇ KPTABLE.NFF
- ◇ LIGHTS.NFF
- ◇ LOBBY.NFF
- ◇ MEGURO.NFF
- ◇ OPLAN.NFF
- ◇ SANFRAN.NFF

This demonstration program supports the following features:

- ◇ Loading NFF, 3DS, DXF, or OBJ model files
- ◇ Interactive texturing of surfaces

◇ Drag and drop of models and textures

◇ Changes to ambient light

◇ Changes to background color

◇ Moving objects

WorldToolKit for Windows is very dependent on the floating-point performance and bus type of your computer. It is recommended that WorldToolKit for Windows be run on a PC with at least a 486DX2 50 MHz processor and an SVGA video board with at least 1M of VRAM. This will give you 800 x 600 pixels at 64,000 colors. Also, an SVGA board with a VESA or PCI local bus will give you about 30 percent faster display speed than an equivalent board with ISA or EISA bus.

Other, more detailed, issues and requirements are covered in one of the read me files that accompanies this demo.

In addition to the Windows version, WorldToolKit is available for the following platforms:

◇ Silicon Graphics, Inc., workstation

◇ Sun Microsystems workstations

◇ DEC ALPHA workstations

◇ Intel-based PCs with a SPEA Fire graphics board and DOS software

Impressive as the demonstration files clearly are, there is more to WorldToolKit than that. WorldToolKit is actually a development environment that includes a rich set of over 400 functions written in C that you can use to build 3-D graphical and virtual reality applications.

▣ VISTAPRO DEMO

VistaPro is a three-dimensional landscape simulation program. It uses data derived from the United States Geological Survey (USGS) digital elevation model (DEM) files. These DEM files contain coordinate and elevation data at 30 meter (roughly 100 feet) increments. It uses a combination of artificial intelligence, chaos math, and a user-definable set of values to simulate landscapes in their natural state. Each small VistaPro DEM file is a complex file. How complex? Well, it actually contains about 65,000 elevation data points and generates 130,000 polygons. Using this data, VistaPro can accurately re-create real-world landscapes in vivid detail.

VistaPro is a single frame generator, meaning that it acts like a camera; every time you point the camera and click, it renders a new view of the landscape. You can view the landscape from a practically infinite combination of heights, angles, and distances. Using the combination of user-controllable values and VistaPro's built-in functions, you can make landscapes as realistic or as surrealistic as you want. It is easy to alter tree and snow lines, haze, exposure, rivers, lakes, and light sources to customize the appearance of the landscape.

VistaPro also can be used as a fractal landscape generator. Used in this fashion, VistaPro can create landscapes from a random seed number. VistaPro supports over four billion different fractal landscapes!

Because VistaPro allows extraction of a certain amount of data from the DEM files, including exporting landscapes as 3-D modeling applications, it can be a useful tool. You can use the output either as an educational tool or as a research tool for the study of topography. Because of its excellent user interface, by simply clicking on VistaPro's topographic map with various tools, you can create rivers and lakes in a landscape where none existed previously. Unfortunately, for the purpose of this demonstration, some of those tools are not available.

Installation Procedure

There are two directories on the disk that accompanies this book. The first is WTKDEMO and the second is VPDEMO. Because one is a Windows program and the other is a DOS program, each has its own installation procedure.

WORLDTOOLKIT FOR WINDOWS DEMO

Sense8 Corporation
4000 Bridgeway, Suite 104
Sausalito, CA 94965
(415) 331-6316

As the title suggests, WorldToolKit for Windows Demo is a Windows program. To install this program, you need to be in the Windows Program

Manager. Put the demo disk into drive A, click on the File menu, and select the Run option.

Select drive A and type **Install** in the box marked Run. The installation program will automatically install the demo onto your hard disk. It even copies two additional files, IGL.DLL and IGLSYS.DLL, into your Windows System.

To start the demo, activate the WTKDemo window; click on the WTKDemo icon.

You are presented with the information about WTKDemo. Click the Do It option to activate the demo. The default universe is OPLAN.NFF. By clicking on the navigating arrows located just underneath the window, you can move right into the universe. To view other universes or objects, click on the Universe or Object menu and choose the appropriate program.

LOADING OBJECTS

If you examine the models subdirectory, you will find a dozen files with the .NFF extension. These are Sense8 Neutral File Format models. You can load any of these into WorldToolKit by either dragging them from the File Manager window and dropping them into the graphics window, or by using the Universe Load or Object Load menu items.

The difference between a universe and an object is very simple. Universes are static, they cannot be moved, scaled, or stretched, and you can only have a single universe entity loaded at one time. Objects, on the other hand, can be moved and manipulated. You can also have as many objects as performance and memory permits.

LOADING A STATIONARY UNIVERSE

1. First, you load a new universe. Select Load from the Universe menu. This displays a file selection dialog box.

2. Next, you pick a model. Select the models directory. This should show you the list of all the .NFF files included with this demo. You can double-click on a listed file to load it into the graphics window.

LOADING AN OBJECT

1. First, you clear the universe. Select New from the Universe menu. This should clear the Universe of any existing objects.

2. Next, you load a new object. Select Load from the Object menu. This displays a file selection dialog box.

3. Finally, you pick a model. Select the models directory. This should show you the list of all the .NFF files included with this demo. You can double-click on a listed file to load it into the graphics window.

NAVIGATING WITH THE MOUSE

You can use either the push-buttons to fly your viewpoint, or you can use the mouse directly. If you are using the mouse directly, your viewpoint will change based on the position of the cursor in the WorldToolKit graphics window. To move closer to an object, for example, you click with the left mouse button near the top of the graphics window.

The following table explains the behavior of your viewpoint if you are using the mouse or the push-buttons:

Push-button	Result Mouse Equivalent
Move forward	Click left button near top of window
Move backward	Click left button near bottom of window
Turn (rotate) left	Click left button near left side of window
Turn (rotate) right	Click left button near right side of window
Move up	Click right button near top of window
Move down	Click right button near bottom of window
Pan (shift) left	Click right button near left side of window

Pan (shift) right	Click right button near right side of window
Pitch (look) up	Click both buttons near top of window
Pitch (look) down	Click both buttons near bottom of window
Reset pitch	NA
Reset initial viewpoint	NA

You can accelerate your speed when using the push-buttons by clicking with the right mouse button instead of the left. This should more than double your speed.

If you are navigating using the mouse directly (instead of the push-buttons), you can adjust your mouse sensitivity by using the dialog box under the View menu.

VistaPro

Virtual Reality Laboratories, Inc.
2341 Ganador Court
San Luis Obispo, CA 93461
(800) 829-VRLI

VistaPro is a DOS program. To use this program, simply copy the VP3DMO.EXE program from the VPDEMO directory on the enclosed disk onto a directory on your drive C. If you want to store this program in its own directory on drive C, you first must create that directory. You do this while you are at the C:> prompt by typing the following:

```
MD VPDEMO
```

You copy the VP3DMO.EXE file from drive A to the VPDEMO directory on drive C by typing the following

```
COPY A:\VPDEMO\VP3DMO.EXE C:\VPDEMO
```

After you finish copying this program, you can expand it. But, first, you must be inside that directory. To get into the directory, simply type

```
CD\VPDEMO
```

When you are inside the directory, you can expand this file by typing

```
VP3DMO
```

Because the file VP3DMO.EXE is a self-expanding file, after it is fully expanded you will see four separate files in that directory, the original VP3DMO.EXE plus VPDEMO.EXE, VPDEMO.TXT, and TROUBLE.TXT.

To see the demo, type **VPDEMO**. After a notice about VPDEMO, there will be an on-line tutorial on what some of the controls are. You can bypass this tutorial by pressing Esc. Now you're ready to use the program. Some of the features have been disabled for purpose of this demo, but what's there are still very powerful stuff. Change the camera angle or reposition the object, then select **Render** and enjoy the vista of the Yosemite Valley.

Glossary

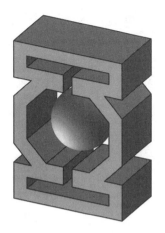

By Joe Psotka and Sharon Davison

6DOF - Six degrees of freedom: Yaw, pitch, roll, up-down, left-right, front-back (or pan, zoom, swivel).

A-Buffering - Keeping track of the Z-depth of pixels to cull them before rendering.

Accelerator - specialized hardware to increase speed of graphics manipulation.

Accommodation - Change in the focal length of the eye's lens.

Actors - CAD representations of players performing actions for them, as in the Mandala system (see Agent, Character).

Accelerator - Specialized hardware to increase speed of graphics manipulation.

Affine - Any transformation composed from rotations, translations, dilatations (expansions and contractions) and shears.

Agents - CAD representations of human forms capable of guiding (Guides) navigators through a VR (see Actor, Character).

Aliasing - An undesirable jagged edge on many 3D renderings on bitmapped displays. Creates jaggies along the sides of objects and flickering of objects smaller than a pixel. (see Anti- Aliasing)

Allocentric - Other than egocentric, such as a bird's eye view, or adopting another person's viewpoint.

Ambient light - General non-directional illumination.

Anti- Aliasing removes jagged edges on bitmapped displays by interpolating neutral colors or intermediate intensities.

Articulation - Objects composed of several parts that are separably moveable.

Artificial Intelligence - The attempt to mimic and automate human cognitive skills through rules and knowledge representation techniques (e.g., understanding visual images, recognizing speech and written text, solving problems, making medical diagnoses, heuristic knowledge, etc.).

Artificial Reality - Introduced by arts and computer visualization scholar Myron Krueger in the mid-1970s to describe his computer- generated responsive environments. Krueger has emphasized the non-intrusive (Second - Person VR) systems that track people with pattern recognition techniques and display them and the surround on projection systems (see CAVE). As realized in his VIDEOPLACE and the Vivid Group's Mandala system, it is a computer display system that perceives and captures "a participant's action in terms of the body's relationship to a graphic world and generates responses (usually imagery) that maintain the illusion that his actions are taking place within that world." (M. Krueger, Artificial Reality, 1992) (See Virtual Reality and Cyberspace)

Aspect ratio - Ratio of width to height of the field of view.

Augmented Reality - This is the use of transparent displays worn as glasses on which data can be projected. This allows someone to repair a radar, for example, and have the needed data displayed on the glasses while walking around the radar.

Back clipping plane - A distance beyond which objects are not shown.

Backface Removal - The elimination of those polygons that are facing away from the viewer.

Backward raytracing - From the eye to the object (currently how most raytracing is done).

Binaural - Stereo sound incorporating information about the shadows at human ears and heads.

Biosensors - Special glasses or bracelets containing electrodes to monitor muscle electrical activity. One interesting VR use is for tracking eye movements by measuring muscle movements.

BOOM - A 3-D display device suspended from a weighted boom that can swivel freely about so the viewer doesn't have to wear an HMD; instead, it steps up to the viewer like a pair of binoculars. The boom's position communicates the user's point of view to the computer.

Browser - Overviews such as indexes, lists or animated maps to provide a means of navigating through the physical, temporal, and conceptual elements of a VR.

CAVE - A VR using projection devices on the walls and ceiling to give the illusion of immersion.

Character - A being with a virtual body in virtual reality. (Walser, 1991.) (See Agent, Actor.)

Concept Map - A browser or terms, definitions, or icons arranged in semantic proximity.

Convergence - The angle between the two eyes at a fixation point. This changes for objects at varying depths in the real world and on 3-D displays.

Convolvotron - A system for controlling binaural sound production in a VR.

Consensual Reality - The world, or a simulation of a world, as viewed and comprehended by a society. (Walser, 1991.)

Culling - Removing invisible pieces of geometry and only sending potentially visible geometry to the graphics subsystem. Simple culling involves rejecting objects not in the view frustum. more complex systems take into account occlusion of some objects by others, e.g. a building hiding trees behind it.

Cybernetic Simulation - Dynamic model of a world filled with objects that exhibit lesser or greater degrees of intelligence.

Cyberspace - 1. A place filled with virtual "stuff" populated by people with virtual bodies. A special kind of virtual space which promotes experiences involving the whole body. (Walser, 1991). 2. A term coined by William Gibson in his book Neuromancer (1984 a coincidental date!) to describe a shared virtual universe operating within the sum total of all the world's computer networks. (See Artificial Reality and Virtual Reality)

Cyberspace Playhouse - Social center or place where people go to play roles in simulations. (Walser, 1991).

Cyberia - see Cyberspace and a pun on Siberia; an Autodesk project and the first VR project by a CAD company.

DataGlove - A glove wired with sensors and connected to a computer system for gesture recognition. It is used for tactile feedback and it often enables navigation through a virtual environment and interaction with 3-D objects within it.

DataSpace - A visualized representation of complex information.

DataSuit - Same as a DataGlove, but designed for the entire body. Only one DataSuit has yet been built, with limited capabilities.

Deck - A physical space containing an array of instruments which enable a player to act within, and feel a part of, a virtual space. (Walser, 1991).

De-rez - Techniques to make pixels less visible in a display.

Depth Cuing - Using shading, texture, color, interposition (or many other visual characteristics) to provide a cue for the z-coordinates or distance of an object.

Direct Manipulation - A term coined by Shneiderman to reflect the use of computer icons or text as if they were real objects.

Disorientation - Confusion about distances and directions for navigation.

Dreaming - A state of mind during sleep where vivid colored imagery becomes realistic and immersive. A natural counterpart to VR.

Droid - Puppet that embodies a human intellect (as in android). (Walser, 1991.)

Dynamics - The way that objects interact and move. The rules that govern all actions and behaviors within the environment.

Dynamic Lighting: Changes in lighting effects on objects as they and the observer move.

Force Feedback - Representations of the inertia or resistance objects have when they are moved or touched.

Effectors - The output techniques that communicate a user's movements or commands to the computer and to the VR.

Egocenter - The sense of self and personal viewpoint that determines one's location in a VR. See projection point.

Electromagnetic Forces - Effects of emf on human tissues are poorly understood and may constitute an important hazard from tracking and display devices.

Endoscopic - Part of a family of new surgical procedures that avoid cutting open major portions of the patient in favor of making small holes through which tools and sensors are inserted and the surgery performed. In a VR or telepresence application, the surgeon manipulates the tools by observing the surgery site on a monitor via optical fibers and a tiny video camera.

Environment - This a computer-generated model that can be experienced from the "inside" as if it were a place.

Eyeball in the Hand - A metaphor for visualized tracking where the tracker is held in the hand and is connected to motion of the projection point of the display.

Eyephone - An HMD made by VPL that combines visual and auditory displays.

Eye Tracking - Devices that measure direction of gaze. Most HMDs do not currently support eye tracking directly.

Exoskeletal Devices - In order to provide force feedback designers have added rigid external supports to gloves and arm motion systems.

Field of View (FOV) - The angle in degrees of the visual field. Most HMDs offer 60 to 90 degrees FOV. Since our two eyes have overlapping 140 degree FOV, binocular or total FOV is roughly 180 degrees in most people. A feeling of immersion seems to arise with FOV greater than 60 degrees.

Finite element modelling - Decomposition of complex structures into small, simple elements so that engineering computations are manageable.

Fish Tank VR - With stereographic display systems attached to a monitor and the scene's virtual image behind the screen, the egocentric projection is called a fish tank.

Flat Shading - A uniform shading in which one value is applied to each facet of a polygon.

Force Feedback - The computer guides a machine to offer just the degree of resistance to motion or pressure a situation would offer in real life.

Fractal - Any function that contains elements of self-similarity (after the work of Benoit Mandelbrot).

Frustum of Vision - 3-D field of view in which all modelled objects are visible.

Gesture - Hand motion that can be interpreted as a sign or signal or symbol.

Goggles - Often used to refer to HMD or other displays.

Gouraud - Shading polygons smoothly with bilinear interpolation.

Haptic Interfaces - that use all the physical sensors that provide us with a sense of touch at the skin level and force feedback information from our muscles and joints.

Head-coupled - Displays or robotic actions that are activated by head motion through a head tracking device.

Head Tracking - Monitoring the position of the head through various devices.

Head-related transfer function - A mathematical transformation of sound spectrum that modifies the amplitude and phase of acoustic signals to take into account the shape effects of the listener's head.

Heads Up Display(HUD) - A display device that lets users see graphics superimposed on their view of the world. (Created for aviators to see symbols and dials while looking out the window.)

Hidden Surface - Parts of a graphics object occluded by intervening objects.

Holodeck - Virtual reality simulation system and place used primarily for entertainment by the crew of the Enterprise in Star Trek: The Next Generation television series.

HMD (Head Mounted Display) - A set of goggles or a helmet with tiny monitors in front of each eye that generate images, seen by the wearer as being 3-D. VPL Research refers to the HMDs they sell as Eyephones.

Hypermedia - The combination of digital text, video, and sound with navigation techniques like buttons, links, and hotspots into one system.

HyperSpace - The space of hypertext or hypermedia documents.

Immersion - The feeling of presence, of "being there", surrounded by space and capable of interacting with all available objects that is the hallmark of good VR.

Impressionists - A 19th century group of artists whose paintings were directed at capturing color and mood, rather than exact perspective outlines.

Interactive Fiction - Dramatic creations that encourage user and viewer participation through computer technology, e.g. hypertext, group feedback, or VR.

Interaural Amplitude - Differences between a person's two ears in the intensity of sound.

Interaural Time - Differences between a person's two ears in the phase of sound.

Interface - A set of devices, software, and techniques that connect computers with people to make it easier to perform useful activities.

Inverse kinematics - A specification of the motion of dynamic systems from properties of their joints and extensions.

Internet - A world wide digital network.

Jack - To connect to the matrix of virtual space. (see Gibson).

Joysticks - Graphic interface devices.

Kinaesthetic Dissonance - Mismatch between feedback or its absence from touch or motion during VR experiences..

Lag - Delay between an action and its visual, acoustic, or other sensory feedback, often because of inherent delays in the tracking devices, or in the computation of the scene.

Laparoscopy (also laparoscopic surgery) - Less invasive forms of surgery that operate through small optics and instruments; lending themselves to robotic manipulation and VR training.

LBE (location based entertainment) - A VR game that involves a scenario based on another time and place; filling a studio or space with VR games.

LCD - (Liquid Crystal Display) Display devices that use bipolar films sandwiched between thin panes of glass. They are lightweight and transmissive or reflective, and ideal for HMD.

LOD (level of Detail) - A model of a particular resolution among a series of models of the same object. Multiple LOD's are used to increase graphics performance by drawing simpler geometry when the object occupies fewer pixels on the screen. LOD selection can also be driven by graphics load, area-of-interest, gaze direction,

Magic Wand - A 3D interface device used for pointing and interaction; an elongated 3D mouse.

Metaball - A kind of "equipotential surface" around a point. You specify a point, a radius, and an "intensity" for each ball; when balls come close, their shapes blend to form a smooth equipotential surface. They seem to be very useful for modelling shapes like animals and humans. They can be rendered by most raytracing packages (also "blobs" or "soft spheres" or "fuzzy spheres").

Microsurgery - A form of surgery that lends itself to robotics and VR. See also Laparoscopy.

MIDI (Musical Instrument Digital Interface) - A digital sound standard for music.

MOO - A MUD, object-oriented.

Monitor - Display, HMD, Goggles, HUD, LCD

Motion parallax - Objects at different distance and fixation points move different amounts when the viewpoint is dollied along the x axis (left- right).

Motion Platform - A controlled system that provides real motion to simulate the displayed motion in a VR.

Motivation - A psychological need, drive, or feeling that raises the intensity of an action.

MRI - Magnetic Resonance Imaging; a way of making internal organs and structures visible by analyzing radio frequency emissions of atoms in a strong magnetic field. Can be made 3D with rendering of large amounts of data.

MUD - A multiuser dungeon; a place on the Internet where people can meet and browse (also a MOO).

Multiperson Space - 1. Multiplayer space involving 2 or more human players. 2. A type of interactive simulation which gives every user a sense that he/she, personally, has a body in a virtual space. (Walser, 1991).

Multiplayer Space - Cyberspace that emerges from simulation that is generated simultaneously by two or more decks. Players can be made up of one human and the rest AI. (Walser, 1991).

Nanomanipulation - Ability to visualize and affect objects in the nanometer range.

Navigation - Moving through virtual space without losing one's way.

Objects – Graphical entities that can be dynamically created or loaded from model files. Many functions act upon them...

> **Tasks**: each *object* performs a task per frame
>
> **Hierarchies**: *objects* can be "linked" together
>
> **Sensors**: *objects* can be connected to sensors
>
> **Modify**: color, texture, scale, etc.
>
> **Collision Detection**: between *objects* and polygons

Vertices: these can be dynamically created along with the definition of a vector normal for Gouraud-shading.

Occipital Cortex - The back of the brain receiving retinotopic projections of visual displays.

Occlusion - Hiding objects from sight by interposition of other objects.

Pan - The angular displacement of a view along any axis or direction in a 3D world; or a move through translation in a 2D world.

Parietal Cortex - An area of the brain adjacent and above the occipital cortex, thought to process spatial location and direction.

Paths: objects or viewpoints can follow predefined paths that can be dynamically created and interpolated.

Perspective - The rules that determine the relative size of objects on a flat page to give the impression of 3D distance.

Phong Shading - A method for calculating the brightness of a surface pixel by linearly interpolating points on a polygon and using the cosine of the viewing angle. Produces realistic shading.

Photorealism - An attempt to create realistic appearing images with much detail and texture.

Pitch - The angular displacement of a view along the lateral axis (front - back).

Pixel - The smallest element of a display that can be adjusted in intensity.

Polygons - An ordered set of vertices connected by sides: these can be dynamically created and texture - mapped using various sources of image data. Various hardware platforms support different texturing methods and quantities. Rendering is performed in either wireframe, smooth-shaded or textured modes.

Pop. When an object's visible appearance suddenly changes or an object appears out of nowhere. Usually an undesired artifact of poor LOD.

Portals - Polygons that once passed thru, automatically load a new world or execute a user-defined function.

Position trigger - A hotspot, or sensitive spot, or button, that begins a computation when touched in some way.

Presence - A defining characteristic of a good VR system, a feeling of being there, immersed in the environment, able to interact with other objects there.

Projected Reality - A VR system that uses projection screens rather than HMDs or personal display monitors.

Radiosity - A diffuse illumination calculation system for graphics based on energy balancing that takes into account the multiple reflectances off many walls.

Raytracing - A rendering system that traces the path of light from objects to light sources (see Backward Raytracing).

Real projection - A VR projection system (a pun on rear projection).

Real-time - Appearing to be without lag or flicker (e.g. 60 cps displays; highly interactive computation).

Renaissance - A period of art dominated by the exploration of perspective.

Render - Convert a graphics object into pixels.

Resolution - Usually the number of lines or pixels in a display, e.g., a VGA display has 640 by 480 pixels.

Roll - The angular displacement of a view along the longitudinal axis (left- right).

Scan Conversion - The change of video signals from one form (e.g. RGB) to another (e.g. NTSC).

Scintillation. The "sparkling" of textures or small objects. Usually undesirable and caused by aliasing.

Second Person VR - The use of computational medium to portray a representation of you that is not realistic, but still identifiable. E.g., in the Mandala system a video camera allows you to see yourself as another object over which you have control by your own bodily movement.

Sensor Lagtime - Delays in the feedback or representation of your actions caused by computation in the tracker or sensor.

Sensors - Mechanisms or Functions that act to change objects in response to multiple devices connected to lights, objects, viewpoints, etc., in the real world.

Sensory Substitution - The conversion of sensory information from one sense to another; e.g. the use of auditory echoes and cues to "see" the shape of your surroundings.

Sequence (keyframe animation) - Interpolate images between stored frames (tweening).

Shared Worlds - Virtual environments that are shared by multiple participants at the same location or across long distance networks.

Shutter Glasses - LCD screens or physically rotating shutters used to see stereoscopically when linked to the frame rate of a monitor.

Simnet - A prototype networked simulation system built by BBN for training military skills in tanks, helicopters, and other vehicles. Using networked graphics and displays built into physical mock-ups, it has been called a vehicle-based VR or synthetic environment.

Simulator sickness - The disturbances produced by simulators, ranging in degree from a feeling of unpleasantness, disorientation, and headaches to nausea and vomiting. Many factors may be involved, including sensory distortions such as abnormal movement of arms and heads because of the weight of equipment; long delays or lags in feedback, and missing visual cues from convergence and accommodation. Simulator sickness rarely occurs with displays less than 60 degrees visual angle.

Sound - Accurate localization of sounds without individualized head transfer functions remains a problem.

Spatial superposition - In augmented reality displays, accurate spatial registration of real and virtual images remains difficult.

Spatial navigation - Accurate self localization and orientation in virtual spaces is not as easy as real world navigation. Techniques for embedding navigational assists in complex dataspaces remain important research goals.

Spatial Representation System - The cortical structures and functions that maintain spatial orientation and recognition.

Spreadsheets - Early spreadsheets made the computer a valuable tool for accounting, and helped spread computers throughout industry. What is the "spreadsheet" or commercial application that will make VR a success?

Star Trek - The fantasy rich series offers a widely known example of a VR in its "Holodeck". Plans are also underway to use VR in a Star Trek LBE (location based entertainment).

Stereopsis - Binocular vision of images with horizontal disparities. The importance of stereopsis for immersion is not established.

Striate Cortex - Visual cortex (see Occipital, Parietal).

Supercockpit - An Air Force project led by Tom Furness that advanced the engineering and human factors of HMDs and VR. It used digital displays of instruments and terrain.

Synthetic Environments - VR displays used for simulation.

Tactile displays - Devices like force feedback gloves, buzzers, and exoskeletons that provide tactile, kinaesthetic, and joint sensations.

Tactile stimulation - Devices like force feedback gloves, buzzers, and exoskeletons that provide tactile, kinaesthetic, and joint sensations.

Tele-existence - Remote VR.

Telemanipulation - Robotic control of distant objects.

Teleoperation - see Telemanipulation.

Telepresence - VR with displays of real, remote scenes.

Telerobotic - Robotic control of distant objects (see Telemanipulation, Teleoperation).

Telesurgery - Surgery using Teleoperation.

Terrain - Geographical information and models that can be either randomly generated or based on actual data. Dynamic terrain is an important goal for current SIMNET applications.

Texture mapping: A bitmap added to an object to give added realism.

> Detail Texture: A texture superimposed on another texture to increase the apparent resolution of the original texture image. Used when the eyepoint is so close to the textured object that the base texture is being magnified (i.e., one texel in the texture image being mapped to many pixels on the screen). A detail texture, typically a noise image, is blended into the image at a higher resolution adding a gritty realism to the appearance of the object.

Texture Swimming - Unnatural motion of static textures on the surfaces of objects as they are rotated. Caused by quick and dirty texture interpolation in screen coordinates. Correctable by subdividing polygons sufficiently or by doing perspective correction.

Theater - VR opens new metaphors to explore with interactive theater.

Tracker - A device that emits numeric coordinates for its the changing position in space.

Transparency - How invisible and unobtrusive a VR system is.

Trompe l'Oeil - Perspective paintings that deceive viewers into believing they are real (e.g., a painting of the sky and clouds on the inside of a dome).

Universe - This is the "container" of all entities in a VR. Entities can be temporarily added or removed from consideration by the simulation manager. The sequence of events in the simulation loop can be user-defined.

VRactors - Virtual actors, either autonomous or telerobotic in a VR theater.

Viewpoints - Points from which raytracing and geometry creation occurs. The geometric eye point of the simulation. You can have multiple viewpoints. They can be attached to multiple sensors.

Virtual Cadaver - A current NIH project to slice and digitize a complete human body.

Virtual patient - Telerobotic or digitized animations of humans with accurate disease models.

Virtual Prototyping - The use of VR for design and evaluation of new models.

Virtual Reality - An immersive, interactive simulation of realistic or imaginary environments. (Jaron Lanier.)

Virtual Environments - Realistic simulations of interactive scenes.

Visualization - Use of computer graphics to make visible numeric or other quantifiable relationships.

Voxel - A cubic volume pixel for quantizing 3D space.

Waldo - A remotely controlled mechanical puppet (Heinlein).

Windows - On some hardware platforms, you can have multiple windows and viewpoints into the same virtual world.

Wire Frame Outlines - Displays of the outlines of polygons, not filled in.

World - Whole environment or universe.

World in the hand - A metaphor for visualized tracking where the tracker is held in the hand and is connected to motion of the object located at that position in the display.

Yaw - The angular displacement of a view around the vertical, y axis (up - down).

Glossary Resources

We thank many people for their help and input, particularly all the users of virtu-l and sci.virtual.worlds. Latham's dictionary was particularly useful.

Latham, R. (1991) The dictionary of Computer Graphics Technology and Applications. New York: Springer - Verlag.

Benedikt, M. (Ed.), (1991) Cyberspace: First Steps. Cambridge, MA: The MIT Press.

Earnshaw, R. A., Gigante, M. A., Jones, H. Virtual Reality Systems, New York: Academic Press.

Ellis, S. R. (Ed.), (1991) Pictorial Communication in Virtual and Real Environments. London: Taylor and Francis.

Kalawsky, R. (1993) The Science of Virtual Reality and Virtual Environments New York: Addison-Wesley.

Laurel, B. (1991) Computers as theater. New York: Addison-Wesley Publishing Co.

Pimentel and Teixeira (1992) Through the looking glass. Intel.

Rheingold, H. (1991) Virtual Reality. New York, Simon & Schuster.

Bibliography

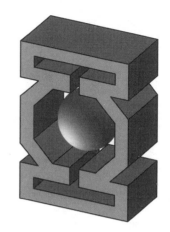

▣ GENERAL ARTICLES

Antonoff, Michael and Stover, Dawn. "Living In A Virtual World." *Popular Science* June, 1993:82
General overview of VR but with a bit more meat than most other introductory articles. Includes discussion of VR applications in medicine and entertainment and the military.

Bacard, Andre. "Welcome To Virtual Reality." *Humanist* March-April, 1993:42

Tries to define the appeal of VR experiences. Says that experiencing 'multisensory' data (sight, sound and touch) and the interactivity are what make VR appealing to many people.

Bird, Jane. "When A Fantasy Leaps Into Life." *Times* April 2, 1993:35
Says that while VR was first developed for training pilots, it is now being used for such applications as product promotions and scientific modeling. Describes the technology and computer resources necessary in order for VR systems to work.

Bletter, Nathaniel. "The virtues and vices of virtual reality." *Design Quarterly* Spring, 1993:38 General discussion of VR. Says it will benefit humankind if developers concentrate on practical applications such as training and medicine rather than fantasy.

Corliss, Richard. "Virtual, Man!" *Time* Nov 1, 1993:80 General overview of VR including some of its history and financial data. This is primarily for the curious and casually interested.

Coxeter, Ruth. "Virtual Reality Could Mean Real Eye Trouble." *Business Week* July 26, 1993:74 Briefly discusses vision problems (inability to focus) that VR users sometimes suffer after prolonged exposure the VR experiences.

Davis, Bob "Getting (Virtually) Real Is 'way Cool.'" *The Wall Street Journal* Sept 22, 1993:A18(E) Describes VR show at the World Trade Center, Boston.

de Jager, Peter. "Oceanic Views And A Visit To The Holodeck." *Computing Canada* Jan 4, 1993:20 General discussion on how VR may be put to use in business applications. VR can assist users to more quickly and easily understand the significance of data. Quotes Christopher Dede, a professor at George Mason University, on his definition of VR.

DeFanti, Thomas A. et al. "A 'room' with a 'view.' IEEE *Spectrum* Oct, 1993:30 Technical overview of the work done at the University of Illinois at Chicago on Cave Automatic Virtual Environment (CAVE) environments. Describes advantages of CAVE versus immersive VR and mentions possible uses for CAVE systems.

Eliot, Lance B."Reality Into Virtual Reality. " *AI Expert* Dec, 1993:9. Describes the advantages of augmented reality, where the view sees the victual world superimposed on the real world. Describes a project in which augmented reality was used to help users change toner in a laser printer.

Ellis, Stephen R. "What Are Virtual Environments?" IEEE Computer Graphics and Applications Jan, 1994:17 Good, detailed general description of what VR is and how it can be used. Points out that the term virtual reality may be an oxymoron; a better term may be virtual environment displays. Describes area for further research.

Englebardt, Stanley L. "Get Ready For Virtual Reality." *Reader's Digest* Dec, 1993:127 General discussion of what VR is and how it may change our lives.

Freeman, David. "Physical Engineering: Endowing The Physically Challenged With A Wealth Of New Capabilities." *Popular Mechanics* Dec, 1993:33
Describes new devices and technologies such as: a walking chair, which can go where a wheel chair cannot, new sports equipment, and VR systems.

Galatowitsch, Sheila. "Defense 2010; Ten Technologies That Will Change The Way We Build Systems, Fight Wars And Envision Defense. *Defense Electronics* Dec, 1992:49
The technologies predicted to affect defense include: VR, high-definition TV, computer communications, speech and graphic recognition systems and artificial intelligence.

Greenfield, Richard. "Simulator Sickness." *Computer Weekly* March 17, 1994:38
Symptoms resulting from spending too much time in a simulation include: disorientation and nausea

Hamilton, Joan O'C. "Trials Of A Cyber-Celebrity. " *Business Week* Feb. 22, 1993:95

Profiles VR pioneer Jason Lanier and his new company, Domain Solutions. Also ,describes the history of VPL Research Inc, which was founded by Lanier in 1984 and from which he was ousted shortly before the company went bankrupt in 1993.

Hamit, Frances. "The Cyberspace Race. " *Information Week* August 23, 1993:44
Provides a general discussion of what VR is and the applications to which it has been put to use. Also makes the point that Japan is ahead of the U.S. in VR research.

Heath, Jenny. "Virtual reality resource guide." *AI Expert* May, 1994:32.
Excellent guide that contains list of products along with brief descriptions and company names and addresses.

Holusha, John"Carving Out Real-Life Uses For Virtual Reality." *New York Times* Oct 31, 1993:11
Overview of various applications to which VR technology can be put. Includes discussion of VR for training doctors, researchers, and astronomers. Discusses a Cine-Med system for training doctors in laproscopic surgery.

Isdale, Jerry. "What Is Virtual Reality; A Homebrew Introduction and Information Resource List" *Version2.1*, Oct 8 1993
An excellent overview and resource list. Avaialbe from on-line resources. Isdale can be reached through the Internet (or CompuServe) at 72330.770@compuserve.com

"Jaron Lanier Is Virtually Sure." *New Yorker* Dec 27, 1993:59
Profile of VR pioneer Lanier.

Johnson, R. Colin. "VR Becoming Reality For Everyone. *Electronic Engineering Times* Jan 10, 1994:31
General introduction including brief discussions of software, and hardware including head-tracking devices

Lewis, Peter H. "Building Virtual Reality For The Smithsonian." *The New York Times* July 25, 1993:F12

An interview with Allison, David K. about the Smithsonian's plans to include VR exhibits.

Louderback, Jim. "Emerging Technologies To Look At But Not To Touch." *PC Week* August 30, 1993:67

Describes computer technologies that will beam important by the end of 1995 including natural language querying systems and VR.

McCluskey, Jim. "A Primer On Virtual Reality." *T H E Journal* Dec, 1992:56.
General description of VR and how it might be applied to educational applications.

Metcalfe, Robert M. "Virtual Reality Could Revolutionize Business, Or Be '90s LSD." *InfoWorld* Oct 5, 1992:51
Relatively early description of VR. Describes an potential teleconferencing application in which users in remote areas would, through immersive VR, seem to be seated in the same room.

Patch, Kimberly"Virtual Reality Becoming More Real." *PC Week* Oct 4, 1993:147
Interviews with industry experts who predict the future acceptance of VR. Points to the Clinton Administration's VR Technology Task Group (part of the High Performance Computing, Communications and Information Technologies Committee.)

"Point Me Toward The Beginner's Slope." *CIO* June 15, 1992:30
Provides a general discussion on VR and describes a an exhibit on computer simulations held at the Computer Museum in Boston, MA, which included a relatively early VR system.

Pool, Bob. "Virtual Volleyball. "*Los Angeles Times* Feb 5, 1994:B1
Describes VR exhibit, 'Liquid Vision' at The California Museum of Science and Industry in Los Angeles

Robertson, George G. et al. "Nonimmersive Virtual Reality. " *Computer* Feb., 1993:81
Offers the argument that non-immersive VR provides many of the advantages (even some of the illusion) of immersive VR, but does not have the technical problems inherent in immersive VR. Also non-immersive (window on the world) systems are more familiar and easier to learn than HMD-based VR.

Rosenthal, Steve. "Neurons And Artificial Reality." *MacWeek* June 21, 1993:30

   Describes how research into the functioning of the human brain may result in data on how users may respond to VR technologies. For example: the human cannot deal with rapidly changing images and people exposed to them may experience stress.

Ryan, Michael. "Go anywhere! But Don't Leave Your Chair." *Parade* March 21, 1993:18(virtual reality)

   A very general and easy to read explanation of VR. Says if TV is a window, VR is a door. Mentions entertainment as well as research applications.

Schmitz, Barbara. "Virtual Reality: On The Brink Of Greatness." *Computer-Aided Engineering* April, 1993:26

   Good general overview of VR technology includes: types of VR systems, hardware and software and specific applications.

Schroeder, Ralph. "Virtual Reality In The Real World: History, Applications And Projections." *Futures* Nov, 1993:963

   Traces the history of VR and follows its use in education and entertainment. Also looks to the future.

Sheridan, Thomas B.;and Zelter, David. "Virtual Reality Check." *Technology Review* Oct, 1993:20

   Good overall discussion of VR, including mention of applications for which it may be put to use and current problems with the technology.

Skurzynski, Gloria. "The Best Of All (Virtual) Worlds" *School Library Journal* Oct, 1993:37

   The article attempts to debunk the idea that VR and other entertainment technologies may be bad for children. The author points out that when she was younger, radio was suspected as being bad for children.

Snyder, Howard A. "The Cybergeneration." *Christianity* Today Dec 13, 1993:17

   This editorial warns that while VR can be put to good uses, it could also be more addictive than video games. The editorial advises parental supervision.

Stevens, Tim. "Virtual Reality: Is It Really Real?" *Industry Week* May 17, 1993:30

   Makes the point that while VR is excellent for industrial and medical applications, the general user, expecting to be transported to a virtual world, will be disappointed with the low quality graphics, jerky annimations and high cost.

Studt, Tim. "Virtual Reality: From Toys To Research Tools." *R & D* March, 1993:18

   Provides a concise overview of VR and looks at how it can be applied to scientific studies.

Swain, Bob. "Better than the real thing?" *Guardian* June 15, 1993: E14
Describes in general terms what VR is, what hardware is needed and what applications VR can be pout to. Distinguishes between 'immersive' and 'non-immersive.' VR.

Taylor, Nigel. "A virtual solution? (computer-aided design meets virtual reality)." *Cadcam* March, 1994:13
Discusses advantages as well as limitations in present day immersive and non-immersive systems. Discusses expense, low-resolution, lag time, etc.

"The Technology Previews." *Telephone Engineer & Management* Sept 1, 1992:63
Describes demonstrations of new technologies presented at the National Communications Forum in 1992. Technologies presented included speech recognition, and VR.

Tierney, John. "Jung In Motion, Virtually, And Other Computer Fuzz" *New York Times* Sept 16, 1993:B1
Profile of VR artist Brenda Laurel (author of 'The Art of Human-Computer Interface Design' and 'Computers as Theater'). One of her most famous projects takes participants into a virtual cave

Wellner, Pierre et al. "Computer-Augmented Environments" *Communications of the ACM* July, 1993:24
Makes the case that VR cuts people off from the real world and so have limited applicability to real world tasks. Discusses the advantages of augmented reality systems

"Why not?" *Maclean's* July 5, 1993:30
The article profiles eleven Canadians who it considers creative visionaries. Among those profiled are . software designer Daniel Langlois and VR artist Graham Smith.

Wilson, J.R. "Virtual Reality Benefits May Prove Illusory." *Interavia Aerospace World*"April, 1993:34
Makes the point that VR may not prove to be the panacea for flight training that had been predicted. Cites the benefits of traditional flight simulators and training in the actual aircraft. Mentions the problem of VR motion sickness.

Wintrob, Suzanne. "Visual Computing: Beyond The Lab". *Computing Canada* Dec 20, 1993:1
Defines visual computing as 3D graphical representation of data, including the use of VR to depict data. Discusses new applications for visual computing including s simulated surgery.

Wirbel, Loring. "'virtual Audio' Finally Sounds Like Music To The Ears.". *Electronic Engineering Times* Oct 28, 1992:9
  Reviews research into virtual audio, or 3-D sound. Discusses how humans know the direction sound comes from. Profiles Crystal River Engineering Inc , which makes products for producing 3D sound.

VR Applications

Articles that describe VR in action

Bain, Brian. "Lasers Strike Home." *Leisure Management* April, 1993:71
  Discusses technological advances in laser games. Says that in the future laser game technology will merge with video and VR games.

Bandrowski, Paul. " Try Before You Buy: Virtually Real Merchandising." *Corporate Computing* Dec, 1992:209
  Discusses modeling and visualization system (including VR systems) to help designers and merchandisers build a prototype store.

Barry, Jim. "Stealth Video." *Video Magazine* April, 1993:98
  Describes how, because of the end of the Cold War, defense firms are applying technologies to video-related consumer electronics including VR.

Bauer, Claude J. "War Zones No Barrier To Multimedia." *Government Computer* NewsJuly 19, 1993:S12
  Describes how the US government has brought multimedia technology, including VR simulators, to Somalia and Croatia for training and medical purposes. Also discusses NASA Ames Research Center's Virtual Wind Tunnel.

Bauer, Claude J."Future Soldiers Train On Virtual Battlefield" Government *Computer* Sept 20, 1993:43
  Describes he Army's VR combat simulator. This simulation for foot soldiers will include sound, 3D visual effects, tactile responses and physical exertion

Bellinger, Robert. "Can Virtual Reality Aid Disabled?" *Electronic Engineering Times* April 26, 1993:101
  Includes quotes from Jaron Lanier (who is generally credited with inventing the term 'virtual reality) from his talk at the Technology and Persons With Disabilities conference. He discusses advantages and limitations of current VR systems.

Blanchard, David. "NASA Uses VR To Explore Antarctica. " *AI Expert* March, 1994:7

Very brief description of the use of WorldToolKit for Windows (Sense 8 Corp)to create VR program for NASA.

Booker, Ellis. "Go back in 'virtual time.'" *Computerworld* June 28, 1993:28

Describes Benjamin Britton's (professor of fine arts at Cincinnati's College of Design, Architecture, Art and Planning) VR gallery tour of France's Cave of Lascaux. Also describes a project at the Carnegie Mellon University's Studio for Creative Inquiry called "Virtual Egypt."

Bradshaw, Della. "Grabbing The Elusive Protein." *The Financial Times.* July 9, 1993:18

Describes work done by a team led by Rod Hubbard at York University, England, to demonstrate the usefulness of VR in molecular modeling and drug design. Glaxo, the pharmaceutical company, is interested.

Brady, Diane. "Virtual Virtuosity" *Maclean's* July 5, 1993:60A:

Describes the use of VR by artists and musicians CD-ROM and VR technology to experiment with new art forms.

Braille, Louis. "Art Meets Cyberspace In A VR Museum." *Computer Graphics World* Dec, 1992:14

Describes Carnegie-Mellon University's and Research Fellow Carl Eugene Loeffler's work creating a Networked Virtual Reality Museum at the school's Studio for Creative Inquiry. At the time the article was written, Loeffler had established a connection between Munich and Pittsburgh that allows users in both locations to share a VR experience.

Bulkeley, William M. "Virtual Reality Is No Longer In The Future." *Wall Street Journal* June 28, 1993:B4

Describes the use of VR in non-entertainment, real world applications including: training astronauts working on the Hubble Space Telescope.

"Cadd Theater Offers New Visualization Technique." *Building Design & Construction* July, 1993:12

Describes CAD system in which five computer-controlled projectors simultaneously provide images above and on all sides of viewers.

Cahill, Philip. "True, Fair, Virtually Real. "*Accountancy* August, 1993:52

Describes how companies are seeking ways to apply VR to commercial applications. Cites British Telecom's joint effort with SheffieldUniversity and Ipswich Hospital to develop a VR system for surgeons and the Tokyo Electric Power Co.'s effort with The University of Tokyo to create a VR system to monitor information flows.

Cantor, Murray et al. "Computers That Make Friends With You." *Design News* August 16, 1993;75

Looks at how multimedia graphics technology, including VR, will aid design engineers.

Carlson, Shawn. "Virtual Mars?" *Ad Astra* Jan-Feb, 1993:59

Analyzes VR and cites ways in which it may be used for planetaryexploration.

Carr, Clay. "Is Virtual Reality Virtually Here?" *Training & Development* Oct, 1992:36

Describes what VR is and then looks at how it can be applied to training. Says that the high cost of VR can be justified when training mistakes would be very costly.

Cheek, Martin "Voicing An Opinion." *Computer Weekly* Nov 25, 1993:44

Describes various products for the disabled displayed at the Science Museum in the United Kingdom. Includes description of The Speaking Hand, which allows deaf and blind people to communicate using a VR glove

Coull, Tom and Rothman, Peter. "Virtual Reality For Decision Support Systems." *AI Expert* August, 1993:22

Describes a scheme in which decision support systems (used to analyze multidimensional data) can be improved though visualization techniques created by VR systems. The advantage of VR systems is that it reduces the need to work with two dimensional grids

Delaney, Ben. "Long Time Coming, Long Way To Go." *IEEE Computer Graphics and Applications* Sept, 1993:89

Reports on the discussions of VR at the 1993 Technology and Persons with Disabilities Conference. Describes two prototypes presented at the conference: a scavenger hunt game that teaches children with severe emotional disabilities the value of cooperation and Virtual Workstation, which helps designers create handicapped-friendly interior spaces.

Englert, Ken. "Future Shock. " *Boating* June, 1993:58

Describes possible ways in which VR may be used in boating including: training for boat handling, understanding radar signals and map reading. Also discusses current VR applications.

Enrado, Patty. "Diving into VR." *AI Expert* May, 1994:48.

Describes a VR system that simulates the Eagles Nest cave system in Hernando County, one of the largest and most dangerous cave systems in the world.

Feiner, Steven et al. "Knowledge-Based Augmented Reality." *Communications of the ACM* July, 1993:52

Begins with a description of augmented reality. Then the article discusses how Intent-Based Illustration System (IBIS), rule-based graphics, can be used to support t augmented reality. Describes in detail the KARMA proto-type, which was used to create the well-known augmented reality system to help users change toner in printers.

Ferrell, Keith. "The Society For Literature And Science: A ConferenceDedicated To Connecting The Two Cultures." *Omni* Jan, 1993:9

Describes The Society of Literature and Science, which views science and the humanities as two sides to a single culture. Recently, the Society expressed an interest in VR.

Fingersh, Julie. "Future Technology Displayed At Virtual Reality Exhibition." *Amusement Business* April 12, 1993:19

Describes the Virtual Reality Systems 1993 Conference & Exhibition. In attendance were about 1,500 officials from different industries ranging from motion pictures and amusement parks to medical and defense.

"Getting A Virtual Education. " *AI Expert* August, 1993:48

Profiles a UK educational program for learning-disabled children in which VR is used for vocabulary-building. For example, one program allows children to 'drive' through the virtual world.

Gilbert, Evelyn. "Virtual Reality, Laser Beams Fight CTD Claims." *National Underwriter Property & Casualty-Risk & Benefits Management* Nov 9, 1992:12

Describes new treatments for cumulative trauma disorders (CTDs). Mentions the use of a VR system to test for CTD and other, related conditions.

Hanrahan, Michael J. "Computerization 2000." *Journal of Property Management* Jan-Feb, 1993:57

Describes new software and technologies that can be used in property management. Brief discussion of VR.

Haverson, Debra Sheer. "Reflections On A Revolution. " *MIDRANGE Systems* Feb 25, 1994:38

Discusses recent trends and innovations in manufacturing technologies. Most of the discussion in on computer-aided manufac-turing/computer-aided engineering (CAE/CAD) products, but VR applications.

Hedberg, Sara "See, hear, learn. " *Byte* July, 1993:119

Show how adding Knowledge-based systems (KBS) to VR ("Hybrid KBS") will provide tools for banking, education and troubleshooting.

Heichler, Elizabeth. "BT Puts Virtual Reality Spin On Network Management" *Network World* August 9, 1993:1
Profile of BT Laboratories' use of Dimension Ltd's Superscape VR software to build virtual worlds that simulate parts of BT's network, thus making it easier to manage.

Helsel, Sandra. "Virtual Reality And Education." *Educational Technology* May, 1992:38
Begins with a general discussion of VR. As an educational tool, it looks at VR as a means of shifting from text-based to imagery- and symbol-based education.

Hodgkinson, Neville. "Showing In A Theatre Near You: Robodoc." *Sunday Times* April 11, 1993:39
Describes work being done by the US DoD on telemedicine. The articles describes the technology as combining VR and endoscopic surgery. Says that the surgical installation of the future will include a video display, stereo sound and hand controllers.

Holusha, John. "Carving Out Real-Life Uses For Virtual Reality" *The New York Times* Oct 31, 1993:F11
Describes the use of VR to train surgeons and help them develop new techniques. Mentions Cine-Med's VR system for endoscopic surgery and work by the National Institutes of Health's National Library of Medicine to produce a standard digitized cadaver.

"How GM Targets Mature Market Niche." *Advertising Age* Jan 11, 1993:26
Describes GM's use of technology to create products for and to market to the baby boomers. VR will be used for product testing in order to create autos that are comfortable and safe.

Kurzweil, Raymond. "The Virtual Village." *Library Journal* June 15, 1993:49
Discusses the use of communications technology to provide information to students. Says that VR can provide an easy and interesting means of accessing historical information.

Lazar, Jerry. "The Best Of All Virtual Worlds." *Federal Computer Week* April 12, 1993:F26
Describes how simulation software is increasing in use at federal agencies for testing and training. Discusses SIMMOD (the F.A.A.'s modeling of traffic control systems and the Defense Department's Close Combat Tactical Trainer (CCTT) and Simulation Development Lab

Leibs, Scott "Virtual reality 101" *Information Week:* August 23, 1993:38
Describes the advanatges of VR in manufacturing. Profiles Rockwell International Corp's use of VR software that can exports CAD data files into VR environments.

Leibs, Scott. "It's virtually educational." *Information Week* March 28, 1994:36.
Interview with Bill Winn of the Human Interface Technology Lab at the University of Washington about VR as a teaching tool.

Leibs, Scott. "Virtual reality 101." *Information Week* August 23, 1993:38
Depicts the use of VR in manufacturing and design. Profiles Rockwell International Corp.'s explorations into VR, including developing software that allows CAD drawings to be represented as VR environments.

Mahoney, Diana Phillips. "Exploring Mars, Virtually." *Computer Graphics World*, April, 1994:50.
A VR system created by the NASA Ames Research Center using Sense8's WorldToolKit software and Carnegie Mellon University's Task Control Architecture (TCA) that models planetary exploration.

Mahoney, Diana Phillips. "Easing Access. " *Computer Graphics World* Sept, 1993:68
Describes an immersive VR-system by Prairie Virtual Systems which specializes in helping architects design spaces that provide barrier-free work areas for the disabled.

Mahoney, Diana Phillips. "Volvo Sells Safety With VR." *Computer Graphics World* Feb, 1994:57
Describes a project in which Volvo AB is using VR technology (from Division Ltd and Virtual Research to sell its cars safety. Volunteers at trade shows will be invited to experience a crash though VR.

Maloney, Janice. "Location-based entertainment: is it the movie house of the next century?" (virtual reality) *Digital Media* July 26, 1993:45
Describes various cockpit simulators and points out their failings and advantages vis-a-vis both movies and traditional amusement park rides.

Marsan, Carolyn Duffy. "Fed Agencies Navigate Virtual Worlds" *Federal Computer Week* June 7, 1993:1
Describes how Federal law-enforcement agencies are considering VR applications to help in f computer-aided design (CAD), scientific visualization and training.

McCarthy, Shawn P. "The Undersea World Of NASA Scientists." *Government Computer News* Jan 4, 1993:29
Describes a NASA project in Antarctica to test technology planned to be used in the exploration of Mars. The project involves a telepresence system

using an HMD, an Apple Macintosh computer, and a remote guidance system from Polhemus Inc.

McCarthy, Shawn P. "Virtual Reality Isn't All Just Fun And Games" *Government Computer News* Sept 13, 1993:70
Discusses the Department of Energy's Virtual Reality Laboratory and its work studying computer-human interaction through situational training and activities in harsh environments.

McCarty, W. Dean; et al. "A Virtual Cockpit For A Distributed Interactive Simulation. " *IEEE Computer Graphics and Applications* Jan, 1994:49
Describes a project by the Advanced Research Projects Agency and the Air Force Institute of Technology (AFIT) to develop networked VR flight simulators. The project should result in simulation that can run on SIMNET, the Defense Department's simulation network.

McNatt, Robert. "Virtual Reality Gets Real: Firms Explore Practical Uses Of Technology." Crain's New York Business Nov 15, 1993:3
Describes down to earth uses of current VR systems.

Mitchell, David H. "Being Here And There." *Byte* March, 1993:132
Describes in technical terms what telepresence is and outlines its advantages. Explains how telepresence works with immersive VR systems.

Moshell, Michael. "Virtual Environments In The Us Military." *Computer Feb,* 1993:81
Provides brief mention of the history of simulations in the U.S. military; describes current simulations, and goes into detail on VR projects including SIMNET

Muradian, Vago."U.S. Army Targets Development Costs; Aims To Speed Arms Production Through Virtual Reality Prototyping." *Defense News* August 23, 1993:24

Muroff, Cindy. "Warehouse Layouts:" *Chilton's Distribution* March, 1993:84
Describes the use of computer simulation, including VR, in designing an efficient warehouse. Simulators help in the development of facilities that are ready for new storage strategies such as cross-docking and just-in-time.

Naj, Amal Kumar. "Virtual Reality Isn't A Fantasy For Surgeons." " *Wall Street Journal* March 3, 1993:B1
Describes a project in which General Electric Co and surgeons from Brigham and Women's Hospital of Boston are working together to create a VR approach to viewing l magnetic resonance images

Naj, Amal Kumar. "Virtual Reality Isn't A Fantasy For Surgeons."*The Wall Street Journal* March 3, 1993:B1

Describes a project in which General Electric Co scientists have joined forces with doctors from Brigham and Women's Hospital of Boston on a VR approach to surgery. 2D l magnetic resonance images of a volunteer's brain was compiled into a 3-D computer simulation.

Nwoke, Ben U. and Nelson, Del R."An overview of computer simulation in manufacturing." *Industrial EngineeringJuly*, 1993:43
Discusses the advantages and availability of the use of Computer simulation in place of traditional design and testing methods. Describes the use of VR in car design. Includes very good bibliography on the subject

Olsen, Florence. "Prof drives computers in new dimensions." *Government Computer News* Jan 24, 1994:18
Description of the work of Ben Shneiderman and the University of Maryland's Human-Computer Interaction Laboratory, which he heads. Describes work in progress on developing non-immersive VR systems as an interface to databases.

Oppenheim, Charles. "Virtual Reality And The Virtual Library." *Information Services & Use* May, 1993(215)
Describes possible ways to use VR in libraries. For example: for handling data and to provide users easy access to information banks.

Orr, Joel N. "Light From Shadow: The Virtues Of Virtual Reality." *Computer-Aided Engineering* May, 1993:64
Describes the potential benefits of VR to engineers. Mentions: simulation to test the effects of pressure and temperature and the advantages of 'Buffering', is the use of VR to protect the testers from potentially harmful occurrences.

Pantelidis, Veronica S. "Virtual Reality In The Classroom." Educational Technology April, 1993:23
Provides a brief history and overview of VR, points out potential benefits of VR to educators and gives practical suggestions on how to use Virtus Corp's Virtus WalkThrough software in the classroom. package and specific classroom

Penrose, Paul. "When Operations On TV Become The Real Thing." *Times* March 19, 1993:31
Describes work by researchers from British Telecom, Sheffield University and Ipswich Hospital to develop a VR system to help surgeons. The first stage is a VR system that models the lower intestines. Future systems will allow surgeons to operate from remote locations.

Pesek, William, Jr."Abd's Global Traders Test Virtual Reality." *American BankerMay* 24, 1993:4A
Profiles ABD Securities Corp., which has been using a VR securities tracking system created with Maxus Systems International Inc's Metaphor Mixer. Dealers at the firm can more quickly understand the securities data.

Porush, David. "Cyberspace: Portal To Transcendence?" *Omni* April, 1993:4
Postulates that VR may eventually be used for spiritual transcendence. By electronically stimulating the brain, meditation may be enhanced.

Quinnell, Richard A."Virtual Reality Enlivens High-Tech Games." *EDN* Dec 23, 1993:30
Describes use of VR in location-based games such as Virtual World Entertainment Inc 's BattleTech. Also discusses desktop VR games that can be played on Apple Macintosh and l Commodore Amiga microcomputers.

Ribarsky, William, et al. "Visualization And Analysis Using Virtual Reality." *IEEE Computer Graphics and Applications* Jan, 1994:10.
Describes work being done at the Georgia Institute of Technology Graphics, Visualization, and Usability Center and the Office of Information Technology Scientific Visualization Lab to explore how VR can be used for data analysis. Describes "Glyphmaker", a VR interface for data analysis.

Ridout, Graham. "Chaos Theory. " *Building* Dec 3, 1993:46
Describes the use of Vegas (Virtual Egress Analysis and Simulation), a VR program to help building designers learn the likely behavior of people in case of an emergency.

Roblyer, M.D. "Technology In Our Time: Virtual Reality, Visions, And Nightmares." *Educational Technology* Feb, 1993:33
Presents the argument that educators should resist the temptation to latch on to the latest in instructional technology instead of first determining what teaching and learning should accomplish and then finding the best technology to met that goal.

Rosenbaum, Sharyn. "Robotics, Virtual Worlds Meet Medicine." Health Industry Today Nov, 1992:1
Discusses new and proposed uses of robotics and VR in medicine including medical training.

Sawyer, Christopher A. "Virtual Reality." *Automotive Industries* June, 1993:85
Describes work being done at the Army's Tank-Automotive Research, Development and Engineering Center(TARDEC). The Army used VR for prototyping during the Gulf war. Don Sarna, a director, believes that similar VR systems could be used in the commercial automotive industry.

Schmitz, Barbara. "Watching The Trends." Industry WeekJuly 19, 1993:C28
> Discusses computer trends that will have an impact on CAD/CAD systems. VR is noted as one of those trends and .

"Shopping As Virtual Reality" *Chain Store Age Executive* Sept, 1993:64
> Describes Visionary Shopper (from MarketWare Corp), which allows consumers to shop using a trackball and touch screen. Goodyear Tire and Rubber Co was the first company to Pilot the product.

Sikorovsky, Elizabeth. "Software 'scalpel' promises medical advances. " *Federal Computer Week* March 7, 1994:22
> Describes the possible use of Teleos software, VR software from High Techsplanation Inc' and VR hardware to train military surgeons.

Sims, Dave "Multimedia Camp Empowers Disabled Kids." *IEEE Computer Graphics and Applications* Jan, 1994:13
> Describes nine-week summer day camp for students with disabilities at the High MacMillan Rehabilitation Center in Toronto, Canada in which children, teenagers and adults use VR development tools to create VR artistic environments.

Smith, Carrie RE."VirtuaL Reality: Immerse Yourself." *Wall Street & Technology* Dec, 1993:10
> Describes use of VR systems to help in the visualization of real-time financial data. Discusses Maxus Systems International's MetaphorMixer which uses VR to help traders monitor 10,000 stocks simultaneously.

Smith, James M. "Space Center's Rising Star Says His Job Is A Real Blast." *Government Computer News* Oct 26, 1992:16
> Profiles Marvin L. LeBlanc, head of the NASA Johnson Space Center Flight Planning and Pointing Section. Discusses his work on the Distributed Earth Model and Orbiter Simulation System (DEMOS).

Smith, James M.. "NASA honors engineers for 'right stuff' in virtual reality. " *Government Computer News* June 7, 1993:78
> Describes how the team of engineers who developed a VR visualization system (Distributed Earth Model and Orbiter Simulation System) was honored by NASA at the Lyndon B. Johnson Space Center. The engineers were: Scott McClanahan, Marv LeBlanc, Erik Geisler and Gary Smith.

Sprout, Alison L. "Reality Boost: Headset Displays Make It Easier To Build A Plane Or Tend A Laser Printer." *Fortune* March 21, 1994:93
> Discusses work at Boeing Co to develop augmented reality systems to help in the manufacturing process.

Tapscott, Mark. "Paradigm Changing From Simulators To Simulation" *Defense Electronics* Sept, 1993:33
Describes the differences between simulators and synthetic training devices, which can be altered to provide training on various weapons. Points out that Distributed Interactive Simulation (DIS) based systems is based on a simulation environment and that the move to this method of training represents a trend.

Temin, Thomas R. "DoD Trains Soldiers With Virtual Battlefield." *Government Computer News* August 30, 1993:68
Describes work done through the Naval Postgraduate School and the Air Force Institute of Technology on VR landscape for training soldiers

Thornton, Emily and Schlender, Brenton R. "New Products From - And Still Stuck In - Japan's Pipeline." *Fortune* Jan 11, 1993:14
Discusses three Japanese inventions including a VR skiing program from NEC Corp.

Valovic, Thomas S. "Corporate Networks: Future Directions For The Emerging Virtual Marketplace." *Telecommunications* Oct, 1993:47
Primarily, the article deals with ways in which wide area networks and new networking technologies may restructure communications and even the organizations themselves. Technologies include videoconferencing, group-ware and VR(which is discussed very briefly).

Van Lenten, Barry. "Electronic Retailing." *Daily News Record* Dec 20, 1993:24
Argues that in the future electronic retailers will have to sell their wares in a VR shopping center

Williams, Gurney, III. "Virtual Reality: Enter The World Of Simulated Reality." *American Legion* Feb, 1993:24
Describes test at the HInes Rehabilitation Research and Development Center in which disabled veterans are experimenting with a VR system that determines wheel-chair accessibility of indoor spaces.

Winn, William and Bricken, William. " *Designing Virtual Worlds* For Use In Mathematics Education." Educational Technology Dec, 1992:12
Proposes a use for VR in the teaching of elementary algebra.

Winter, Drew. "These Games Aren't For Kids." *Ward's Auto World* Dec, 1993:86
Describes how VR has been put to use in the manufacturing of automobiles. Outlines how some programs simulate objects eliminating the need to create "mock ups."

Yam, Philip. "Surreal Science: Virtual Reality Finds A Place In The Classroom." *Scientific American* Feb, 1993:103
Discusses work of physicist R. Bowen Loftin, who developed a VR system to help high school physics students to perform mechanics experiments.

VR Hardware

Articles about hardware which can be used in VR systems.

Adam, John A."Virtual Reality Is For Real." *IEEE Spectrum* Oct, 1993:22
Discusses the advances as well as limitations in the current crop of VR hardware. Also points out the massive computational power needed to run VR worlds at 30 frames per second.

Azuma, Ronald. "Tracking Requirements For Augmented Reality." *Communications of the ACM* : July, 1993:50
Points out the special tracking requirements of augmented reality systems including: speed, long distance and accuracy.

Barlow, M. Andrew. "Of Mice And 3d Input Devices." *Computer-Aided Engineering* April, 1993:54
Describes how 3D mice work and provides directory containing thirteen suppliers.

Bolas, Mark T."Human Factors In The Design Of An Immersive Display." *IEEE Computer Graphics and Applications* Jan, 1994:55
Describes in detail Fakespace Inc.'s BOOM (Binocular Omni-Orientation Monitor). Discusses advantages of BOOM versus HMDs in terms of ergonomics

Cash, Debra. "Touching is believing." *Technology Review August*-Sept, 1993:9
Discusses work being performed at the Massachusetts Institute of Technology to provide a sense of touch to VR systems. Mentions practical applications for a sense of touch in such fields as industrial design and medicine.

Cotter, Patrick. "More That Meets The Eye." *The New York Times* June 20, 1993:F9(N)
Describes work being done at the University of Washington on Virtual Retina Display, a technology that projects an image directly ont0o the user's retina. The technology may eliminate the computational problems related to producing a high-resolution image on an HMD.

Fischetti, Mark"The sound of data." *Technology Review* July, 1993:17
Describes 3D audio systems. Discusses potential applications in air-traffic control, teleconferencing, robotics and navigational aids for the blind

King, Douglas. "Heads up." *Computer Graphics World Nov*, 1993:41.
Comprehensive discussion of head of HMDs, comparative review of six HMDs (ranging from $6,000 and $100,000), directory of HMD and non-HMD VR displays. Good resource material.

Leibs, Scott. "Welcome to the next level." *Information Week* July 26, 1993:46
Discussion of "ubiquitous computing," and interview with Rich Gold, a researcher at Xerox Parc, who has been a composer, toy designer and cartoonist. He was partly responsible for designing the Data Glove, Mattel's low-cost data input glove often used in home-brew VR projects.

McDowall, Ian. "3D stereoscopic data for immersive displays." *AI Expert* May, 1994:18

Meilach, Dona Z. "Giving Life-Like Dimension To Computer Graphics With 3-D Stereo Systems." *Computer Pictures* Nov-Dec, 1993:44
Discusses how stereographics can be used in business, art and entertainment, and scientific analyses, Includes brief description of technology and companies that make tools for it.

O'Reilly, Richard. "Reality Of Flight Simulators Takes Off." *Los Angeles Times* Dec 2, 1993:3
Discussion of Applied Emerging Technologies International's $1,999 Fly-It personal motion simulator. The device, meant for use in flight simulators, provides up-and-down pitch and side-to-side roll

Ryan, Bob. "Three Ways to 3-D. " *Byte Nov*, 1993:215
Describes hardware requirements for VR systems. Discusses high-end graphics engines and workstations from companies like Hewlett Packard, Sun Microsystems, and Silicon Graphics, Inc.

Shandle, Jack. "Sensors Start To Catch Up With Systems' Needs." *Electronic Design* June 24, 1993:55
Cites increasing power of sensing devices and how that will affect VR. Says that university and corporate researchers are developing sensors possess aural and visual ability.

Shandle, Jack. "Virtual Reality Needs Better Sensors." *Electronic Design* Sept 17, 1992:18
Says that while VR has the potential to help engineers, it still lacks optimum position-sensing technology. It points out that products that do deliver relatively good accuracy are expensive, and less expensive products lack accuracy and speed.

Sturman, David J.; and Zeltzer, David. "A Survey Of Glove-Based Input." *Computer Graphics and Applications* Jan, 1994:30
Describes in detail how glove-based input for VR systems work. Also describes applications for glove-based input devices including. Discusses how some specific gloves work including : Mattel Power Glove, Sayre, DataGlove and Dexterous HandMaster

"Virtual Vision: A View Of Things To Come?" *Consumer Reports* Dec, 1993:764
   A (mostly negative) review of Virtual Vision Sport, television receivers that
   are worn like glasses. Virtual Vision has been used in some VR projects. The
   article complains about poor resolution, focusing and contrast.

Zeidenberg, Jerry. "Multimedia Computing: A Virtual Reality By 2001."
   Computing Canada Nov 9, 1992:S17
   Describes the future of multimedia systems (including VR). Discusses new
   multimedia technologies such as synthesis and speech recognition.

■ ARTICLES ABOUT THE DEVELOPMENT OF VR SYSTEMS

Andrew, Ian and Ellis, Sean. "Bringing virtual worlds to life. *AI Expert* May,
   1994:15
   Describes VR) development systems and how they work. Also describes different levels of VR environments.

Arthur, Kevin W. et al. "Evaluating 3d Task Performance For Fish Tank Virtual
   Worlds." *ACM Transactions on Information Systems* July, 1993:239
   Technical article which discusses "fish tank" (also known as "window on the
   world") VR systems, which uses a monitor rather than HMD. Evaluates pros
   and cons of fish tank versus immersive VR.

Brill, Louis M."Kicking The Tires Of VR Software." *Computer Graphics* World
   June, 1993:40
   Describes VR application development software and points oput how it differs from traditional 3D applications: it incorporation the ability to create
   immersive systems and must include interactivity.

Emmett, Arielle. "An Operating System For Virtual Reality." *Computer Graphics
   World* Jan, 1993:14
   Describes the Virtual Environment Operating System (VEOS), an interactive
   environment that provides VR developers with a number of tools meant to
   assist in the design of virtual worlds. VEOS was created by the Human interface Technology Laboratory (HIT Lab) of the University of Washington.

Fitzmaurice, George W.; et al. "Virtual Reality For Palmtop Computers." *ACM
   Transactions on Information Systems* July, 1993:197.
   Technical article which proposes ways to equip palmtop computers with 3D
   displays for VR applications.

Johnson, Andrew. "How virtual reality can broaden your horizons." *PC User* March 9, 1994:31.
  Describes the use of Superscape 3.5 virtual reality application to design military and factory simulations

Johnson, R. Colin. "Mercury on the rise at Hit Lab." *Electronic Engineering Times* Jan 18, 1993:35
  Describes Mercury, a user interface to VR, developed by the Human Interface Laboratory. The interface links VR software and hardware.

Nicolaisen, Nancy. "Creating Vision In A Virtual World." *Computer Shopper* April, 1994: 578
  Discusses how to create 3-D graphics for use in virtual worlds. Explains modeling and rendering, and how images in virtual worlds differ from those in traditional computer graphics.

Pimental, Ken; and Blau, Brian. "Teaching Your System To Share." *IEEE Computer Graphics and Applications* Jan, 1994:60.
  Describes work by researchers at Sense8 Corp. and the Institute for Simulation and Training at the University of Central Florida to develop "Workroom," a VR system that allows two users to build a house collaboratively and walk around in it.

Porter, Stephen. "A Peek Into The Future." *Computer Graphics World* Dec, 1992:42
  Describes results of poll taken by Computer Graphics World during its 15-year anniversary in Dec 1992. The majority of responses showed that the next five to 10 years will see an increase in desktop computing power which will allow for, among other things, VR.

Shaw, Chris, et al. "Decoupled Simulation In Virtual Reality With The MR Toolkit." *ACM Transactions on Information Systems* July, 1993:287
  Very technical and comprehensive tutorial on how to create VR user interfaces to traditional applications. Proposes a "Decoupled Simulation Model using a Minimal Reality (MR) toolkit as a VR development tool.

Swaine, Michael. "Psychedelic Technology." *Dr. Dobbs Journal* April, 1993:99
  Describes the elements of a good VR system.

Wintrob, Suzanne. "Visual Computing: Beyond The Lab." *Computing Canada* Dec 20, 1993:1
  Lists and describes scientific applications for VR including surgery Also provide a good overview of what VR is and describes some animation software (including software from Alias research) that can be used to create VR worlds.

◙ ARTICLES ABOUT **VR** ENTERTAINMENT

Ash, Neville. "Get Real." *Leisure Management* July, 1993:39
    Describes the VR entertainment market in the UK. Discusses major players:
    W Industries, Division and Dimension. Also discusses VR television and
    describes 'Cyberzone," BBC VR TV program.

Champagne, Christine. "Virtual Reality." *Back Stage-SHOOT* March 19, 1993:29
    Discusses the state of technology and the application for computer-generat-
    ed images (CGI). One application: synthetic actors, which can be used in
    VR experiences.

Codrington, Andrea. "High-Tech Sex." *Self Nov*, 1993:82
    Describes VR sex, outlines the technological improvements needed before
    VR sex is possible and predicts the advent of computer sex sometime after
    the year 2000.

Davenport, Kate. "Virtually real." *Leisure Management* March, 1992:23
    Announces that Rediffusion Simulation Ltd,, Virtual Reality Design and
    Leisure Ltd and Quasar have launched new simulation, VR and laser games.

Denselow, Robin. "Virtually Without Frontiers." Guardian July 31, 1993:23
    Describes work by rocker Peter Gabriel to promote audio-visual compact
    discs and VR interactive experiences as the replacement for the LP record.

Dorozynski, Alexander. "Computers Bring Back A Long-Lost French Abbey."
    Science July 30, 1993:544
    Describes a VR simulation of an abbey that was destroyed after the French
    Revolution. The exhibit was in the Ochier museum in Cluny, France.

Douglas, J. Yellowlees. "Where The Senses Become A Stage And Reading Is
    Direction: Performing the Texts Of Virtual Reality And Interactive Fiction."
    Drama Review Winter, 1993:18
    Describes how VR and interactive texts can change aspects of theater aes-
    thetics. For example, VR allows the viewer to physical sensations of the char-
    acters. But most VR plays have a limited number plot narrations.

Evans, David. "Trivial Pursuits." *Computer Weekly* Jan 28, 1993:28
    Describes the British Broadcasting Corporation's TV show: 'Cyberzone', a
    quiz show in which contestants play VR games.

Fingersh, Julie. "CNE Wants To Redefine Midway" *Amusement Business* July 26,
    1993:32
    Describes plans of the Canadian National Exhibition (CNE) in Toronto,
    Canada to include VR games in the midway in 1995.

Gill, Andy. "He's Got The Whole World In His Laptop." *Independent* July 15, 1993:16
Discusses Pete Townshend's (of the Who) interest in VR, which he says dates back to the 1970s.

Gottschalk, Mark A. "Infrared Tracking System Senses Velocity, Speed, Spin:" *Design News* Feb 1, 1993:62
Describes work on a VR golf system.

Hirschorn, Michael "The PC Porn Queen's Virtual Realities." *Esquire June,* 1993:57
Profiles Lisa Palace, who has recorded erotic material on 3D audio compact discs, which she calls Cyborgasms. Her magazine, Future Sex looks ahead to a time when VR sex will be possible.

Hsu, Jeffrey. "Virtual Reality." *Compute* Feb, 1993:100
Defines VR then describes the Virtuality product line of entertainment-oriented VR systems.

Keizer, Gregg. "Out-Of-House Experiences." *Omni* Dec, 1993:12
Describes arcades that include VR rides such as Sega' 'Virtual Racing' or Virtuality's 'Dactyl Nightmare.'

Kelly, Paul. "Simulators: Boom Or Bust?" *Leisure Management* July, 1993:34
Projects the five-year market for simulators used in entertainment. Says that while at present simulators are mostly found in amusement parks, soon dedicated simulator centers will be established in the UK.

King, Douglas. "Virtual Basketball: A Sign Of Things To Come." *Computer Graphics World* June, 1993:21
Describes Jumpshot , a VR arcade game from Corporate Communication Group. It says the game eliminates a major problem with other VR arcade games: the bulky and unhygienic HMD. Instead Jumpshot uses a large-screen display.

Langberg, Mike. "Virtual Reality Center Will Bring Mars To Main Street." *San Jose Mercury* News May 21, 1993:1C
Describes Virtual World, a VR entertainment center in Walnut Creek, California.

McConville, James A. "Reality Tested." *HFD-The Weekly Home Furnishings* Newspaper August 9, 1993:61
Describes home-based VR games and their manufacturers. Mentions Sega of America Inc and VictorMaxx Amusements.

Newquist, Harvey "Reach Out And Touch Someone." *AI Expert* August, 1993:42
Describes how VR technology might be used for sexual gratification

301

Quinnell, Richard A. "Virtual Reality Enlivens High-Tech Games." *EDN* Dec 23, 1993:30
  Describes VR games both location-based (eg. Virtual World Entertainment Inc's BattleTech) and desktop (eg. those that run on Macintosh and Amigas)

Sanders, Lauren "A day at the park." *Back Stage-SHOOT* August 20, 1993:23
  Discusses visual effects on motion-based rides. Describes challenges for special effects film and mentions a few ground-breaking rides.

Schuytema, Paul. "Inside A Virtual Robot." *Omni* Sept, 1993:27
  A first-person account of a BattleTech player.

Shaffer, Richard A. "Playing Games." *Forbes* August 16, 1993:108
  Analyzes the video game market. Says that CD-ROM and VR games will soon seriously challenge cartridge systems.

Smith, Anthony. "The Electronic Circus." *Economist* Sept 11, 1993:F78
  Predicts the future of entertainment, which it divided into high-tech communal events and personal experiences. VR, it predicts, will be a part of both types of experiences.

Walker, Karen. "Fantastic Voyages." *Leisure Management* Jan, 1993:50
  Describes how the end of the cold war and the decline in the aerospace industry has encouraged a technology transfer to entertainment simulators. But the article points out that while the technology for developing simulators is available from firms which used to serve aerospace, imaginative applications are also needed.

Weber, Jonathon. "Playing Around In The Future." *Los Angeles Times* Feb 28, 1993:A1
  Discusses how VR will affect the computer game market. Describes the types of games for which VR is best suited: flight simulators, war and racing games. Also mentions games based on movies: 'Back to the Future' and 'Star Trek'

ARTICLES ABOUT BUSINESS INVOLVED IN VR

Aho, Deborah and Teinowitz, Ira. "Cutty Sark sets a virtual sail." *Advertising Age* May 9, 1994:16
  Describes VR promotional system for Cutty Sark which Hiram Walker & Sonsscotch used at the 1994 National Restaurant Association show. The company plans to take the promotion to a road show which encompasses 22 US cities.

Aragon, Lawrence. "Money Games." *PC Week* July 26, 1993:A1
    Presents the argument that entertainment, not business or scientificuses, will be the dominant VR application. Provides market figures from market-research firm 4th Wave

Bevan, Mike. "Seeing Is Believing." *Computer Weekly* Nov 4, 1993:50
    Discusses UK companies which are marketing or developing hardware and software products for the VR industry.

Brandt, Richard and Gross, Neil; and Coy, Peter. "Sega! It's Blasting Beyond Games And Racing To Build A High-Tech Entertainment Empire." *Business Week* Feb 21, 1994: 66
    Feature story about Sega Electronics Ltd plan to broaden its market share through a number of means including developing VR theme parks.

Cane, Alan. "Growing Enthusiasm For Electronic Imagery." *The Financial Times* Oct 12, 1993:20
    Cites trend of investors to take interest in companies involved in VR. But states that many investors still don't appreciate how important VR is likely to become before the end of this decade. Cites specific VR applications including: entertainment, computer aided design and production and simulation and training.

Davies, Hunter. "Dr. Waldern's Dream Machines." *Independent* Nov 23, 1993:21
    Profile of Dr. Jonathan Waldern, the founder of Virtuality(Leicester, UK), a leading British VR company.

Eisenstodt, Gale. Virtual Disney." *Forbes* Feb 28, 1994:46
    Profiles Sega Enterprises, whose earning have dropped but which may rebound by creating virtual theme parks

Encarnacao, Jose; and Gobel, Martin; and Rosenblum, Lawrence. "European Activities In Virtual Reality." *IEEE Computer Graphics and Applications* Jan, 1994:66
    Describes European businesses and institutions involved in VR research and development. Includes discussion of:) technology. The Fraunhofer Institute for Computer Graphics (Germany); Division Ltd, Advanced Robotics Research Ltd and Virtuality Entertainment Systems (UK).

Enders, Deborah G. "Industry, Military Team Up For Interactive Technology." *Amusement Business* Nov 8, 1993:61
    Points out that with the end of the Cold War many military simulation makers are seeking to bring their products to the entertainment market. Mentions joint ventures and how many simulation companies are spinning off entertainment divisions.

Georgianis, Maria V. "Carol Bartz: Autodesk Inc." *Computer Reseller News* Nov 8, 1993:128
Profile of Autodesk Inc's President, Chairwoman and CEO Carol Bartz. Her strategy for her company is to improve its VR software.

Gross, Neil and Carey, John. "Japan's Liquid-Crystal Gold Rush." *Business Week* Jan 17, 1994:76
Says that Japanese companies control 95 percent of the growing market for liquid-crystal displays (LCD), which are often used in VR display devices such as HMDs.

Guyon, Janet. "Virtual Center: A British Company Looks To Lead The Way In A New Form Of Arcade Entertainment. " *Wall Street Journal* March 21, 1994:18
Profile to Virtuality Group PLC, the world's leading vendor of (VR arcade systems

Hamilton, Joan O'C. "Trials Of A Cyber-Celebrity." *Business Week* Feb 22, 1993:95
Interview with VR pioneer Jason Lanier who was newly at Domain Solutions after his ouster from VPL Research Inc (which later went bankrupt). Mostly covers business of VPL but also some technology issues.

Hartnett, Michael"Fun And Games." *Stores* Oct, 1993:62
Discusses trend of placing VR simulations in shopping malls. Mentions shopping malls. Profiles Edison Brothers Mall Entertainment, which offer an interactive Starship Enterprise re-creation.

Hotten, Russell. "Inventor's Dream Becomes Reality. " *The Independent* Oct 19, 1993:31
Profile of Dr Jon Waldern, the founder of Virtuality, which manufacture hardware and software for VR) for entertainment. Discusses the company from a business (stockholder's) perspective.

Jefferson, David J. "Head trip; virtual Reality Is Coming." *Wall Street Journal* March 21, 1994:14
Discusses he VR arcade video game industry. Describes some games but also discusses problems the industry has including expensive and immature technology such as low resolution devices.

Kahaner, David. "Japanese Activities In Virtual Reality." *IEEE Computer Graphics and Applications* Jan, 1994:75
Describes activities of Japanese companies, schools and research groups (many government-sponsored) in VR. Says that there are about 20 major and 80 small-scale projects in the works. Describes projects of some companies and institutions including: Matsushita, Nippon Electric Co, The Kyoto

Systems Research Laboratory and The Institute of Engineering Mathematics at the University of Tsukuba

Keebler, Jack. "Cyberspaced out." *Automotive News* Oct 25, 1993:81
Describes Ford Motor Co 's use of VR in the designing and engineering process. Discusses the work of John Lafond, manager of energy analysis for advanced vehicle systems, a leading proponent of VR at Ford.

Kellar, David. "Virtual Reality, Real Money." *Computerworld* Nov 15, 1993:70
Describes work by Matsushita Electric Works Ltd to place its famous Kitchen World kitchen design system for customers in product showrooms around Japan. In order to create a cost effective system, the company will move the product to Pentium-based microcomputers.

Lieberman, David. "Kopin, Honeywell Mount Display Push." *Engineering Times* Dec 20, 1993:4
Announces plans of Kopin Corp and Honeywell Technology Center to develop HMDs. Honeywell will design and build the units; Kopin will license Honeywell's optics technology (developed as part of a Defense Advanced Research Projects Agency project.)

Machover, Carl; and Tice, Steve E. "Virtual Reality." IEEE Computer Graphics and Applications Jan, 1994:15
Describes the outlook for VR both from a business as well as technology perspective. Notes what needs to be done if VR is to be usable by the masses

Mead, Gary. "Future Growth Is Virtually Certain." *The Financial Times* Sept 1, 1993:20
Profile of W Industries, the U.K.'s largest VR company. Says the company's products have become industry standards, mentions agreements and joint efforts with Sega, and project earnings.

Santo, Brian. "Inching Closer To Reality." *Electronic Engineering Times* Jan 31, 1994:70
VR lived in research labs for 20 years and is finally beginning to provide the basis of commercial products. This article looks at likely market for VR products over the next few years.

Smith, Rebecca. "Real Woes Hit Virtual Reality Firm" *San Jose Mercury News* Dec 8, 1992:1G
Good history of the final hours of VPL Research Inc. Discusses how it lost its patents to its creditor, French firm Thomson CSF.

Tetzeli, Rick. "Videogames: Serious Fun." *Fortune* Dec 27, 1993:110
Videogame business is worth $6.5-billion-a-year according to the article. Describes major players and trends, including moving VR games into the home.

Traherne, David et al. "Artificial Look Into The Real World." *The Financial Times* Nov 18, 1993:1

How VR is being used in design and development process. Discusses joint efforts among UK research companies, universities and industry. For example, Rolls-Royce has joined a research effort run by Advanced Robotics Research.

"Trains, planes and automobiles." *Economist* Dec 25, 1993:96

Describes how Renault used a CAD-VR program to design its new 'Raccoon' vehicle.

"Virtual Theme Parks: We Are Not Amused." *CIO* Oct 15, 1993:18

Describes a few VR theme parks (Virtual World, the Other World) and takes the view that they the concept in general is not working and that most parks are foundering.

Waddell, Ray "Cutting-Edge Technology To Liven Family Entertainment Center." *Amusement Business* Sept 13, 1993:39

Profiles Edison Brothers Entertainment, which is says is the leader in the family amusement center industry. It says the company has recently ventured intoVR.

Index

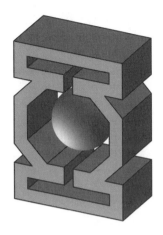